Atheist Exceptionalism

Due to its Constitution, and particularly to that Constitution's First Amendment, the relationship between religion and politics in the United States is rather unusual. This is especially the case concerning the manner with which religious terminology is defined via the discourse adopted by the United States Supreme Court, and the larger American judicial system. Focusing on the religious term of Atheism, this book presents both the discourse itself, in the form of case decisions, as well as an analysis of that discourse. The work thus provides an essential introduction and discussion of both Atheism as a concept and the influence that judicial decisions have on the way we perceive the meaning of religious terminology in a national context.

As a singular source on the Supreme, Circuit, and District Court cases concerning Atheism and its judicial definition, the book offers convenient access to this discourse for researchers and students. The discursive analysis further provides an original theoretical insight into how the term 'Atheism' has been judicially defined. As such, it will be a valuable resource for scholars of religion and law, as well as those interested in the definition and study of Atheism.

Ethan G. Quillen is an Independent Scholar whose research interests are in the areas of Religion, with a particular focus on Atheism and Secularism, Ethnography and Literature, and Discourse Analysis. He has published on these and related areas.

ICLARS Series on Law and Religion

Series Editors:

Silvio Ferrari, University of Milan, Italy; Russell Sandberg, Cardiff University, UK; Pieter Coertzen, University of Stellenbosch, South Africa; W. Cole Durham, Jr., Brigham Young University, USA; and Tahir Mahmood, Amity International University, India

The *ICLARS Series on Law and Religion* is a new series designed to provide a forum for the rapidly expanding field of research in law and religion. The series is published in association with the International Consortium for Law and Religion Studies, an international network of scholars and experts of law and religion founded in 2007 with the aim of providing a place where information, data and opinions can easily be exchanged among members and made available to the broader scientific community. The series aims to become a primary source for students and scholars while presenting authors with a valuable means to reach a wide and growing readership.

Other titles in this series:

Islam, Law and the Modern State
(Re)imagining Liberal Theory in Muslim Contexts
Arif A. Jamal, National University of Singapore, Singapore

Religious Freedom and the Australian Constitution
Origins and Future
Luke Beck, Western Sydney University, Australia

Free Exercise of Religion and the United States Constitution
The Supreme Court's Challenge
Mark P. Strasser, Capital University Law School, USA

Law and International Religious Freedom
The Rise and Decline of the American Model
Pasquale Annicchino, European University Institute, Italy

Proportionality, Equality Laws, and Religion
Conflicts in England, Canada, and the USA
Megan Pearson, University of Southampton, UK

Islam and Women's Income
Farah Deeba Chowdhury, Queen's University, Canada

Blasphemy, Islam and the State
Stewart Fenwick, University of Melbourne, Australia

www.routledge.com/ICLARS-Series-on-Law-and-Religion/book-series/ICLARS

Atheist Exceptionalism

Atheism, Religion, and the United States Supreme Court

Ethan G. Quillen

Routledge
Taylor & Francis Group
LONDON AND NEW YORK

First published 2018 by Routledge

2 Park Square, Milton Park, Abingdon, Oxfordshire OX14 4RN
52 Vanderbilt Avenue, New York, NY 10017

Routledge is an imprint of the Taylor & Francis Group, an informa business

First issued in paperback 2020

British Library Cataloguing-in-Publication Data
A catalogue record for this book is available from the British Library

Library of Congress Cataloging-in-Publication Data
Names: Quillen, Ethan G, author.
Title: Atheist exceptionalism : atheism, religion, and the United States Supreme Court / Ethan G. Quillen.
Description: Abingdon, Oxon ; New York, NY : Routledge, 2018. |
Series: ICLARS series on law and religion
Identifiers: LCCN 2017057252| ISBN 9781138242418 (hbk) |
ISBN 9781315278377 (ebk)
Subjects: LCSH: Atheists—Legal status, laws, etc.—United States. |
Atheists—Legal status, laws, etc.—United States—Cases.
Classification: LCC KF4868.A84 Q55 2018 |
DDC 342.7308/5222—dc23
LC record available at https://lccn.loc.gov/2017057252

ISBN: 978-1-138-24241-8 (hbk)
ISBN: 978-0-367-59059-8 (pbk)

Typeset in Galliard
by Florence Production Ltd, Stoodleigh, Devon

Dedicated to the enduring work ethic of the beavers of Lake Morey, Vermont, whose singular devotion to their task is the ultimate yardstick against which we might best measure the true spirit of America.

Contents

Acknowledgments

I am sincerely indebted to a number of people for their influence and support in the writing of this book.

I owe great thanks to Professor Randal Balmer and the Department of Religion at Dartmouth College for granting upon me the distinction of Visiting Scholar, and thus providing me access to the scholastic grandeur that is the Baker-Berry Library.

In that this book's genesis began at Baylor University, I am also grateful to my colleagues there who suffered and survived with me the demise of the J.M. Dawson Institute of Church-State Studies.

Likewise I am equally grateful to the advisement, support, and camaraderie of the Department of Religious Studies at the University of Edinburgh.

I also owe great thanks to Professor Jon R. Stone, whose unrelenting encouragement and advisement all these years has been a benefit to my work beyond mere description.

As well, I would like to thank the Aloha Foundation in Fairlee, Vermont for providing me the perfect retreat in which to write this book. And in that same way I wish to thank Kelden Smith – as well as his fellow members of Samurai Soul Food: Shawn, Travis, Neil, Amy, Gretchen, Linnea, Michelle, Tiriq, both Abby-1 and Abby-2, Corey, and Riley – for providing me the monetary, as well as libationary, support needed for this venture.

Of course, I must convey my thanks to my parents for their undying encouragement.

And lastly, I owe immeasurable affection and appreciation to Andrea.

The same, as well, to Josephine.

Cases

Statutes

Federal Legislation

State Legislation

Introduction

The exceptionalism of American Atheism

> Lastly, those are not at all to be tolerated who deny the being of a God. Promises, covenants, and oaths, which are the bonds of human society, can have no hold upon an atheist. The taking away of God, though but even in thought, dissolves all; besides also, those that by their atheism undermine and destroy all religion, can have no pretence of religion whereupon to challenge the privilege of a toleration.
>
> — John Locke, *A Letter Concerning Toleration*, 1689

Atheism in America

The Atheist is no longer a stranger in America.

Since the 1940s, Atheist-Americans have played an important role in re-shaping American religion. They have successfully removed sectarian religious education and prayer from American public schools. They have changed State laws that once required a person testifying or swearing an oath to also proclaim a belief in God. They have guaranteed that the right to absent oneself from military service as a conscientious objector was not limited to Christians. And though in recent years they have been unsuccessful in removing 'under God' from the Pledge of Allegiance, ending federal funding for faith-based social programs, and eliminating prayer invocations from legislative meetings, even in their failures they have succeeded in initiating a nationwide conversation about the changing relationship between church and state in America.

Their influence can be measured in more discursive ways as well.

Popular Atheists, such as Madalyn Murray O'Hair, George Carlin, and Bill Maher have commercialized their Atheisms to a broadening American audience. Atheist legal organizations, such as American Atheists and the Freedom from Religion Foundation, have fought judicial battles since the 1960s. Four financially successful texts (three written by Americans) have introduced the world to 'New Atheism.' Billboard and bus ad campaigns have told Americans they could 'be good without God.' Even Atheist congregations have begun to materialize in cities throughout the country, offering a Sunday morning alternative for those Americans who identify as 'religiously unaffiliated.' And in addition to all of this, academic interest has piqued as well. There are now numerous 'handbooks,' 'short histories,' 'dictionaries,' 'companions,' and 'short introductions,' on the subject, as well as research organizations devoted to the study of the same, such as the Nonreligion and Secularity Research Network, the International Society for Historians of Atheism, Secularism, and Humanism, and the International Society for Heresy Studies.

Compare all of this with the results of the Pew Forum's 'Changing Landscape Study,' that in 2014 measured a 1.5% increase (1.6 to 3.1) from 2007 of Americans who identify as 'Atheist,' and it begins to look less like a fringe subject in the study of religion, and more like a topic worthy of further analysis.

This book will provide such an analysis.

It will also break new ground.

This book will bring together, for the first time, the seven Supreme Court decisions (up to the time of this writing) that have directly dealt with Atheism in America. Spanning sixty-six years, from the middle of the twentieth century, to the beginning of the twenty-first, these decisions represent a unique two-part discourse: on one hand, they provide an insight into how the Federal Judiciary has interpreted the manner with which the religious rights and protections guaranteed by the United States Constitution have been applied to Atheist-Americans, while on the other, they offer a unique perspective on the significant role played by these Atheists in re-shaping the American religious landscape.

As such, it will tell two stories.

Atheism and American religion: two stories

Like American Christianity, American Judaism, American Islam, et al., American Atheism is exceptional to the religions of the world, because American religion is exceptional to the religions of the world. And this is because the American citizen is given free and absolute access to an ever-expanding religious marketplace, a retail environment that offers a seemingly unending stockpile of worldviews, all protected by the two religion clauses of the First Amendment to the United States Constitution:

> *Congress shall make no law respecting an establishment of religion, or prohibiting the free exercise thereof.*

As a governing document, the Constitution was a radical experiment. Not only did it establish an unprecedented federal union of free and independent states, but after the ratification of the Bill of Rights in 1791, it also bestowed upon the American people, through ten distinct amendments, a certain number of inalienable rights. These included such revolutionary ideas as the freedom of speech and of the press, the right to protest, to bear arms, and to protect oneself against perjury, the right of a public trial, of the due process of law, and rights against illegal searches and seizures, against the illegal quartering of soldiers, and against cruel and unusual punishment. All of which addressed sincere issues concerning eighteenth century America. And at the forefront of these were the right to freely exercise one's religious beliefs – to an extent – and a safeguard against any governmental endorsement of any one, particular worldview.

While these two clauses for the first time provided a sense of religious freedom not before espoused by a governmental body of this caliber, and because of the diversity that characterized the religious beliefs of the American people at the time, they likewise exposed the need for administrative regulation. On two fronts.

First, in an environment wherein a people are granted permission to freely practice their religion, there are bound to arise conflicts between the deeply held beliefs that exemplify those religions, and the ethics instrumental to maintaining a civilized society. At the same time, when a government is made up of officials elected by, and from within, those same people, there are bound to arise similar conflicts between the beliefs of those elected, and the secularism required of them in order to ensure that government remains religiously disestablished.

It is the Judicial Branch of the United States Government that is responsible for overseeing such regulations, at the top of which sits the Supreme Court. Which also means that the discourses embodied by the Federal Judiciary's decisions in this regard are ripe for interpretation, not only in order to better understand how this particular government entity addresses issues pertaining to religious free exercise and disestablishment, but in order to better clarify what is meant by the very concept of 'American religion' as well.

And it is the same for American Atheism.

If we wanted to understand the place of American Atheism in the context of American religion, these discourses offer an equal, but by no means exclusive, means of doing that. After all, it is through the Federal Judiciary that the religious beliefs and practices of the American people are filtered, and then emulsified, into the 'melting pot' that for generations has defined the proud diversity of the United States.

Which, of course, appropriately leads to a series of essential thesis questions:

> If American Atheists are granted the same First Amendment religion protections as other Americans, whose religious beliefs are defined by their adherence to the doctrine, myths, and rituals of ideologies such as Christianity, Judaism, Islam, et al., would American Atheism, by means of these protections, be transformed into an equally accepted American religion? And if so, how would that transformation alter the very meaning of the concept 'American religion,' when the doctrine, myths, and rituals that define an Atheist's adherence to Atheism appear antithetical to the meaning that we have always imparted upon that concept?

This book will address these questions by following a specific structure.

The plan of the book

As it is with any book of this size and content, a few preliminary details must first be illuminated.

In Chapter One I will briefly discuss Atheism in a general capacity, as well as present the methodology that I have chosen to dictate my treatment of it within the book. In this way, the discursive analysis that I will provide within my discussions of the seven decisions themselves, as well as in the Conclusion, will maintain a sense of continuity throughout.

Chapters Two and Three will then tell two characteristically American stories. The first will provide the necessary history of the United States, dictated by the creation and implementation of the four documents that gave birth to America: the Continental Association, the Declaration of Independence, the Articles of Confederation, and the Constitution of the United States. This story, with its infamous cast of characters and its oft-mythologized plot, is discursively crucial in understanding that of the origins, process, and functions of the American Judiciary, which I will tell in Chapter Three. This Chapter will also better clarify the relationship between the Supreme Court and American religion, and will conclude with a description of how I will present to you the seven decisions herein:

- *McCollum v. Board of Education* (1948)
- *Torcaso v. Watkins* (1961)
- *Abington School District v. Schempp* (*Murray v. Curlett*) (1963)
- *Welsh v. United States* (1970)
- *Elk Grove v. Newdow* (2004)

- *Hein v. Freedom from Religion Foundation* (2007)
- *Town of Greece v. Galloway* (2014)

Each of these deals with American Atheism in their own unique ways. Three of them (*McCollum v. Board of Education*, *Abington v. Schempp*, and *Elk Grove v. Newdow*) discuss Establishment Clause issues at American public schools, a common battleground for many of the 'landmark' Supreme Court cases concerning the complexities intrinsic to the First Amendment's two religion clauses. *Torcaso v. Watkins* discusses both the legality of demanding an American individual acknowledge the existence of God while taking an oath, as well as the significance of the Supreme Court's ability to overrule the rights and privileges of a state constitution in its application of those commanded by the federal one. *Welsh v. United States* discusses not just the permissibility of allowing an Atheist-leaning agnostic the right to conscientiously object to war, when that distinction is predicated on the applicant's relationship to a belief in a 'Supreme Being,' but how such permissibility might entirely alter the meaning of religion when doctrines based on wholly secular ideologies are considered equal to those based on sacrosanct ones. *Hein v. Freedom from Religion Foundation* discusses the constitutionality of providing federal funding to faith-based social service programs, and how the justification of doing so might additionally modify the Federal Government's re-evaluation of the relationship between church and state. And *Town of Greece v. Galloway* discusses a similar re-evaluation in the Court's permissibility, by means of 'history' and 'tradition,' of the policy of opening a legislative meeting with a prayer, and the consequences of doing so when it might be imbued with secular or 'Atheist' content.

Each decision will be presented in full, free from emendations or abridgements, aside from some grammatical anomalies and legal abbreviations. I have removed and altered these for the benefit of readers not readily familiar with judicial language, and placed them into a series of endnotes at the end of each discussion.

I have also designed each decision's presentation for the same sake of readability. Each one will begin with a preliminary discussion of its 'background,' detailing the story of how it came to the Supreme Court, including specifics about the individuals involved, the perceived unconstitutional issues at the heart of the initial lawsuit, and the antecedent case decisions that led to the Court's ultimate ruling. Following the transcript of each decision, I have provided a discussion of its 'importance,' wherein I will detail the decision's discursive influence on the broader meaning of American Atheism, as well as the similar effects it has had on American religion.

In addition to the structure of these sections, each of these 'chapters' will tell an isolated story about the case decision at its center, so that two additional points must be made here about the content of each. First, within my background descriptions and discussions of their importance, I will also provide a valuable introduction to the process and function of the American Judiciary, so that though this book's focus will be on American Atheism and the Supreme Court, it might also act as a primer for anyone interested in the Judiciary itself. Especially with respect to how it has addressed First Amendment religion questions from its inception to the early 2000s.

Second, because there was a thirty-four year gap in cases that came before the Supreme Court dealing with the First Amendment rights of American Atheists between *Welsh v. United States* and *Elk Grove v. Newdow*, and because in that time the Court itself underwent a number of ideological changes, there will be a noticeable difference in the length and content of the first four 'chapters' and the latter three. This is in large part due to the different complexities inherent in the questions that came before the Court in these two groups. In *McCollum v. Board of Education*, *Torcaso v. Watkins*, *Abington v. Schempp*, and *Welsh v. United States* the questions were rather straightforward, while in *Elk Grove v. Newdow*, *Hein v. Freedom from Religion Foundation*, and *Town of Greece v. Galloway* they dealt with much more complicated issues. My overall treatment of these complexities will thus be equally as detailed.

The Conclusion of the text as a whole will then provide a deeper analysis of this overall discourse, wherein I will more directly address the two thesis questions specified above.

Atheist exceptionalism

Atheism, like the concept religion, is a complex thing.

And like religion, we could spend a lifetime debating the 'definition' of the term, how it is 'lived,' how it is 'expressed,' and the best ways to examine these dimensions. We could build 'schools of thought' devoted to our different methodological approaches, and these could in turn dictate the narratives of scholarly departments or research institutes on the subject. Out of these could rise predominate voices whose seminal works on the subject would be studied for a generation, and then wholly deconstructed by the next.

As a companion discipline to Religious Studies, that might be the future of Atheist Studies, but for now these are merely the first steps. And that, perhaps more than anything else, describes my intentions with this book.

I have written the following pages in order to provide for you a preliminary and objective introduction to one aspect of American Atheism. And as such I have endeavored to ensure that every detail and fact presented herein is unfiltered by my personal opinion on the subject. Which is why I have chosen to provide the discourse at the heart of this book, as it is, without commentary beyond the necessary facts needed to fully understand it.

It is my belief that the best way to understand such ambiguous subjects as 'religion' or 'Atheism' is to see how people have either defined those things in their own words, or how others have defined them on their behalf. And these Supreme Court decisions do just that. In these discourses we are able to see the face-to-face process of identity construction play out in a wonderfully exceptional fashion. Here are American Atheists, defining themselves as such in reflection of the ways in which they have felt 'injured' or 'outcast' or 'set apart' by constitutional violations wherein government entities have breached the wall of separation erected by the First Amendment. And here also is a Federal body describing their Atheisms within its consideration of their injury or offense, equally in reflection of the religious beliefs and practices against which they have found themselves opposed. In these ways, this discourse not only offers the perfect case study with which to examine one aspect of American Atheism, but an ideal boundary marker as well. For it would be utterly irresponsible not to limit one's scope in the study of such an ambiguous topic.

More than that, though, this book will raise a number of important questions. Questions about the exceptionalism of American Atheism, about what it means to be an American Atheist, about its relationship to American religion, and whether or not it should be proportionately defined as such. And in that same way, these questions will examine the possibility that perhaps the study of Atheism is actually the study of religion, just from a new vantage point not yet applied.

It is my intention herein to consider these things.

Bibliography

Julian Baggini, *Atheism: A Very Short Introduction* (Oxford: Oxford University Press, 2003).
Stephen Bullivant and Michael Ruse, eds. *The Oxford Handbook of Atheism* (Oxford: Oxford University Press, 2013).
George Jacob Holyoake, *Among the Americans and a Stranger in America* (Chicago: Belford, Clarke, & Co., 1881).
Gavin Hyman, *A Short History of Atheism* (London: I.B. Tauris, 2010).
International Society for Heresy Studies: http://heresystudies.org/
International Society for Historians of Atheism, Secularism, and Humanism: https://atheism secularismhumanism.wordpress.com/
Lois Lee and Stephen Bullivant, *Oxford Dictionary of Atheism* (Oxford: Oxford University Press, 2016).
Michael Martin, ed. *The Cambridge Companion to Atheism* (Cambridge: Cambridge University Press, 2009).
Non-Religion and Secularity Research Network: https://nsrn.net/
Pew Forum, *Changing Landscape Study*: www.pewforum.org/2015/05/12/americas-changing-religious-landscape/

Part I

Methodology and histories

1 Discourse analysis and the definition of Atheism

> Atheism is that system of thought which is formally opposed to theism. Since its first coming into use the term atheism has been very vaguely employed, generally as an epithet of accusation against any system that called in question the popular gods of the day. Thus while Socrates was accused of atheism and Diagoras called an atheist by Cicero, Democritus and Epicurus were styled in the same sense impious (without respect for the gods) on account of the trend of their new atomistic philosophy. In this sense too, the early Christians were known to the pagans as atheists, because they denied the heathen gods; while, from time to time, various religious and philosophical systems have, for similar reasons, been deemed atheistic.
>
> — Francis Aveling, 'Atheism' in *The Catholic Encyclopedia*, 1907

Religious terminology, Atheism, and the problem with 'definitions'

Religious terminology offers a special challenge.

The words that people use to discuss religion and religious beliefs, either their own or someone else's, are deeply imbued with meaning. Especially on an individual-to-individual level. What one person might think of when they read a religious term like 'Christianity' could have a completely different meaning to someone else. For example, consider what that term meant to you as you read it here. Does it conjure within your mind certain imagery? Rituals? Dress? Historical figures? Do you think of denominations? Protestant? Catholic? Orthodox? Does it have a personal meaning to you? Do you attach it to a particular culture? When you read the term 'Christianity' do you think of American Christianity, or Chinese, or Latin American, or African? And as you read those words does the image in your mind change to accommodate those cultures? What do those images look like, and where did you first begin thinking of them that way? What inspired your own personal definitions of these different types of 'Christianities'?

Now consider even further how a term like 'Christianity' might conjure different images between two people when one of them identifies as a 'Christian,' and the other does not. Do these two personal definitions represent an 'insider' and 'outsider' perspective, and if so, which one might we regard as more 'complete' or 'accurate?' Would the insider's definition be too personal? Would the outsider's be too disconnected? Or, would it be easier to accept them both and then try to find between them a common denominator in order to form a more comprehensive understanding of 'Christianity-in-general'?

These are just a few of the challenges faced by the scholar of religion. Challenges that become even more complex as we turn from specific terms like 'Christianity,' to broader ones, like 'religion.'

So how do we proceed? How do we move forward with our research, when even at the start we find ourselves already bogged down by terminological complexities? In other words, what is the proper methodology? Do we simply dismiss these sorts of terminological discussions and focus solely on statistical numbers? Or do we focus entirely on the words used by individuals? Should we even try to define religious terminology, and if so, how? Do we try to produce 'general' definitions? Is that unfair to our subjects? Does it betray their own definitions, or does it bolster them? What approach works best?

Before laying out the methodology that I have chosen for this book, let us first consider some questions more relevant to its interests, as based on this definition:

> *Atheism is not believing in God.*

This is a fairly straightforward definition, is it not? It's simple, and short, and to the point. But, do you think that it's accurate? Is it fair? At this point in a book on American Atheism, would you argue that this definition benefits or weakens my intentions going forward?

If we look at it a bit closer, deconstruct it and break it down, that simplicity begins to look a lot more complex. For example, consider these questions, which I have focused solely on the two words, 'not believing':

> Would you agree that an Atheist is the exact opposite of someone who *does* believe in God? If so, would that bind together the believer and the non-believer in some type of relationship? Would those two individuals then represent the two sides of a debate about 'God's existence'? And if so, again, would this further mean that Atheism is a belief based on that relationship? Might we even say that because it is based on this relationship, and because that relationship is based on the question of God's existence, that it represents a theological conclusion? Is Atheism then merely a reflection of the believer's belief that God exists? It's all part of the same discourse, is it not? Or, might we look at the whole thing a different way. Didn't not having a belief come before having one? Weren't we all 'non-believers' at some point? We weren't born believing the things we believed, were we? If we weren't, and if Atheism is simply not believing in God, then weren't we all born Atheists? Did we convert to believing in God's existence? And if so, are we merely converting back to Atheism when we reject the existence of God?

I could go on.[1]

Questions like these complicate definitions, or rather, they complicate our attempts at trying to provide definitions in books like this one, because there are always more and more questions to be asked. Which also means that no matter how hard we try to construct complete, or even workable, definitions, we always fall short.

To make my point here even clearer, consider these examples, proposed by three prominent scholars in the field of Atheist Studies.

The first comes from Michael J. Buckley's *At the Origins of Modern Atheism*, published in 1987:

> Forensic theology had divided Athens since Anaxagoras of Clazomenae had introduced philosophy into this center of Hellenic culture. Anaxagoras had been indicted under the city's decrees against those 'who do not believe in the divine or who teach

> *logoi* about matters transcendent' and had fled for his life to Lampascus. A Bronze tablet displayed on the Acropolis publically proscribed Diagoras of Melos, and a reward of one talent was posted for those who would kill him and two talents for those who would bring him captive into Athens. Diagoras was an 'atheist.' Indeed, his fame was to rank him among the great classical atheists in the ancient world, with his name heading the canonical catalogues of the godless. The tablet explains his atheism: he had ridiculed the Eleusinian Mysteries and spoken about what occurred within them. Around the same time, 415 B.C., Protagoras of Abdera was reportedly banished from Athens and his books burnt in the *agora* for theological skepticism: 'About the gods, I do not have [the capacity] to know, whether they are or are not, nor to know what they are like in form; for there are many things that prevent this knowledge; the obscurity [of the issue] and the shortness of human life.' Whatever solid ground of actual event and word lies beneath the mist and haze of story, allegation, and maxim surrounding Anaxagoras, Diagoras, and Protagoras, Athens was never the territory of untrammeled inquiry that the Enlightenment projected [emphases in original].[2]

The second comes from Stephen Bullivant's *The Salvation of Atheists and Catholic Dogmatic Theology*, published in 2012:

> For the purposes of this study, then, the word 'atheist' will signify the following: *a person who is without a belief in God (or gods)*. This encompasses both those who believe that God does not exist, and those who, while not necessarily disbelieving, do not possess a belief in God's existence either [emphasis in original].[3]

The third comes from the Nonreligion and Secularity Research Network, an organization committed to further discussions of nonreligion and secularity, and its glossary of terms:

> Atheism: A conscious or unconscious lack of commitment to god(s).[4]

Each of these is an exceptional definition. They provide clear and coherent descriptions, are well written, and offer the same sort of simplicity as my own example above. But they also vary quite a lot in their answers to the question, 'what is Atheism,' and it is within those differences where we once again find their simplicity turning toward complexity.

For example, Buckley's definition gives us a different perspective from both Bullivant's and the NSRN's, simply because it is context-bound to his discussion of the 'origins' of Atheism in the ancient world. His is what we might call a *lexical* definition, a description of something that had a particular meaning to a particular person or people at a particular time.[5] We find these types of definitions most often in dictionaries. And while they provide excellent illustrations of how a term has been used by a specific group of individuals in a specific time and place, and though we might be able to cull more general meaning from those illustrations, they tend to differ drastically from later lexical definitions, such as this one from Gavin Hyman's (2010) *A Short History of Atheism*:

> Atheism is an accomplice of modernity in that it shares its fundamental conviction that the truth of the world is, in principle, accessible to human beings through the exercise of their rational, experiential and experimental capacities. [. . .] Atheism is inseparably connected not only to modernity, but also to the theism against which it reacts and defines itself.[6]

In comparison, we might define Bullivant's definition as a *stipulation*, a way of defining something in order to support an argument or discussion. We might also call this a 'functional definition,' in that it provides a sense of utility to his endeavor. Which, of course, begs the question: is it then useful beyond his usage? Or in other words, could we remove his definition from the context of his using it and apply it universally to the notion of 'Atheism-in-general'? Moreover, could we do this with Buckley's or Hyman's?

It is here where the short simplicity of the NSRN's definition stands out amongst these three examples. Like Bullivant's, it was designed for a distinct purpose, but unlike his, that purpose extends well beyond the context of a specific study. In fact, it could be argued that the NSRN's definition is an attempt at finding the 'essence' of each and every definition of the term, so as to present a universal one that could speak on behalf of any and all Atheists. And while it is not usually the best scholastic policy to attempt these sorts of *essential* definitions, especially given the sometimes-misconstrued bias often underscoring the intent of such things, this example is remarkably well designed. In fact, it works so well that it likewise supports my larger argument here that Atheism is not, actually, an easy term to define.

It does this by combining certain signifying terms, which we could readily use to plot the many ways in which the word itself has been defined across the history of its usage. For instance, both 'lack of commitment' and 'god(s)' refer directly to two lexical definitions. The first, because of the use of the word 'lack,' speaks to the idea that an 'Atheist' is someone 'missing' something, an absence signified by the alpha privative prefix 'A,' that etymologically translates the word as 'a' (without) 'theos' (god). And second, the parenthetical nod to the Atheist's 'lack of commitment' to the belief of both a monotheistic and/or polytheistic deity is a signifying reflection of the differences between the ancient and modern examples of Atheism, respectively illustrated by my two samples above by Michael Buckley and Gavin Hymen.

And this works the same with the definition's use of the words 'conscious' and 'unconscious.' Where 'lack of commitment' and 'god(s)' demonstrate historical descriptions, these two words reflect the term's more theoretical background. This dichotomous split between two types of either explicit or implicit Atheisms, or what is more often referred to as 'positive' and 'negative' types, can be traced back to the earliest theoretical stipulations of the term's meaning, best exemplified by Francis Aveling's initial contribution in the 1907 *Catholic Encyclopedia*:

> The most trenchant form which atheism could take would be the positive and dogmatic denial existence of any spiritual and extra-mundane First Cause. This is sometimes known as dogmatic, or *positive* theoretic, atheism. [. . .] A second form in which atheism may be held and taught, as indeed it has been, is based either upon the lack of physical data for theism or upon the limited nature of the intelligence of man. This second form may be described as a *negative* theoretic atheism [emphases mine].[7]

A century later, Michael Martin repeated this same determination – albeit with a few slight emendations – in his introduction to *The Cambridge Companion to Atheism*:

> Negative atheism in the broad sense is then the absence of belief in any god or Gods, not just the absence of a belief in a personal theistic God, and negative atheism in the narrow sense is the absence of belief in a theistic God. Positive atheism in the

> broad sense is, in turn, disbelief in all gods, with positive atheism in the narrow sense being the disbelief in a theistic God.[8]

Martin's repetition here of Aveling's positive and negative, as well as his addition of 'broad' and 'narrow' types, reflect even further the comprehensiveness of the NSRN's definition. But it is also here where we begin to find the type of precariousness that often detracts from the quality of these kinds of essentialisms. That is, where definitions like these provide for us a workable description of a term that can speak for entire generations, even millennia, of that term's usage, they also lack a certain sense of nuance, particularly in regard to what might have driven the individual-to-individual definitions that they have essentialized.

The best example of this comes from Antony Flew's definition in his *The Presumption of Atheism*, published in 1976. By using this positive and negative dichotomy in order to support his argument that people are 'born Atheists,' which would then shift the 'onus of proof' of the existence of God from the Atheist to the theist, Flew defined the term as such:

> What I want to examine is the contention that the debate about the existence of God should properly begin from the presumption of atheism, that the onus of proof must lie upon the theist. [. . .] In this interpretation an atheist becomes: not someone who positively asserts the non-existence of God; but someone who is simply not a theist. Let us, for future ready reference, introduce the labels 'positive atheist' for the former and 'negative atheist' for the latter.[9]

In contrast to Martin's more objective definition, Flew's here is imbued with bias and intention, with his overall conclusion that people 'convert' to a belief in the existence of God, only to re-convert later back to their original Atheism. This argument is repeated by George H. Smith in his 1989 book, *Atheism: The Case Against God*,[10] as well as in Julian Baggini's more widely disseminated *Atheism: A Very Short Introduction*, wherein he uses a colorful metaphor about the existence of the Loch Ness Monster to argue that Atheism, as a lack of belief, came before theism, which espoused one.[11]

Of course, that these examples offer a less impartial description of Atheism than the others who likewise adopted the positive and negative dichotomy in their own definitions should not be understood here as my reproaching them for doing so, or for faulting the NSRN's definition as a whole. That this discourse found representation in its own definition is indeed quite laudable.

Rather, my point in leading you down this semantic detour was instead to briefly introduce you to the difficulties and consequences that are often found in such endeavors, by using examples directly sourced from the discourse in which this has been attempted.

With all of this in mind, then, I would like to proceed here toward a description of the methodology that I have chosen for this book, as well as an explanation as to why I believe it will prove more beneficial to my intentions herein, by supporting my decision not to offer you a definition of Atheism at all.

Discourse analysis and the 'definition of Atheism'

In the pages that follow, you will find a type of 'discursive Atheism,' related examples bound within an explicit context, which I have provided here so that you might gain an insight into how that discourse influences the 'meaning of Atheism' independent from the discourse above about the 'definition of Atheism.' What you will not find is a definition. And it is vitally important that before turning to a description of that discourse, and the discourse itself, that I explain here the methodological reasoning behind my decision in doing that.

At its core, *discourse analysis* is the study of 'language in use,' or rather, of the discourse or discourses that people use when they describe themselves, their beliefs, their culture, and so on. From an a-religious perspective, discourse analysis might best be understood as a research paradigm in which the researcher allows his or her subjects to 'speak for themselves,' a sort of anthropological tactic meant to maintain a clear and untarnished representation of the subject's cultural self-description. When it comes to studying religion, however, it works the same way, but more specifically in a manner that alleviates the scholar's responsibility in interpreting, and by that way influencing, his or her subject's religious self-description with an external definition, like we saw above.

While in the former, a-religious sense, discourse analysis has enjoyed a healthy upbringing, it has also, of course, suffered some of the same growing pangs as other research paradigms. For instance, we could easily ask what is 'discourse,' and given that term's equal ability to mean a number of different things to a number of different people, answering that question would likely bog us down even further. This is not to say, however, that there have not been attempts at answering it, so that I could easily present here a list similar to the one above concerning 'Atheism':

- An analysis of the way language use impacts the communication of beliefs within interactions between individuals;[12]
- An approach aimed at specific patterns of language use across differing textual media;[13]
- An analysis of language reflecting and/or shaping social order.[14]

But this would merely lead us down yet another semantic detour. Fortunately, though, the term 'discourse' is not as heavily imbued with the sort of personal and sacrosanct meaning as is 'religion' or 'Atheism,' so I have no issue stipulating here my own definition, for the benefit of this book:

> 'Discourse' means a collection of language usage, focused on a particular term, in order to provide a means with which we might better understand how that term is used within, and only within, the context of that language usage.

In other words, I am using the term 'discourse' here in order to set up a boundary that will keep my discussion herein limited to a particular type of Atheism, rather than to 'Atheism-in-general.' This does not mean, of course, that it is somehow separate from that larger discussion. Rather, this is simply my way of saying: this is how Atheism is understood within this milieu, not in all milieux.

As it pertains to the study of religion, though, discourse analysis offers more than just a boundary-marker. Since its inception, the field of *religious studies* has been home to a diversity of theoretical methodologies, as those engaged with the 'science of religion' or 'comparative religions' have found ways to examine their subjects between 'substantive' and 'functionalist' routes. And, to their credit, these approaches have provided countless answers to the question, *what is religion*, in relation to both what people believe, and how they practice those beliefs. However, those answers have most often come in the form of 'definitions of religion,' and while this has provided a healthy discourse for debate, it has in many ways turned the steadfast chorus of the study of religion into an out-of-tune gabble. This is perhaps most apparent when we interpret the division between the 'substantive' and 'functionalist' routes as the difference between theological and secular approaches.

And this is where discourse analysis becomes essential for my own intentions herein.

First introduced by Kocku von Stuckrad in 2003, a discursive approach to the study of religion acts as an escape from the process of offering definitions by providing instead a 'theory of discourse.' How this works is rather simple: in lieu of stipulating a definition of the religious term at focus – such as I described above – the scholar instead treats that term as an *empty signifier*, a word devoid of meaning, that is then filled, depending on the use of it by his or her subjects.[15] What this also does is shift the focus of the inquiry from defining terms in general to simply allowing the discourse to speak for itself.

Thus, by beginning here with the conception that the term, ATHEISM, is an empty signifier, and is thus nothing more than a series of seven letters that over the course of this book will eventually be filled by the discourses presented, I can avoid defining for you what it might mean either in general, or to the Atheists at focus. The 'definition,' if we wish to call it that, will appear in time.

Of course, one might make the valuable argument here that no word, especially one like 'religion' or 'Atheism,' could ever be truly 'empty,' as the history behind the creation and implementation of these things can never be truly removed. And I would agree with that. Which is why, even when we adopt the discursive approach of pre-emptively stripping our terms to their bare minimum, I would argue that we are still obliged to, if nothing else, set a terminological stage on which to present our research.

Which I have done, albeit in a rather devious manner.

My above discussion about the difficulties and consequences in playing the 'definition game' with terms like 'Atheism,' and in critically analyzing examples of the ways in which scholars have defined that term over time, did just that. In fact, what I actually did was provide for you a discursive analysis, writ small of course, corralled within a boundary demarcated by three definitional categories: lexical, stipulative, and essential. Which also means that alongside my not needing to define that term for the benefit of this book, I also provided a decent background of its meaning for those entirely unfamiliar with it. Such is the overall benefit of a discursive analysis.

This also means that you are not required to alter your own perception of the term in order to match my preliminary description. Nor are you forced to agree or disagree with me. Rather, in providing you with a basic background of the term's meaning according to a particular discourse, and then in offering you the additional discourse herein merely as supplementary data about how the term has been used in a distinct way, I have additionally provided for you the opportunity to interact *only* with that data. Any agreement or disagreement that you may feel will be the result purely of that interaction.

With this methodology fully explained, then, I will turn now toward a short description of that supplementary discourse itself.

American Atheism and the First Amendment

One final requirement of conducting a discourse analysis is the specification of the 'field' in which you intend to study. This sort of boundary-marking works to ensure we do not over-extend our reach, and in that way, produce an examination so broad that the point of doing it becomes incomprehensible. Additionally, as discourse analysis essentially means that anything – so long as language usage is involved – is accessible as a discursive field, then setting the scene, so to speak, keeps our discussion within a set of practical restrictions.

The discursive field presented herein is exemplified by seven United States Supreme Court case decisions, spanning from 1948 to 2014.

- *McCollum v. Board of Education of School District 71* (1948)
- *Torcaso v. Watkins* (1961)
- *Abington School District v. Schempp* (*Murray v. Curlett*) (1963)
- *Welsh v. United States* (1970)
- *Elk Grove v. Newdow* (2004)
- *Hein v. Freedom from Religion Foundation* (2007)
- *Town of Greece v. Galloway* (2014)

American Atheists have played a significant role in each of these decisions, acting as either plaintiffs or defendants, appellants or appellees. For those unfamiliar with these distinctions, I will explain them in detail later.

With respect to their discursive affiliation with one another, it should be noted that they share a few content-based similarities. First, aside from quotes taken from testimonies or briefs submitted to the Court for further details, each is written in a third-person narrative voice, which means the discourse itself will be presented by an external description, rather than by individuals describing themselves. Second, each decision deals with the *Establishment Clause*, the first of the two religion clauses of the First Amendment to the United States Constitution – the other being the *Free Exercise Clause.* What that means, and why it is important, will be better explained in the following two chapters. And third, these decisions, as well as the discourse that they collectively define, offer us two essential insights.

The first, of course, deals with American Atheism. Each of these decisions offers a unique look at that concept, particularly because they each deal with singular American Atheists, who are themselves dealing with constitutional issues, at singular times. In this way, they also offer us the chance to see how the Atheism of each individual (or group of individuals), defined by their interactions with the individual or group against whom/which they have filed suit – as well as the Court – might act as an exceptional representative for American Atheism at a certain time. Thus, in reading these descriptions, in context, we are additionally provided the opportunity to better understand, discursively, the elements that have contributed to the larger judicial description of American Atheism.

Second, because these decisions each represent instances of perceived Establishment Clause violations, and because these perceived violations involve American Atheists, they also offer us the opportunity to see how these same Atheists have influenced, and continue to influence, the larger judicial description of American religion. That is, because each of these decisions involve the Supreme Court considering constitutional questions that pertain to issues of religious establishment, and because Supreme Court decisions become the 'law of the land,' the repercussions that stem from them are felt on a federal level. So that, when a Supreme Court decision is announced wherein the Court has ruled in favor of the First Amendment rights of an American Atheist, and in that way placed restrictions on the religious practices of the individual or group against whom/which they have filed suit, that Atheist has, through the Court, changed the very character of the American religious landscape.

I will devote a good deal more to this discussion in Part Three.

For now, however, I will turn here toward the more historical foundation of this book's discussion, in two parts. The first will provide the necessary story of America's genesis, and the second will do the same for the Supreme Court, detailing how it was designed, how it functions, and how its decisions have altered the discourse of religion in America.

Notes

1 See Ethan G. Quillen, 'Discourse Analysis and the Definition of Atheism' (*Science, Religion, and Culture*, Vol. 2, Issue 3, 2015).
2 Michael Buckley, *At the Origins of Modern Atheism* (New Haven: Yale University Press, 1987), 2–3.
3 Stephen Bullivant, *The Salvation of Atheists and Catholic Dogmatic Theology* (Oxford: Oxford University Press, 2012), 16.
4 The Nonreligion and Secularity Research Network's Glossary of terms, accessible at: http://nonreligionandsecularity.files.wordpress.com/2011/11/nsrn-glossary-28-aprl-2011-lois-lee1.pdf (accessed 7 July 2014).
5 See Robert D. Baird, *Category Formation and the History of Religions* (Paris: Mouton & Co., 1971).
6 Gavin Hyman, *A Short History of Atheism* (London: I.B. Tauris, 2010), xviii.
7 Francis Aveling, 'Atheism' in *The Catholic Encyclopedia*, Volume 2 (New York: Robert Appleton Company, 1907).
8 Michael Martin, 'Introduction' in Michael Martin, ed., *The Cambridge Companion to Atheism* (Cambridge: Cambridge University Press, 2007), 2.
9 Antony Flew, *The Presumption of Atheism & Other Philosophical Essays on God, Freedom and Immortality* (New York: Barnes and Noble Press, 1976), 13–14.
10 See George H. Smith, 'The Scope of Atheism' in George H. Smith, *Atheism: The Case Against God* (New York: Prometheus Books, 1989).
11 See Julian Baggini, *Atheism: A Very Short Introduction* (Oxford: Oxford University Press, 2003), 8.
12 Teun A. van Dijk, 'The Study of Discourse' in Teun A. van Dijk, ed. *Discourse Studies: A Multidisciplinary Introduction*, Volume 1 (London: Sage, 1997).
13 Brian Paltridge, *Discourse Analysis: An Introduction* (London: Continuum, 2006).
14 Adam Jaworski and Nikolas Coupland, 'Introduction: Perspectives on Discourse Analysis' in Adam Jaworski and Nikolas Coupland, eds., *The Discourse Reader*, Second Edition (New York: Routledge, 2006).
15 Kocku von Stuckrad, 'Discursive Study of Religion: Approaches, Definitions, Implications' (*Method and Theory in the Study of Religion*, Vol. 25, No. 1, 2013), 12.

Bibliography

Francis Aveling, 'Atheism' in *The Catholic Encyclopedia*, Volume 2 (New York: Robert Appleton Company, 1907).

Julian Baggini, *Atheism: A Very Short Introduction* (Oxford: Oxford University Press, 2003).

Robert D. Baird, *Category Formation and the History of Religions* (Paris: Mouton & Co., 1971).

Michael Buckley, *At the Origins of Modern Atheism* (New Haven: Yale University Press, 1987).

Stephen Bullivant, *The Salvation of Atheists and Catholic Dogmatic Theology* (Oxford: Oxford University Press, 2012).

Antony Flew, *The Presumption of Atheism & Other Philosophical Essays on God, Freedom and Immortality* (New York: Barnes and Noble Press, 1976).

Gavin Hyman, *A Short History of Atheism* (London: I.B. Tauris, 2010).

Adam Jaworski and Nikolas Coupland, 'Introduction: Perspectives on Discourse Analysis' in Adam Jaworski and Nikolas Coupland, eds., *The Discourse Reader*, Second Edition (New York: Routledge, 2006).

Michael Martin, 'Introduction' in Michael Martin, ed., *The Cambridge Companion to Atheism* (Cambridge: Cambridge University Press, 2007).

The Nonreligion and Secularity Research Network's Glossary of terms, accessible at: http://nonreligionandsecularity.files.wordpress.com/2011/11/nsrn-glossary-28-aprl-2011-lois-lee1.pdf (accessed 7 July 2014).

Brian Paltridge, *Discourse Analysis: An Introduction* (London: Continuum, 2006).

Ethan G. Quillen, 'Discourse Analysis and the Definition of Atheism' (*Science, Religion, and Culture*, Vol. 2, Iss. 3, 2015).

George H. Smith, *Atheism: The Case Against God* (New York: Prometheus Books, 1989).

Teun A. van Dijk, 'The Study of Discourse' in Teun A. van Dijk, ed., *Discourse Studies: A Multidisciplinary Introduction*, Volume 1 (London: Sage, 1997).

Kocku von Stuckrad, 'Discursive Study of Religion: Approaches, Definitions, Implications' (*Method and Theory in the Study of Religion*, Vol. 25, No. 1, 2013).

2 The story of America

A government of our own is our natural right: And when a man seriously reflects on the precariousness of human affairs, he will become convinced, that it is infinitely wiser and safer, to form a constitution of our own in a cool deliberate manner, while we have it in our power, than to trust such an interesting event to time and chance. [. . .] Should the government of America return again into the hands of Britain, the tottering situation of things, will be a temptation for some desperate adventurer to try his fortune; and in such a case, what relief can Britain give? Ere she could hear the news, the fatal business might be done; and ourselves suffering like the wretched Britons under the oppression of the Conqueror. Ye that oppose independence now, ye know not what ye do; ye are opening a door to eternal tyranny, by keeping vacant the seat of government. There are thousands, and tens of thousands, who would think it glorious to expel from the continent, that barbarous and hellish power, which hath stirred up the Indians and Negroes to destroy us, the cruelty hath a double guilt, it is dealing brutally by us, and treacherously by them.

— Thomas Paine, *Common Sense*, 1776

The complexities of the First Amendment

America is exceptional because of the First Amendment to the United States Constitution.

More specifically, though, America is exceptional because of the first sixteen words of the First Amendment. Yes, the freedom of speech, of the press, of the people to peaceably assemble, and the right to petition the government for a redress of grievances, are all essential safeguards of liberty, but it's the two religion clauses that stand out as especially profound:

> *Congress shall make no law respecting an establishment of religion, or prohibiting the free exercise thereof.*

In these two clauses, the American experiment broke ground where no other government body had before. When first drafted, these sixteen words conveyed the idea that not only would the United States be free from an established religion, it would likewise become a place open to all religions; a federal government, representative of the people elected to run it, that would ensure each and every American citizen the right to freely exercise their religious beliefs, exclusive of governmental endorsement.

And yet, while the rights and protections of the First Amendment were meant to promote, and have promoted, such an environment, the business of applying them has been less than simple.

For instance, we might consider these questions: what is meant by 'free exercise?' Does this mean any and all religious beliefs and practices? What about female circumcision, animal sacrifice, plural marriage? What about arranged marriages to, and between, minors? If these sorts of rituals are protected by the Free Exercise Clause of the First Amendment, are they likewise endorsed by the Constitution? Do they contribute to a definition of 'American religion,' or do we regulate such rituals in consideration of the larger political, ethical, or moral standards against which they compete? And if so, how?

Or, we might also ask: what does 'an establishment' mean? Does a disestablishment of religion mean a secular government, or a secular country? Does it promote an a-religious government, or a non-religious government? And what about the differences between a federal disestablishment and a state-to-state one? Are state constitutions that support or promote certain religious beliefs overruled by the United States Constitution? Moreover, how does the U.S. Government enact and uphold this separation between 'church' and 'state'? In other words, how does it safeguard each from each, so that the government is protected from the people's religious beliefs, and the people's religious beliefs are protected from the government?

It is the job of the Supreme Court, and in a larger way, the American Judiciary as a whole, to answer these questions. Which means that it holds the singular and unique power of dictating and determining the larger meaning of 'American religion' by means of the protections and limitations that it administers via its judicial review. For the sake of better understanding that concept, then, its case decisions with respect to the constitutional rights and privileges of the American people, and thus the discourse that these decisions collectively create, become the perfect apparatus with which to do this.

And it works the same with American Atheism.

For these reasons, and before fully delving into this discourse, it is important to understand how the Judiciary came to hold this power. In other words: how it came to exist, how it functions, and what it does.

The Judicial Branch of the United States Government was created by the Constitution, and since a constitution is, in essence, a government's founding document, it is itself derived from a number of catalysts and antecedents. In this way, the story of the American Judiciary is inherently bound to the story of the Constitution, a document built on a history of war and taxes and revolution, of altering and abolishing destructive governments, of declaring independence, and allying free and independent states into a nation of its own.

This chapter will tell that story.

The story of America

When Abraham Lincoln gave his First Inaugural Address on March 4th, 1861, the'union' of the United States was facing a terminal crisis. Shortly after his election in November of 1860, and between December and February, seven states (South Carolina, Mississippi, Florida, Alabama, Georgia, Louisiana, and Texas) seceded and formed their own government: the Confederate States of America. Arguing that such a secession and government was constitutionally illegal, and thus void, Lincoln directed his address toward those states specifically, declaring that, regardless of their perceived separation, the union remained 'unbroken.'

As part of his argument, he provided a description of that union through a brief recounting of America's origin story, made manifest through four documents:

> Descending from these general principles, we find the proposition that, in legal contemplation, the Union is perpetual, confirmed by the history of the Union itself. The Union is much older than the Constitution. It was formed in fact, by the Articles of Association in 1774. It was matured and continued by the Declaration of Independence in 1776. It was further matured and the faith of all the then thirteen States expressly plighted and engaged that it should be perpetual, by the Articles of Confederation in 1778. And finally, in 1787, one of the declared objects for ordaining and establishing the Constitution, was 'to form a more perfect union.'[1]

These four documents mark narrative points within the genesis of the United States, indicating moments when the American 'founding fathers' put into words their grievances against their King, their justifications for independence, their first unionization of each independent state into a cohesive whole, and their own notions of good government. I will use them here, just as Lincoln did, in order to tell the story of that genesis.

The Continental Association

The Continental Association (also known as the Articles of Association) was, in all ways but name, a boycott: a non-importation, non-consumption, and non-exportation of British goods in the colonies. Drafted by the First Continental Congress in October 1774, it was one of three measures adopted in response to the 'Intolerable Acts,' a series of retributive laws passed earlier that year by Parliament as punishment for the Boston Tea Party. And while it was the first declaratory document drafted by a congressional gathering of colonial representatives, and in that way signaled an early shift toward complete independence, it was predominately a statement about unfair taxation, and a unionized protest over a lack of parliamentary representation in regard to that taxation. It would be inaccurate, then, to assert here that it arose simply out of colonial antagonism toward just the Intolerable Acts. In fact, to really understand how this first of America's four founding documents came to be, it is essential to understand the impetus for drafting it in the first place. The origins of this reach back to the Seven Years War, a global conflict that in the North American colonies was known colloquially as the 'French and Indian War.'

Between 1754 and 1763, Great Britain and France battled each other along the colonial frontier, fighting for control of the Ohio River Valley, as well as the point where the Allegheny and Monongahela rivers met, at what would become Pittsburgh, Pennsylvania. And these battles were fought, in short, over land disputes, the French fearing the growing size of the British colonies, as well as their monopoly on trade with the native tribes in the area. At times brutal and violent, echoing in many ways the conflicts erupting between Austria and Prussia in Europe, the war ended with the Battle of Signal Hill in 1762. Militarily, Britain was victorious, and gained in the process territory far beyond their previous colonial borders, land that extended east to the Mississippi River, as well as south to Florida, and north to the Great Lakes region. What it also gained was debt. Lots of debt: from roughly 75 million pounds in 1754 to 130 million in 1764.

Parliament's answer to settling this debt came in the form of an indirect tax on the British colonies, a Sugar Act designed to raise revenue by levying a duty on white or clayed sugars, foreign indigo, foreign coffee, wine from Madeira, Spain, or Portugal (but not France), and cloths and fabrics from Persia, China, or East India. It also dictated that lumber, which could only be exported to Great Britain, would require a bond payment made to a customs official before exportation.

But the Sugar Act had a second benefit on top of just subduing colonial debt. It also acted as a means to fund the necessary defense and protection of post-war America:

> Whereas it is expedient that new provisions and regulations should be established for improving the revenue of this kingdom, and for extending and securing the navigation and commerce between Great Britain and your Majesty's dominions in America, which, by the peace, have been so happily enlarged: and whereas it is just and necessary, that a revenue be raised, in your Majesty's said dominions in America, for defraying the expences of defending, protecting, and securing the same; we, your Majesty's most dutiful and loyal subjects, the commons of Great Britain, in parliament assembled, being desirous to make some provision, in this present session of parliament, towards raising the said revenue in America, have resolved to give and grant unto your Majesty the several rates and duties herein after-mentioned.[2]

The colonial response to the Sugar Act was not as Parliament had hoped. Instead of raising revenue, it instead stoked a growing spirit of revolution, driven by the notion that taxation, without proper representation, was oppression. After all, colonial Americans were British citizens, expected to pay their proper due in taxes, but they were not permitted to discuss, or voice opposition to, either the amount that they were taxed, or their government's usage of those taxes.

Nevertheless, the taxation continued.

In September of 1764 Parliament passed the Currency Act, which restricted the colonies from issuing paper money, and in March of 1765 it passed the Stamp Act, a duty perceived as the most egregious taxation imposed on colonial America up to that time.[3]

The Stamp Act required a levy paid for every use of paper, parchment, or vellum in the colonies, essentially placing a direct tax on everything from legal documents to playing cards, again in the name of building revenue, and 'defraying the expences' of defending, protecting, and securing British America. The Americans were enraged, and their response was totally unprecedented. For the first time in its history, elected delegates from nine colonies (Massachusetts, Rhode Island, Connecticut, New York, New Jersey, Pennsylvania, Delaware, Maryland, and South Carolina) gathered, illegally, in a Stamp Act Congress that convened in New York City from October 7th to October 25th, 1765. They met to draft a document – the Declaration of Rights and Grievances – that would, among other things, declare to their King that as Englishmen, regardless of their being born abroad, they deserved the same rights and privileges as their fellow countrymen in Britain. This was especially true when it came to unfair taxation, particularly when that taxation was imposed upon a people not permitted representation in the Parliament that demanded it.

The Stamp Act was eventually repealed, but it was replaced immediately by the Declaratory Act, which stated that Parliament held absolute legislative powers over colonial America. And then, between 1767 and 1768, Parliament passed the five Townshend Acts: the Revenue Act (1767), the Indemnity Act (1767), the Commissioners of Customs Act (1767), the New York Restraining Act (1767), and the Vice Admiralty Court Act (1768). While the Indemnity, New York Restraining, and Vice Admiralty Court Acts were all met with colonial antagonism, the Revenue and Commissioners of Customs Acts were perhaps the more hated of the five. The former was an amended form of the Stamp Act, an indirect, rather than direct, tax on goods like paper, paint, lead, glass, and tea sent to the colonies from Britain. And the latter set up an American Board of Customs Commissioners to oversee the collection of these taxes, which the colonists saw as nothing more than a legal form of piracy, as commissioners were granted the right to seize possession of any items they deemed 'illegal.'

By 1768, civil unrest in Boston, colonial America's leading port, and thus the location of the American Board of Customs Commissioners, had begun to drastically rise. In response, thousands of British troops were dispatched, and Boston soon became an occupied city.

Four crucial events followed that set the stage for the First Continental Congress: the Boston Massacre on March 5th, 1770; the passing of the Tea Act on May 10th, 1773; the Boston Tea Party on December 16th, 1773; and the passing of the Intolerable Acts from March 31st to June 2nd, 1774.

The fourth, called the Coercive Acts in Britain, were so named by the American colonists because they represented a list of intolerable molestations of their natural human rights. Beginning with the Boston Port Act on March 31st, the British government closed the Port of Boston until the colonists paid for the damage done by the Boston Tea Party, promising to reopen it only after King George III felt order had been restored. Next came the Massachusetts Government Act on May 20th, which altogether removed the Massachusetts Charter, giving the legislative rule of the colony to Parliament as a whole. This meant that only the British Governor, Parliament, or the King was allowed to appoint any lower government positions. On that same day came the Administration of Justice Act, which stated that, because royal officials accused of transgressions within the colony felt they would not receive a fair one in Massachusetts, they were granted leave to go elsewhere to stand trial. This also meant that any colonial witnesses testifying against them would, of course, need to travel to the court of the royal official's choosing, at their own expense. Finally, there was the Quartering Act on June 2nd. This act broadened the requirement that every American colony, as British property, was obliged to quarter soldiers for the benefit of their own defense, declaring that if those soldiers felt their accommodations were not sufficient, improved ones would need to be provided. So hated by the colonists, it in fact became the impetus for the Third Amendment to the U.S. Constitution, which would eventually prohibit such non-consensual accommodation.

America's response was even more unprecedented than its reaction to the Stamp Act.

From September 5th to October 26th, 1774, fifty-six delegates, from twelve of the thirteen colonies, including such notable men as John Adams, Samuel Adams, John Jay, George Washington, Patrick Henry, and Richard Henry Lee, convened at Carpenter's Hall in Philadelphia to address these matters. Along with the Continental Association, they also drafted a Declaration and Resolves and a Petition to the King. The first, also known as the Declaration of Rights, itemized a detailed list of grievances and objections to the Intolerable Acts, many of which repeated the 'rights and grievances' declared by the Stamp Act Congress, that would act as precursors to the assertions made in the Declaration of Independence:

- That as inhabitants of the English colonies in North America, and as the descendants of English-born settlers, they neither 'forfeited, surrendered, nor lost' any of the rights first bestowed on those ancestors, so that they too were entitled to the 'exercise and enjoyment of all such of them, as their local and other circumstances enable them to exercise and enjoy';

- That they were likewise entitled to 'life, liberty, and property,' having never ceded such rights to any sovereign power without consent;
- That they maintained as well the right 'peaceably to assemble, consider of their grievances, and Petition the King';
- And that in consideration of these entitlements they were justified the right of legislative representation.[4]

This final decree epitomized the heart of colonial protestation, that 'taxation without representation' was above all things the catalyst for convening the First Continental Congress in the first place:

> That the foundation of English Liberty, and of all free Government, is a right in the people to participate in their Legislative Council: and as the English Colonists are not represented, and from their local and other circumstances cannot be properly represented in the British Parliament, they are entitled to a free and exclusive power of legislation in their several Provincial Legislatures, where their right of Representation can alone be preserved, in all cases of taxation and internal polity, subject only to the negative of their Sovereign, in such manner as has been heretofore used and accustomed.

In the hope that Parliament, as well as King George III, would be receptive to their declarations, and in order to renew a 'happy and prosperous relationship' with their mother country, they likewise drafted and approved the Continental Association, concluding:

> To obtain redress of these Grievances, which threaten destruction to the Lives, Liberty, and Property of his Majesty's subjects in North America, we are of opinion that a Non-Importation, Non-Consumption, and Non-Exportation Agreement, faithfully adhered to, will prove the most speedy, effectual, and peaceable measure.[5]

This was the first step in forming an autonomous United States, and as a unionized boycott, it signified an early coalition of British citizens drawn together toward the common goal of independence.

The Declaration of Independence

In October of 1774, roughly three weeks prior to the adjournment of the First Continental Congress, members of the recently dissolved provincial assembly in Salem, re-assembled in Concord as the Massachusetts Provincial Congress. Presided over by John Hancock, it became the de facto government of the Massachusetts colony, levying its own taxes, passing legislation, and, most importantly, organizing and supplying a militia. In response, Britain declared Massachusetts as being in an open state of rebellion.

In April 1775, the royal Governor of Massachusetts, Thomas Gage, was ordered to seek out and disarm all organized militias, and on April 19th he sent roughly 700 infantrymen, led by Lieutenant Colonel Francis Smith, toward Concord in order to seize a large cache of military ordnance. During the night of April 18th, Paul Revere and William Dawes rode from Boston to Lexington, just east of Concord, to warn of the assault, so that when the British troops arrived there at sunrise, they were met by armed militiamen. In the tense confusion that followed, a skirmish broke out. The ensuing battles at both Lexington and Concord – the latter receiving the same warning the night before from Samuel Prescott – ended with a tactical British retreat to Boston, and the subsequent siege of the city by a now organized militia force. The Revolutionary War had begun.

Less than a month later, the Second Continental Congress convened in Philadelphia, on May 10th, 1775.

Notable new additions to the delegates in attendance were Benjamin Franklin of Pennsylvania, Thomas Jefferson of Virginia, and John Hancock of Massachusetts, who was elected president on May 24th, 1775. All thirteen colonies sent representatives, with Georgia's delegation arriving last on July 20th.

The immediate concern of the Second Continental Congress was the Revolutionary War. On June 14th, it combined the militias of each colony into a Continental Army, and unanimously elected George Washington as Commander-in-Chief the next day. It also appointed an Ambassador, Silas Deane, who was tasked with petitioning France for aid. In order to further finance the war, it authorized the printing of a currency, colloquially called 'continentals,' that later proved to be quite limited in their monetary value.

Many of the delegates, particularly those from Massachusetts, clashed openly with one another in regard to how they might resolve the War via negotiations with George III, especially after the Battle of Bunker Hill on June 17th, 1775. John Dickinson of Pennsylvania advocated for a peace agreement, and on July 5th, Congress approved and sent his Olive Branch Petition to the King, in which he repeated the charge that, though it had taken up arms to defend itself, colonial America was not, in fact, dedicated to the notion of independence. Rather, he reiterated, it merely sought parliamentary representation. George III's response, in a written declaration on August 23rd, and in an official announcement 'from the throne' on October 27th, dashed any hopes for a peaceful resolution. In the latter he proclaimed:

> The rebellious war now levied is become more general, and is manifestly carried on for the purpose of establishing an independent empire. I need not dwell upon the fatal effects of the success of such a plan. The object is too important, the spirit of the British nation too high, the resources with which God hath blessed her too numerous, to give up so many colonies which she has planted with great industry, nursed with great tenderness, encouraged with many commercial advantages, and protected and defended at much expence of blood and treasure. [. . .] When the unhappy and deluded multitude, against whom this force will be directed, shall become sensible of their error, I shall be ready to receive the misled with tenderness and mercy.[6]

Congress voted for independence eight months later.

The vote for independence itself was actually a vote for the passing of the Lee Resolution, three articles proposed by Richard Henry Lee on June 7th, 1776:

> Resolved, That these United Colonies are, and of right ought to be, free and independent States, that they are absolved from all allegiance to the British Crown, and that all political connection between them and the State of Great Britain is, and ought to be, totally dissolved.

> That it is expedient forthwith to take the most effectual measures for forming foreign Alliances.
>
> That a plan of confederation be prepared and transmitted to the respective Colonies for their consideration and approbation.[7]

The motion to pass was seconded by John Adams, and the Congress as a whole immediately began debating. On Monday, June 10th, the vote was postponed for three weeks, during which time a committee of five was established to prepare a declaratory document, if the vote indeed passed. That committee consisted of John Adams, Benjamin Franklin, Thomas Jefferson, Roger Sherman, and Robert Livingston. Two other committees were likewise created to address the other two articles of the Lee Resolution, one for drafting a Model Treaty to be used in forming foreign alliances, and the other to draft a constitution, which would become the Articles of Confederation.

Of the five members of the committee to draft the Declaration of Independence, Thomas Jefferson was chosen as its chief architect, even though John Adams had previously presented a 'preamble' to support the move toward independence, which the Congress passed on May 15th, 1776. Jefferson delivered his draft for consideration on June 28th. He titled it: 'A Declaration by the Representatives of the United States of America, in General Congress assembled.' On July 2nd, the Congress voted to pass the Lee Resolution, with twelve colonies in favor. New York, not having the approval of its state legislature, abstained from voting. Two days later, Congress voted to approve the final version of Jefferson's draft, which, after the New York delegation passed its vote in favor on July 19th, was given the official title: The unanimous Declaration of the Thirteen United States of America.

The American colonies were now the United States.

As a founding document, the Declaration of Independence was essential in establishing the central creed of the United States, of declaring not just independence, but the ideologies that would form the basis of the American experiment. These are summed up, perhaps best, by this sentence:

> We hold these truths to be self-evident, that all men are created equal, that they are endowed by their Creator with certain unalienable Rights, that among these are Life, Liberty and the pursuit of Happiness.[8]

But the Declaration was limited to only that objective. While it declared the rights and privileges that ought to be bestowed upon the newly United States, it did not dictate how those rights and privileges might be applied. It did, however, state the following with respect to breaking allegiances with its mother country:

> That to secure these rights, Governments are instituted among Men, deriving their just powers from the consent of the governed, That whenever any Form of Government becomes destructive of these ends, it is the Right of the People to alter or to abolish it, and to institute new Government, laying its foundation on such principles and organizing its powers in such form, as to them shall seem most likely to effect their Safety and Happiness.

That, the Congress did, with the Articles of Confederation.

The Articles of Confederation

Like the Declaration of Independence, the Articles of Confederation was the result of a committee, in this instance a committee of thirteen representatives, overseen by John Dickinson. A first draft was presented to Congress on July 12th, 1776, a final draft approved for ratification was delivered on November 15th, 1777, and once fully ratified on February 2nd, 1781, it functioned as the governing document of the United States until the Constitution replaced it on March 14th, 1789.

In contrast to that later Constitution, it was quite simple. The body of the document consisted of a preamble, thirteen articles, and a concluding statement. And because it was designed initially as an agreement between the states, particularly relative to binding them into a 'league of friendship' during the Revolutionary War, the articles themselves were limited to that intention. Seven of them declared explicit assertions about the states themselves: from ensuring they retain their 'sovereignty, freedom, and independence' (Article Two), to defining the union between them as a protective barrier against external forces (Article Three); establishing a right to travel and a system of extradition between them (Article Four); detailing restrictions on their rights of communicating or allying with, and accepting gifts, offices, or titles from, any King, Prince, or State (Article Six); permissions for appointing military officers (Article Seven); determining the amount of expenses paid out to each of them for the sake of 'common defense' and 'general welfare' from a common treasury (Article Eight); and determining that not only would the states be required to 'inviolably observe' each of the Articles, but that the document as a whole could only be amended if every state voted for ratification (Article Thirteen).[9]

Of the Articles that defined the powers and restrictions of Congress, which included details concerning the manner with which delegates would be chosen, how many delegates each state would be allowed, delegate term limits, and the number of votes each delegation would receive (Article Five), as well as the powers and permissions allowed by the Committee of the States, which would meet during times of recess (Article Ten), and a reaffirmation that the war debt accrued by Congress prior to its adoption would be accepted by the states as a whole (Article 12), Article Nine was the most complex.

Here is where the document described both the authority held by Congress, as well as how it functioned in relation to that authority. Congress was given the 'sole and exclusive right and power of determining on peace and war,' including the right of sending and receiving ambassadors, entering into treaties and alliances, establishing rules about the legality of seizing both land and sea property, granting letters of marque, and appointing courts for trying pirates and felons. It would also be the 'last resort on appeal in all disputes and differences now subsisting or that hereafter may arise between two or more States concerning boundary, jurisdiction or any other causes whatever,' as well as being granted the 'sole and exclusive right' of 'regulating the alloy and value of coin struck by their own authority,' fixing the standards of weights and measures of the same, regulating trade and 'managing all affairs with the Indians,' creating and regulating the Post Offices from state to state, appointing officers above the rank of Colonel in both land and naval forces, and appointing a committee of the states to sit in recess of Congress consisting of one delegate from each state. In addition to these, it was also required to keep and publish a journal of the proceedings and votes within each session, excepting those discussions that required secrecy, and submit these publications to the individual state legislatures. With respect to the overall authority that it had in enacting any of these rights and powers it was nevertheless restricted by the larger statewide authority granted by the union itself, as it could not engage in war, grant letters of marque or reprisal (in times of peace), enter into treaties or alliances, coin and regulate the value of money, determine the 'sums and expenses necessary for the defense and welfare of the United States,' emit bills, borrow or appropriate capital, build or purchase vessels of war, raise land or sea forces, or appoint a commander in chief, unless 'nine States assent[ed] to the same,' via a majority vote.

As such, while these Articles granted the Congress – which transitioned from the First Continental Congress to the Congress of the Confederation on March 1st, 1781 – certain governmental rights and powers, it still neither produced, nor supported, a strong federal government. Which meant that there was no president, no Judiciary, and more importantly, no notion of a federal tax system.

This last restriction proved ironically to be its most damaging, as it meant that the new nation had no recourse for paying the debts it accrued during and after the Revolutionary War, beyond asking each individual state for financial assistance, or generating a means of building revenue beyond mere taxation.

One of these latter strategies came in the form of two land ordinances in 1785 and 1787. The first expedited the process by which the United States could sell the land west of the Appalachian Mountains, north of the Ohio River, and east of the Mississippi River. And the second created the Northwest Territory, which would eventually become the states of Ohio, Indiana, Illinois, Michigan, and Wisconsin. Neither of these, however, and with an additional sense of irony, generated the sort of revenue needed to support the new nation, especially as they merely expanded its size, and thus its need for even more income.

And then perhaps the best example of the nation's need for a stronger economy came in the form of Shay's Rebellion, an uprising in Massachusetts which lasted from August 1786 to June 1787, that shed significant light not only on the limitations of the Articles of Confederation, but on the necessity of a more stable government that could economically support it.

The United States Constitution

Though unsuccessful, Shay's Rebellion turned the minds of many political leaders, such as George Washington, toward the value of a centralized, federal government. And this sort of thinking manifested itself physically in a convention of twelve delegates from five states (New Jersey, New York, Pennsylvania, Delaware, and Virginia) between September 11th and 14th, 1786, at Mann's Tavern in Annapolis, Maryland. While the convention failed to achieve its goal of amending the Articles of Confederation, in large part due to a lack of complete representation, it did succeed in calling on Congress to consider holding a larger convention solely for that purpose.

That convention took place between May 14th and September 17th, 1787, at Independence Hall in Philadelphia.

Of the thirteen states in the Union only twelve sent delegations, with Rhode Island being the exception. Seventy-three delegates were appointed, but only fifty-five attended. And only thirty-nine signed the final document.

George Washington was unanimously elected President of the Convention on May 25th.

Almost immediately after it began, its original intention of discussing the necessary revisions to the Articles of Confederation shifted toward writing a new one. This was especially championed by two men: Alexander Hamilton of New York and James Madison of Virginia. And of the numerous issues discussed in this process, much attention was given to the structure of the Senate, the abolition of slavery, and how the executive branch would be designed. Two major 'plans' were submitted for consideration: James Madison's 'Virginia Plan,' which argued for a bicameral congress in which two chambers would represent the population of the elected official's state, and William Paterson's 'New Jersey Plan,' which argued for a unicameral body, with one vote per state.

Four committees were organized across the proceedings, each contributing a major influence on the final document. From May 30th to June 13th, the Committee of the Whole collectively discussed and debated the proposals put forth by the different delegations, including the Virginia and New Jersey Plans. From July 2nd to July 16th, the Committee of Eleven, consisting of a delegate from each state (New Hampshire's delegation would arrive later), met to discuss compromises between the different plans, leading to Roger Sherman's 'Great Compromise' (also known as the Connecticut Compromise), that among other things argued for proportional representation in the House of Representatives based on state population, and equal state representation in the Senate. On July 24th the Committee of Detail, comprised of five elected delegates (John Rutledge of South Carolina, Edmund Randolph of Virginia, Nathaniel Gorham of Massachusetts, Oliver Ellsworth of Connecticut, and James Wilson of Pennsylvania) began the process of drafting a document that would reflect the proposals agreed upon up to that point, and the Convention recessed from July 26th to August 6th. The draft they submitted, which was discussed by the Committee of the Whole from August 6th to September 10th, consisted of a Preamble and twenty-three articles. On September 8th, the Convention appointed five delegates as the Committee of Style and Arrangement: Alexander Hamilton (New York), William Samuel Johnson (Connecticut), Rufus King (Massachusetts), James Madison (Virginia), and Gouverneur Morris (Pennsylvania). They were tasked with constructing a final draft, comprising an amended preamble and seven articles, which they presented on September 12th. This draft was agreed upon by the Convention as a whole, and signed collectively on September 17th.

Not all members of the Convention were satisfied with the final product, however. For example, as the New York delegation was largely against a strong federal government, it had already left the Convention prior to September 17th, so the only signature from that state was Alexander Hamilton, even though he was unable to vote.

Nevertheless, the Congress of the Confederation submitted the Constitution to the states for ratification on September 28th, 1787. Nine states were needed for ratification, which New Hampshire did on June 21st, 1788. The last state to ratify was Rhode Island on May 29th, 1790.

The seven articles of the Constitution provided the infrastructure of the American Government, and Articles One through Three detailed its three branches.

Article One established that:

> All legislative Powers herein granted shall be vested in a Congress of the United States, which shall consist of a Senate and House of Representatives.[10]

It further described how the members of that Congress were to be elected; the length of term they would serve, respectively (Senate: 6 years; Representatives: 2 years); the minimum age requirement for serving in either (Senate: 30; Representatives: 25); the number of Representatives permitted each state based on population; the powers given the Senate, particularly in terms of presidential impeachment; the process of proposing and passing bills for the purposes of raising revenue; the power and right of laying and collecting taxes in order to provide for the 'common defense and general welfare of the United States'; a number of limitations placed on Congress' power, including restrictions concerning the removal of habeas corpus and the granting of titles of nobility; and the limitations placed on the states to enter into a treaty or alliance with each other or a foreign state, instigate import and export taxes, create and keep an army, or enter into war with any entity, without Congress' consent.

Article Two established that:

> The executive Power shall be vested in a President of the United States of America.

It further described the term limitation of that President (four years); the process of appointing electors to the Electoral College; the process with which that College would elect the President and Vice President; that the President must be a 'natural born citizen'; that he must be of a minimum age (35); the process by which the powers and duties of the office would pass to the Vice President in the result of the President's death, resignation, or inability to perform; the compensation the President would receive and the restriction of his receiving any other compensation or 'Emolument' during his term; the oath he must take; his power as the Commander in Chief of the armed forces; his power to make treaties, to nominate and appoint Ambassadors, Public Ministers and Consuls, as well as Judges of the Supreme Court, all under the advice and consent of the Senate, which would need to confirm such nominations and appointments; his obligation to present to Congress a State of the Union Address; and the reasons for impeachment and removal of office, including treason, bribery, and other high crimes and misdemeanors.

Article Three established that:

> The judicial Power of the United States, shall be vested in one supreme Court, and in such inferior Courts as the Congress may from time to time ordain and establish.

It further described the power granted this Judicial Branch, which extended to all cases concerning American law and treaties made under its authority, including those dealing with Ambassadors and other Public Ministers and Consuls; admiralty and maritime jurisdictions; controversies involving both the United States, as well as the individual ones; between individual states and citizens of other states; between citizens of different states; between citizens of the same state; and between citizens of American states and foreign ones. It likewise determined that all trials were to be held within the state where the crime was committed, and that these trials would be heard by a jury. And last, Article Three defined treason as the act of levying war against the United States, or giving aid and comfort to America's enemies, which could only be determined by the testimony of two witnesses.

Where Articles One through Three established the three branches of the American Government, Articles Four through Seven provided supplementary policies, determining many of the rules and restrictions applied by the Articles of Confederation, including the right to travel and extradition policies between states, the permissions and processes of making amendments to the Constitution, the acceptance by Congress of the national debt, and the process by which ratifications might be made. Importantly as well, not only did Article Six declare that 'no religious Test shall ever be required as a Qualification to any Office or public Trust under the United States,' it also defined the Constitution as the 'Supreme Law of the Land,' in essence establishing the stronger federal government missing within the Articles of Confederation. What this also dictated was that the laws defined by each individual state's constitution would not, going forward, be able to conflict with the laws of the United States as a whole:

> This Constitution, and the Laws of the United States which shall be made in Pursuance thereof; and all Treaties made, or which shall be made, under the Authority of the United States, shall be the supreme Law of the Land; and the Judges in every State shall be bound thereby, any Thing in the Constitution or Laws of any State to the Contrary notwithstanding.

The Constitution went into effect on March 4th, 1789, the same day that the Congress of the Confederation became the 1st United States Congress. This First Congress met in three sessions: from March 4th to September 29th, 1789; from January 4th to August 12th, 1790; and from December 6th, 1790 to March 3rd, 1791. George Washington was elected the first President of the United States, and John Adams Vice President, at the start of the first session on April 6th, 1789. The former was inaugurated and took the oath of office twenty-four days later at Federal Hall in New York City on April 30th.

Two important legislative acts, pertinent to the discourse presented herein, also took place during that first session. The first was the Judiciary Act, signed into law on September 24th, 1789. The Judiciary Act established the Federal Judiciary of the United States, as well as created the court system, including the Supreme Court, as determined by Article Three, Section One of the Constitution. More on this in the next chapter.

The second legislative act was the Bill of Rights, a collection of Constitutional amendments approved by a Congressional joint-resolution on September 25th, 1789, and later ratified on December 15th, 1791. This deserves some attention here.

Article Five of the Constitution described the process of proposing amendments as such:

> The Congress, whenever two thirds of both Houses shall deem it necessary, shall propose Amendments to this Constitution, or, on the Application of the Legislatures of two thirds of the several States, shall call a Convention for proposing Amendments, which, in either Case, shall be valid to all Intents and Purposes, as Part of this Constitution, when ratified by the Legislatures of three fourths of the several States, or by Conventions in three fourths thereof.

During the Constitutional Convention, and especially during the ratification period between December 1787 and July 1788, a schism had erupted between members of Congress who were critical of the Articles of Confederation's lack of a strong federal government – and thus in favor of creating one – and those who opposed such measures out of fear of governmental overreach, particularly in granting too much power to the Executive Branch. This division was determined on each side as 'Federalists' and 'Anti-Federalists,' respectively. The latter, such as George Mason of Virginia and Elbridge Gerry of Massachusetts, began calling for a Bill of Rights during the Convention, arguing that such an addition to the Constitution would act as a protector of individual rights. Federalists, such as James Madison and Alexander Hamilton, countered that the

Constitution itself was a Bill of Rights, and that an additional document would prove difficult to support. This debate spilled over into the state-by-state conventions that met to consider ratification, and the notion of a post-ratification addition of a Bill of Rights encouraged many of the votes in favor of doing so.

Occupied by a heavy majority of Federalist-leaning representatives, it was James Madison, once a staunch opponent of such amendments, who made the proposal to the House of Representatives on June 8th, 1789. Partly out of fear that the debate would eventually lead to a second Constitutional Convention, and a re-written Constitution, Madison's nine amendments were taken into consideration by an eleven-member House Select Committee, which enlarged them to twenty. On August 24th, the House of Representatives passed the committee's additions, which they condensed to seventeen. The Senate made its own changes, limiting the Amendments to twelve, which it passed on September 9th.

Given that these Amendments proved so contentious between the two Houses, a Conference Committee of both was convened on September 21st, leading to a joint-resolution of twelve Amendments that were sent to the states for ratification on September 25th. Of those, articles three through twelve were officially ratified when Vermont, having been accepted into the Union on March 4th, 1791, accepted them. These became the ten Amendments of the Bill of Rights.[11]

Many of these deal directly with issues expressed throughout the history of America's founding, including personal freedom rights directly attacked by Britain's Intolerable Acts, and limitations on what the government can and cannot declare concerning judicial actions. Perhaps most pertinent to my interests herein is of course the First Amendment:

> Congress shall make no law respecting an establishment of religion, or prohibiting the free exercise thereof; or abridging the freedom of speech, or of the press; or the right of the people peaceably to assemble, and to petition the Government for a redress of grievances.

As I argued above, it is this Amendment that makes America exceptional, especially considering its two religion clauses. And again, how those might be interpreted in regard to American Atheism is a question better answered via the Supreme Court's decisions on the matter, as it is that entity's duty to interpret and defend the Constitution, including the sometimes-controversial meaning understood in the language of the Bill of Rights. The following chapter will explore this.

One final note here before proceeding, however.

It should be observed that unlike the Declaration of Independence, the Constitution was a wholly secular document. That is, where in the former, Thomas Jefferson wrote eloquently – and with pragmatically vague language – of inalienable rights endowed by a 'creator,' and the separate and equal station to which the 'Laws of Nature' and 'Nature's God' entitled such rights, the latter was entirely void of such things. And aside from the prohibition of a 'religious test' in Article Six and the religion clauses of the First Amendment, it was an entirely a-religious document. Which meant that the government it created would be a-religious as well. How that levied even more responsibility onto the Judiciary in its capacity to define the role of religion in America is something I will discuss in more detail in the next chapter, where I will also introduce the Supreme Court, what it does, how it chooses the cases that it hears, how those cases are decided, and how those decisions – as law – act as a discourse with which we might better understand certain aspects of American religion, such as American Atheism.

Notes

1 Abraham Lincoln, *First Inaugural Address*, March 4th, 1861. http://avalon.law.yale.edu/19th_century/lincoln1.asp
2 The Sugar Act of 1764. http://avalon.law.yale.edu/18th_century/sugar_act_1764.asp.
3 The Stamp Act, March 22nd, 1765. http://avalon.law.yale.edu/18th_century/stamp_act_1765.asp.
4 Declaration and Resolves of the First Continental Congress, October 14th, 1774. http://avalon.law.yale.edu/18th_century/resolves.asp.
5 The Continental Association, October 20th, 1774. www.loc.gov/teachers/classroommaterials/presentationsandactivities/presentations/timeline/amrev/rebelln/assoc.html.
6 King George III, *Address to Parliament*, October 27th, 1775. www.loc.gov/teachers/classroommaterials/presentationsandactivities/presentations/timeline/amrev/shots/address.html.
7 Lee's Resolutions, June 7th, 1776. http://avalon.law.yale.edu/18th_century/lee.asp.
8 The Declaration of Independence, July 4th, 1776. www.archives.gov/founding-docs/declaration.
9 The Articles of Confederation, November 15th, 1777. www.ourdocuments.gov/doc.php?flash=false&doc=3.
10 The Constitution of the United States, September 17th, 1787. www.archives.gov/founding-docs/constitution.
11 The Bill of Rights, September 25th, 1789. www.archives.gov/founding-docs/bill-of-rights. See also, Amendments 11–27, February 7th, 1795–May 7th, 1992. www.archives.org/founding-docs/amendments-11-27.

Further reading

Sydney A. Ahlstrom, *A Religious History of the American People*, 2 volumes (New York: Image Books, 1975).
Eric Foner, *Give Me Liberty! An American History*, Volume 1 (New York: W. W. Norton & Company, 2011).
Robert Booth Fowler, et al. *Religion and Politics in America: Faith, Culture, and Strategic Choices* (Boulder: Westview Press, 2010).
Martin E. Marty, *Pilgrims in Their Own Land: 500 Years of Religion in America* (New York: Penguin Books, 1984).
David McCullough, *1776* (New York: Simon and Schuster, 2005).
Jon Meacham, *Thomas Jefferson: The Art of Power* (New York: Random House, 2011).
Sidney Wilfred Mintz, *Sweetness and Power: The Place of Sugar in Modern History* (New York: Penguin Books, 1986).
Gordon S. Wood, *The Radicalism of the American Revolution* (New York: A.A. Knopf, 1992).
Howard Zinn, *A People's History of the United States* (New York: Harper Collins, 1999).

3 The United States Supreme Court and American religion

> I opposed this bill from the beginning. It certainly is a vile law system, calculated for the expense and with a design to draw by degrees all law business into the Federal courts. The Constitution is meant to swallow all the State Constitutions by degrees, and thus to swallow, by degrees, all the State judiciaries. This, at least, is the design some gentlemen seem driving at. O sweet Candor, when wilt thou quit the cottage and the lisping infant's lips and shed thy glory round the statesman's head? Is it inscribed on human fate that man must grow wicked to seem wise; and must the path of politics be forever encumbered with briers and thorns?
>
> — William Maclay, United States Senator from Pennsylvania, Journal entry concerning the Judiciary Act, July 17th, 1789

The Supreme Court: what it is and what it does

The first notion of American judicial authority appeared in Article Nine of the Articles of Confederation:

> The United States in Congress assembled, shall have the sole and exclusive right and power of [. . .] appointing courts for the trial of piracies and felonies committed on the high seas and establishing courts for receiving and determining finally appeals in all cases of captures, provided that no member of Congress shall be appointed a judge of any of the said courts.[1]

Article Nine also determined that in regard to boundary issues between states, Congress would be the 'last resort on appeal in all disputes,' and was granted the authority of appointing, by joint consent between disputing states, 'commissioners or judges to constitute a court for hearing and determining the matter in question.'

With the Constitution, that judicial authority broadened to reflect the stronger federalized government that it created.

> The judicial Power shall extend to all Cases, in Law and Equity, arising under this Constitution, the Laws of the United States, and Treaties made, or which shall be made, under their Authority;
>
> - to all Cases affecting Ambassadors, other public Ministers and Consuls;
> - to all Cases of admiralty and maritime Jurisdiction;
> - to Controversies to which the United States shall be a Party;

- to Controversies between two or more States;
- between a State and Citizens of another State,
- between Citizens of different States,
- between Citizens of the same State claiming Lands under Grants of different States, and between a State, or the Citizens thereof, and foreign States, Citizens or Subjects.[2]

However, while the language of the Constitution determined the scope of the Supreme Court's authority, neither it nor the Articles of Confederation specifically defined what that court system would look like, how it might function, and what its role would be in defining American law.

These details were determined by the Judiciary Act of 1789.

Under the Judiciary Act, the original Supreme Court consisted of six Justices – a Chief Justice and five Associate Justices – so that a majority opinion, or 'quorum,' would be reached by an agreement of four. The inferior courts were then designated by a 'District' and 'Circuit' court system: the United States as a whole was divided into thirteen 'Districts,' which were overseen by a District Judge, and these districts were further divided into three Circuit Courts, the eastern, the middle, and the southern. In addition to these, three offices were created to oversee the judicial processes between the District, Circuit, and Supreme Courts: a United States Marshall appointed in each district, a United States Attorney for each district, and an Attorney-General, who would oversee the Judicial Branch as a whole, and advise the President and other department heads on questions of law.[3]

The contemporary Federal Judiciary maintains this three-level description, but with some significant changes.

The Supreme Court currently consists of nine Justices, with a single Chief Justice and eight Associates. Throughout the nineteenth century, the number of justices fluctuated from seven in 1807, to nine in 1837, ten in 1863, and eventually back to nine in 1869. In the early twentieth century, and in order to more expediently progress his 'New Deal' policies, President Franklin D. Roosevelt tried to 'pack' the court to fifteen, but that attempt failed.

Each Supreme Court Justice is nominated by the President, and then confirmed by a vote in the Senate. As set by the Constitution, they serve a life term unless they resign, retire, or are removed through impeachment. No Justice has ever been removed.

In its modern form, the Supreme Court itself is the final appellate tribunal in the United States, and maintains definitive jurisdiction over the Circuit Courts of Appeals, the District Courts, and all other inferior courts, including State Supreme Courts. Which means, in contrast to the District Court system, it does not hold its own trials, but instead bases its decisions solely on three things: the opinion of the Court immediately below it, past judicial precedence across the Judiciary as a whole, and 'briefs' submitted on behalf of the two parties involved, that consist of transcripts, notes, and arguments citing such precedence as reasoning for a favorable ruling.

Unlike the original intention for which the Judiciary Act of 1789 created it, the modern Circuit Court serves as the immediate federal appellate court beneath the Supreme Court. Which means of the three courts created by that Act, it has undergone the most changes. At its inception, the Circuit Court represented an intermediary between the District Courts and the Supreme Court, a three-person tribunal that consisted of one District judge from each district, and two Supreme Court Justices who traveled along designated 'circuits.' These 'circuit riders' would hear cases of both original jurisdiction (trial cases) as well as appeals based on District Court decisions. When the Judiciary Act of 1869 broadened the size of the Supreme Court to nine members, it likewise determined that each of the nine Circuit Courts would maintain a Circuit Judge, which alleviated much of the workload of the Supreme Court Justices 'riding circuit.'[4] Then, with the Judiciary Act of 1891 – also known as the Evarts Act – and alongside the creation of the United States Court of Appeals, all appellate cases passed from the Circuit Courts to this new Appeals Court system, which consisted of nine new courts, comprised of two District Judges and one Circuit Judge.[5] The final change came with the Judicial Code of 1911, which on January 1st, 1912 outright abolished the original Circuit Court system, transferring its trial jurisdiction down to the District level.[6] This reorganization ensured a more coordinated federal tribunal. The Court of Appeals then adopted the 'Circuit Court' title, and became the Circuit Courts of Appeals.

Appeals Court judges are appointed by the President, and undergo a confirmation by the Senate. Like Supreme Court Justices, they too maintain lifetime tenure. Each Court likewise has a Supreme Court Justice appointed to it as a 'Circuit Justice,' who acts as a final arbiter on issues such as stays of execution, as well as the granting or denying of numerous other 'writ' applications. Of the thirteen Appeals Courts in existence today, twelve are designated geographically by the District Courts over which they hold appellate jurisdiction. The thirteenth, the United States Court of Appeals for the Federal Circuit, is unique in that it instead hears cases based on subject-matter jurisdiction. As well, Appeals Courts vary in size based on their geographic location, which also dictates the number of appellate judgeships for each Court. For instance, the largest Appeals Court is the ninth, with twenty-nine judgeships who oversee most of the west coast, including the states of Montana, Idaho, Nevada, Arizona, California, Oregon, Washington, Alaska, and Hawaii, as well as the territories of Guam and the Northern Mariana Islands. The smallest is the first, with six judgeships who oversee the states of Maine, Massachusetts, New Hampshire, Rhode Island, and the territory of Puerto Rico. At the time of this writing, Justice Anthony Kennedy serves as the Circuit Justice for the former, and Justice Stephen Breyer for the latter.

As a whole, because they act as the immediate appellate Courts beneath the Supreme Court, and because the Supreme Court is quite selective in the cases that it chooses to hear, the Circuit Courts of Appeals maintain unique power in setting legal precedence and interpreting law for large parts of the United States. As such, the case decisions published by the Courts of Appeals can oftentimes be just as, or even sometimes are more, essential to interpreting American law, particularly concerning religion.

The process by which a case finds its way to the Supreme Court can be complex, and varies from case to case. Moreover, because the Supreme Court holds jurisdiction over appeals from both the federal and state court systems, the number that it receives for each term can range in the thousands. This excessive demand for judicial review proved most problematic during the nineteenth century as the country continued to expand westward, thus equally expanding the Court's workload. In 1925 Chief Justice and former President, William Howard Taft proposed to Congress an amendment to the United States Judicial Code that would alleviate this issue. Known colloquially as the 'Judges Bill,' the Judiciary Act of 1925 altered the requirement of the Court to hear all appeals cases, and granted it the right to choose, via a vote of four Justices, those appeals it felt applied questions directly to issues of federal concern.[7] Then, in 1988, a similar act was passed – the Supreme Court Cases Selections Act – that further amended the United

States Judicial Code to eliminate the same necessity in regard to State Court decisions sent to the Supreme Court on appeal.[8]

Part IV, Chapter 28, section 1254 of Title 28 of the United States Judicial Code now states:

> Cases in the courts of appeals may be reviewed by the Supreme Court by the following methods: (1) By writ of certiorari granted upon the petition of any party to any civil or criminal case, before or after rendition of judgment or decree; (2) By certification at any time by a court of appeals of any question of law in any civil or criminal case as to which instructions are desired, and upon such certification the Supreme Court may give binding instructions or require the entire record to be sent up for decision of the entire matter in controversy.

And section 1257 of the same, states:

> (a) Final judgments or decrees rendered by the highest court of a State in which a decision could be had, may be reviewed by the Supreme Court by writ of certiorari where the validity of a treaty or statute of the United States is drawn in question or where the validity of a statute of any State is drawn in question on the ground of its being repugnant to the Constitution, treaties, or laws of the United States, or where any title, right, privilege, or immunity is specially set up or claimed under the Constitution or the treaties or statutes of, or any commission held or authority exercised under, the United States.[8]

Almost every case that comes before the Supreme Court has been granted what is called a writ of certiorari. A Latin term that means 'to be more fully informed,' certiorari is the means by which the Court chooses the cases it offers judicial review, if it believes those cases reflect a question concerning federal or Constitutional law. As well, certiorari works as a type of court order, demanding that the lower court present the full record of the case that it intends to review.

When a petition for a writ of certiorari arrives at the Supreme Court it enters what is known as the 'Cert Pool.' Created in the early 1970s to further alleviate the heavy workload of the Justices, the Cert Pool is composed of 'clerks' – lawyers employed by the Justices themselves – whose job it is to read the case materials for each petition, draft a summary, and offer an opinion on the qualifications of the case for consideration. The Justices then meet in a 'conference' to discuss these petition summaries, and when four or more of them agree that a case merits review, the writ of certiorari is granted. If certiorari is denied, the case is sent back to either the Appeals Court or the highest State Court, and that decision is affirmed without review.

When a case is granted a writ of certiorari – roughly 1% of those that apply (around one hundred each year) – both parties involved, the petitioner who submitted the request ('appellant'), as well as the respondent ('appellee'), submit briefs. On occasion, parties external to the case itself, but who might offer 'relevant' or 'considerable help,' will submit their own briefs. These are known as 'amicus briefs,' or 'amici curiae,' Latin for 'friend of the court.' The case itself is then scheduled for Oral Review, which takes place during one of the Court's two-week sessions, each month, between October and April.

Advocates for both the petitioner and the respondent are given thirty minutes to argue their case before the Justices, the former going first.

At the end of each week in which oral arguments are made, the Justices confer privately to vote on case decisions, as well as on petitions for certiorari. One Justice is chosen, by the most senior Justice in the majority – when not the Chief Justice – to write the Court's opinion. A first draft of that opinion is circulated amongst the Justices in the majority, who offer amendments and suggestions. Additionally, as the draft opinion is circulated, Justices are permitted to change their personal ruling, which might alter the Court's opinion as a whole. Justices in both the majority and minority are also permitted to write their own concurring or dissenting opinions as supplementary arguments in favor or against the accepted one of the Court. In both instances, these secondary opinions exist *only* for further discussion, as neither carries the same legal weight.

Opinions are written as either affirmations or reversals of lower appellant, District, or state ones.

Once officially drafted and approved, opinions are disseminated to the public via four 'generations' of publication. Bench Opinions, which include the majority opinion, concurrences and dissents, as well as a prefatory syllabus, are provided to the public and the press on the morning in which they are announced. Slip Opinions are provided several days after the Bench Opinion, and often contain grammatical corrections. Preliminary Prints are more finalized versions of the Slip Opinions, but also include additional information, such as announcements, tables, indices, and other features that eventually become the final, bound volumes as dictated by Title 28, Section 411 of the United States Code: 'The decisions of the Supreme Court of the United States shall be printed, bound, and distributed in the preliminary prints and bound volumes of the United States Reports as soon as practicable after rendition.'

Once published, opinion titles are abbreviated and provided citation numbers. For example, the case decision, *People of the State of Illinois ex relatione Vashti McCollum v. Board of Education of School District No.71, Champaign County, Illinois, et al.* was shortened to *McCollum v. Board of Education*, and given the citation, 333 U.S. 203 (1948), which means the case was decided in 1948 and can be found on page 203 of the 333rd volume of the U.S. Report.

The complex nature of decisions on religion

Case decisions like *McCollum v. Board of Education* highlight the type of influence that the American Judiciary, and especially the Supreme Court, have on the broader definition of American religion. This is more explicitly articulated by the fact that decisions such as this one deal with *both* religion clauses of the First Amendment, even though the final decision focused on the Establishment Clause. Which makes them even more complex.

Consider, for example, how both Vashti McCollum and the Board of Education might equally have had constitutional standing.

> In order to promote the traditional value of a religiously educated American youth, the Board of Education of a town predominately populated by Christians of similar mainline protestant denominations offers religious education classes to children who attend public schools in its district. These classes consist of once-weekly, thirty to forty-five minute lessons taught by local clergy members neither employed by the School District, nor compensated for their time, within the children's regular classrooms during normal school hours. Students are not required to attend, and any

parent who does not wish their child to participate may, by written consent, excuse them from partaking. This process, known as 'released time,' provides parents and their children the opportunity to express their First Amendment right of religious Free Exercise, within a safe and inclusive environment.

Vashti McCollum, a taxpaying resident, parent, and Atheist, perceives the Board of Education's religious education policy as illegal for two reasons: though her son, James, is not required to attend, and though she is granted the right to have him excused, doing so makes him an outcast amongst his fellow students; and because these classes take place on school grounds, during school hours, and though the instructors are not compensated by the School District, the classes themselves are still utilizing school materials, which are paid for by taxpayers, such as herself. For these reasons, she believes that the classes, as well as the policy in general, represent a clear violation of the First Amendment's Establishment Clause.

It is the responsibility of the Supreme Court to consider these two sides, and then judge one more constitutionally lawful than the other. In this example, they chose McCollum's. But not every decision is this simple, as each case presents its own unique sets of questions and challenges. Which also means the Court must decide each case individually. And though the Justices often use previous decisions (past precedence) to shape new ones, each case is its own entity. This can sometimes lead to apparent contradictions, as many cases might outwardly 'look' the same. For example, consider the two decisions *Van Orden v. Perry* and *McCreary County v. ACLU*, which were announced on the same day, June 27th, 2005.

Both dealt with public displays of the Ten Commandments. In *Van Orden v. Perry*, the question before the Court asked: does a marble monument, placed on the grounds of the Texas State Capital in 1961, represent an unconstitutional violation of the Establishment Clause? And in *McCreary County v. ACLU*, the question was: does a state statute requiring the posting of the Ten Commandments in courthouses and public schools violate the Establishment Clause of the United States Constitution? While outwardly, these two cases seem analogous to each other, the details of each varied quite significantly. Which is why they were decided differently.

In *Van Orden*, the Court made the distinction that not only did the monument represent a symbolic veneration of the religious foundations on which the United States was built, it was also placed amongst other, secular, monuments in an area designated for such things, where it had stood for forty-four years. In *McCreary County*, the statute requiring the placement of the Ten Commandments was not only new, it was devised with the specific intent of promoting the religious ideologies inherent in the symbolic nature of the Ten Commandments themselves. Which is why, on the same day, and both with a 5–4 vote, the Court ruled that the monument in *Van Orden* was constitutionally permissible, while the placement of the Commandments in *McCreary County* was not.

These different rulings speak to the larger complexity innate to each decision, as well as the reality that though many of the questions brought before the Court might use similar words, they are in fact asking very different things. So that while it would be easy to simply disregard the nuanced distinctions between decisions like *Van Orden* and *McCreary County* as further proof of the Court's continuing equivocation about the relationship between church and state in America, especially with respect to its more conservative narrative in recent years (which I will discuss in detail later), to do so would be to erroneously overlook the fact that the Court is an organic entity. Justices come and go, which means the discourse that their decisions provide is always changing. This is additionally true because there is no set rubric or paradigm that might define its opinions on American religion. And though it has used a number of 'tests' to try to make this job easier, it has not always relied on only one manner of doing so.

But where this might seem like a disadvantage, I would argue that it actually provides the opposite.

From its first decision dealing with American religion in 1879, where it upheld a federal law prohibiting polygamy in *Reynolds v. United States*, to the examples cited above, the Court has undergone significant ideological changes with respect to that concept. Which means my use of its discourse across the seven decisions presented herein offers a broader insight than just that pertaining to American Atheism. It offers me the opportunity to also present to you a glimpse into how the Court's narrative has shifted alongside that of the American culture, which has undergone its own ideological progression since the late 1940s. In this way, and to repeat myself from the introduction, these case decisions will defend my larger argument that the study of American Atheism is, in fact, the study of American religion. But more on that later.

Conclusion and additional descriptions

The seven decisions presented herein span a distance of sixty-six years, from one century to the next.

They are, in chronological order:

- *McCollum v. Board of Education* (1948)
- *Torcaso v. Watkins* (1961)
- *Abington School District v. Schempp* (*Murray v. Curlett*) (1963)
- *Welsh v. United States* (1970)
- *Elk Grove v. Newdow* (2004)
- *Hein v. Freedom from Religion Foundation* (2007)
- *Town of Greece v. Galloway* (2014)

One decision (*Abington v. Schempp*) is the combination of two appeals concerning the same issue, which is similar to the decision in *Welsh v. United States*, which represents a continuation and augmentation of the decision in *United States v. Seeger* (1965). With the latter, I chose to only include the *Welsh* decision, as it more directly addresses the intent of this book. I made a similar decision in not including *Marsh v. Chambers* (1983), even though Earnest Chambers had been described as something akin to an 'Atheist,' as it was overruled, in part, by the decision in *Town of Greece v. Galloway*.

Each decision will be 'bookended' by two points of discussion: 'Background' and 'Importance.' I have placed the first prior to the decision's transcription in order to provide the relevant setting, characters, and history for each one. It should be noted here as well that these descriptions are not meant to persuade your opinion in respect of the Court's, but are merely there to benefit your broader understanding of the facts of each case. Supreme Court rulings can sometimes feel isolated from their roots, mostly because they act to 'overrule' all the events that led up to the Court's final word on the matter. And this can be problematic at times, as they are likewise packed-full with references to the lower Court decisions that led to that final ruling, as well as references to precedence set by similar or relatable case decisions. Knowing this background, or rather, the 'story' of each decision, is just as important as understanding the discourses that they create.

After each transcription I have also included a discussion of its 'importance.' In these sections I will discuss the significance that each decision has had on American Atheism, as well as its influence on American religion.

I will conclude here, then, with one final statement.

* * *

American Atheism and American religion are two concepts bound by a unique relationship, an exceptional affiliation forged by the First Amendment, so that the story of one is, inherently, the story of the other. So that while this might seem like a book devoted to the judicial discourse of American Atheism, it is also devoted to the ways in which that has altered the discourse of American religion. And as such, these seven decisions will act as guideposts along that intertwined story, acting much in the same way as the four founding documents described in the previous chapter, as discursive plot points that together disclose different parts of the story of America.

It is to that particular story that I now turn.

Notes

1 The Articles of Confederation. www.ourdocuments.gov/doc.php?flash=false&doc=3.
2 The Constitution of the United States. www.archives.gov/founding-docs/constitution.
3 The Judiciary Act of 1789. http://avalon.law.yale.edu/18th_century/judiciary_act.asp.
4 The Judiciary Act of 1869. www.fjc.gov/history/legislation/landmark-judicial-legislation-back-historical-note-8.
5 The Judiciary Act of 1891 (Evarts Act). www.fjc.gov/history/courts/u.s.-courts-appeals-and-federal-judiciary.
6 The Judicial Code of 1911. https://ia800207.us.archive.org/7/items/cu31924020607259/cu31924020607259.pdf.
7 The Judiciary Act of 1925. www.fjc.gov/history/legislation/landmark-legislation-judges-bill.
8 The Supreme Court Cases Selections Act, 1988. www.law.cornell.edu/uscode/text/28/1257.

Further reading

Derek H. Davis, ed. *The Oxford Handbook of Church and State in the United States* (Oxford: Oxford University Press, 2010).

Ronald B. Flowers, *That Godless Court: Supreme Court Decisions on Church–State Relationships*, Second Edition (Louisville: Westminster John Knox Press, 2005).

Robert B. Fowler, et al. *Religion and Politics in America: Faith, Culture, and Strategic Choices* (Boulder: Westview Press, 2010).

Marjorie Garber and Rebecca L. Malkowitz, *One Nation Under God? Religion and American Culture* (London: Routledge, 1999).

Philip Hamburger, *Separation of Church and State* (Cambridge, MA: Harvard University Press, 2002).

Phillip E. Hammond, *With Liberty for All: Freedom of Religion in the United States* (Louisville: Westminster John Knox Press, 1998).

Vincent Phillip Munoz, *Religious Liberty and the American Supreme Court: The Essential Cases and Documents* (Lanham: Rowman and Littlefield, 2015).

Martha Nussbaum, *Liberty of Conscience: In Defense of America's Tradition of Religious Equality* (New York: Basic Books, 2007).

Mark P. Strasser, *Free Exercise of Religion and the United States Constitution: The Supreme Court's Challenge* (London: Routledge, 2018).

John Witte Jr. and Joel A. Nichols, *Religion and the American Constitutional Experiment*, Third Edition (Boulder: Westview Press, 2011).

Online judicial sources

www.justia.com/
www.law.cornell.edu/
www.oyez.org/

Part II

Discourse

4 *McCollum v. Board of Education* (1948)

Argued: December 8th, 1947 – Decided: March 8th, 1948.

> We have now arrived at a point in this case at which the cool light of reason may be substituted for the heat of emotionalism which militant atheism has directed against religion. The bitterness of [McCollum]'s complaint, the scorn and contempt of her witnesses for the religious beliefs of others, the rancor of her advocate are stilled.
>
> — John Franklin, attorney representing the Board of Education of School District Number 71, Champaign County Ill., November 20th, 1945

Question before the Court: Does a public school board's support of 'released time,' where students are offered religious classes during normal school hours, violate the establishment clause of the First Amendment?

Decision: 8–1. Yes, such a program violates the First Amendment and is thus unconstitutional.

Antecedent Case Decisions:

- ILLINOIS STATE SUPREME COURT, January 22nd, 1947.

  Ruling: The Judgment of the Sixth Judicial Circuit Court was affirmed, and McCollum petitioned the Supreme Court for a writ of certiorari.

- ILLINOIS SIXTH JUDICIAL CIRCUIT COURT, January 1946.

  Ruling: The Court found in favor of the Defendant, the Champaign, Illinois Board of Education of School District 71.

Background

In 1940, an organization called the Champaign Council on Religious Education was granted permission by the Champaign, Illinois Board of Education of School District 71 to teach religion classes to students between the fourth and ninth grades, on school grounds, during regular school hours. These classes consisted of once-weekly thirty-minute (grade school) and forty-five minute (junior high school) lessons, taught by members of the Council (both clergy and lay), who represented the local Protestant, Catholic, and Jewish churches and synagogues. These instructors were neither officially employed by the School District, nor did they receive monetary compensation for their time.

The classes themselves followed a pre-designed Bible-focused curriculum, created by the Council, under the approval and supervision of the School District's superintendent. Attendance was not compulsory. Parents were asked to sign and submit a permission card that included the designated faith of the child, which would determine whether they attended the Protestant, Catholic, or Jewish classes. Any parent, who did not wish to have his or her child participate, need only refuse to sign the permission card. That child would be removed from his or her classroom and allowed to continue their regular, secular, studies independently. This was a practice called 'released time.'

In 1943, Vashti and John McCollum's son, James, entered the fourth grade at the South Side School within District 71. He did not participate in the religious education classes during his first semester there – alongside five other students – but he did attend, with his parents' permission, during his second. After learning that the curriculum was more sectarian in content than they had initially thought, his parents transferred him to the Dr. Howard School for his fifth grade. They once again requested that he not participate in the religious education classes, and during his second semester he was the only student at the school to do so. During this time, he was placed within the music room to continue his studies under the guidance of his regular teacher, and on one occasion he was put at a desk, alone, in the hallway outside of his classroom. He complained to his parents that he had suffered claustrophobia in the music room, as well as taunts from other children while sitting in the hallway. They brought these concerns to school officials, who discontinued both practices. Nevertheless, his absence from the lessons continued to cause him feelings of ostracism, from both his fellow students and his teacher, who continually pressured him to 'conform.' His parents again expressed their objections to school officials, even arguing that his exclusion, and thus the religious education classes in general, were unfair violations of the rights and protections guaranteed him as a public school student. When the school officials and the School Board refused to terminate the classes, Vashti filed suit against the Board of Education in the Sixth Judicial Circuit Court in June of 1945, requesting a writ of mandamus that would, if granted, discontinue the program entirely.

Like a writ of certiorari, a writ of mandamus is a specialized petition, an official request for a higher public authority (such as a school board) to discontinue a practice performed by a lower public authority (the school) that might be perceived as being in violation of the law. In her initial suit, McCollum argued that the religious education practice did this in three ways: it was in direct violation of the Constitution of the State of Illinois, the School Code of Illinois, and the United States Constitution.

The trial before the Sixth Judicial Circuit was widely publicized, in part because the attorney for the McCollum family, Landon Chapman, used it as an opportunity to 'put religion on trial,' by examining the deficiencies that he found apparent in religion-in-general, as well as by interrogating the local clergy members about their respective faiths. In addition, he also had James McCollum – who was ten years old at the time – testify before the Court about his feelings of exclusion and isolation. And while James' testimony shocked many American readers because he unashamedly described himself as an Atheist, it became even more scandalous once the attorney for the School Board, John Franklin, began questioning his character as such. In fact, Franklin went so far as to argue that any ostracism he might have felt was due solely to his 'troubled' nature, which he confirmed through testimonials given by his fellow students, and teacher, who all agreed that James was a 'non-conformist' and a 'misfit.' Character traits, Franklin declared, that were to be expected from Atheists.

As such, the five-day trial became something of a 'holy war,' with Chapman and Franklin fighting each other from two diametrically opposed fronts. The former called on Vashti's father, Arthur Cromwell, who testified proudly that religion was a 'disease' contracted in childhood, as well as her close friend, and Unitarian Minister, Phillip Schug, who compared Jesus Christ to Santa Claus. Franklin, on the other hand, described the trial as a whole in relation to the Second World War: 'Just as we are concluding a costly and bloody war which ended in victory over unchristian and infidel nations, the struggle of these unchristian and infidel forces against religion is being transferred to this little courtroom in central Illinois.' Responding to this, Chapman countered that Communist Russia was an American ally during the war, which meant so too was Atheism.[1]

On January 26th, 1946, the Circuit Court's three-judge panel unanimously ruled that the religion education classes were permissible, arguing that the doctrine of the 'separation of church and state' did not denote a conflict between these two things.

McCollum appealed her case to the State Supreme Court of Illinois, which on January 22nd, 1947, affirmed the Circuit Court's decision.

In his decision for the State Supreme Court, Justice Charles H. Thompson refuted each of McCollum's claims, repeating the points made by the three-judge panel of the Circuit Court, that not only were the religious education classes voluntary, but because they were not part of the public school's regular curriculum, were not 'worship services,' did not include prayers or the singing of hymns, did not require students to attend or force them to adhere to religious beliefs against their own, were not conducted by school teachers, were not financially supported by the school or school district, and did not demand further expense due to additional 'wear and tear' of school property, they did not violate any of the state or federal statutes that she cited. Furthermore, in addressing the question, 'does either the Federal or State constitution, or both, in their guaranty of religious freedom, prohibit voluntary religious classes in the public schools under the plan as disclosed by this record,' he concluded:

> Certainly, such classes do not violate the freedom of conscience of any individual or group so long as the classes are conducted upon a purely voluntary basis. Freedom of religion as intended by those who wrote the State and Federal constitutions means the right of an individual to entertain any desired religious belief without interference from the State. Our government very wisely refuses to recognize a specific religion, but this cannot mean that the government does not recognize or subscribe to religious ideals. We find such recognition in the very preamble of our State constitution. The government does not recognize a particular faith but this does not mean that it is indifferent to religious faith. To deny the existence of religious motivation is to deny the inspiration and authority of the constitution itself.[2]

McCollum appealed her case one final time to the United States Supreme Court, which noted 'probable jurisdiction' in June 1947, and granted certiorari.

McCollum v. Board of Education was argued on December 8th, 1947, and on March 8th, 1948, in an 8–1 decision, the Supreme Court reversed the Illinois State Supreme Court's decision, ruling in McCollum's favor. The lone dissent was drafted by Justice Stanley F. Reed, who cited concerns about the possible jurisdictional repercussions that might arise from the Court's interpretation of the Establishment Clause.

* * *

McCollum v. Board of Education (1948)

Full Title

People of the State of Illinois ex rel. Vashti McCollum v. Board of Education of School District No. 71, Champaign County, Illinois, et al.

Official Citation

333 U.S. 203
Argued: December 8, 1947
Decided: March 8, 1948

Author

Justice Hugo Black

Syllabus

With the permission of a board of education, granted under its general supervisory powers over the use of public school buildings, religious teachers, employed subject to the approval and supervision of the superintendent of schools by a private religious group including representatives of the Catholic, Protestant and Jewish faiths, gave religious instruction in public school buildings once each week. Pupils whose parents so requested were excused from their secular classes during the periods of religious instruction and were required to attend the religious classes; but other pupils were not released from their public school duties, which were compulsory under state law. A resident and taxpayer of the school district whose child was enrolled in the public schools sued in a state court for a writ of mandamus requiring the board of education to terminate this practice.

Held:

1. A judgment of the State Supreme Court sustaining denial of the writ of mandamus on the ground that the state statutes granted the board of education authority to establish such a program drew into question 'the validity of a statute' of the State within the meaning of [section] 237 of the Judicial Code,[3] and was appealable to this Court.

2. As a resident and taxpayer of the school district and the parent of a child required by state law to attend the school, appellant [the party appealing a lower court decision] had standing to maintain the suit.

3. Both state courts having ruled expressly on appellant's claim that the state program violated the Federal Constitution, a motion to dismiss the appeal on the ground that appellant failed properly to present that question in the State Supreme Court cannot be sustained.

4. This utilization of the State's tax supported public school system and its machinery for compulsory public school attendance to enable sectarian groups to give religious

instruction to public school pupils in public school buildings violates the First Amendment of the Constitution, made applicable to the states by the Fourteenth Amendment.

[*The People v. Board of Education*, (Illinois State Supreme Court, 1947), citation: 396 Ill. 14 71 N.E.2d 161], *reversed.*

The Supreme Court of Illinois affirmed a denial of a petition for a writ of mandamus requiring a board of education to terminate the giving of religious instruction by private teachers in the public schools. On appeal to this Court, reversed and remanded.

Opinion

The appellant, Vashti McCollum, began this action for mandamus against the Champaign Board of Education in the Circuit Court of Champaign County, Illinois. Her asserted interest was that of a resident and taxpayer of Champaign and of a parent whose child was then enrolled in the Champaign public schools. Illinois has a compulsory education law which, with exceptions, requires parents to send their children, aged seven to sixteen, to its tax-supported public schools, where the children are to remain in attendance during the hours when the schools are regularly in session. Parents who violate this law commit a misdemeanor punishable by fine unless the children attend private or parochial schools which meet educational standards fixed by the State. District boards of education are given general supervisory powers over the use of the public school buildings within the school districts.[4]

Appellant's petition for mandamus alleged that religious teachers, employed by private religious groups, were permitted to come weekly into the school buildings during the regular hours set apart for secular teaching, and then and there, for a period of thirty minutes, substitute their religious teaching for the secular education provided under the compulsory education law. The petitioner charged that this joint public school religious group program violated the First and Fourteenth Amendments to the United States Constitution. The prayer of her petition was that the Board of Education be ordered to 'adopt and enforce rules and regulations prohibiting all instruction in and teaching of religious education in all public schools in Champaign School District Number 71, [. . .] and in all public school houses and buildings in said district when occupied by public schools.'

The board first moved to dismiss the petition on the ground that, under Illinois law, appellant had no standing to maintain the action. This motion was denied. An answer was then filed, which admitted that regular weekly religious instruction was given during school hours to those pupils whose parents consented, and that those pupils were released temporarily from their regular secular classes for the limited purpose of attending the religious classes. The answer denied that this coordinated program of religious instruction violated the State or Federal Constitution. Much evidence was heard, findings of fact were made, after which the petition for mandamus was denied on the ground that the school's religious instruction program violated neither the federal nor state constitutional provisions invoked by the appellant. On appeal, the State Supreme Court affirmed. Appellant appealed to this Court under [section 344 of title 28 of the United States Code], and we noted probable jurisdiction on June 2nd, 1947.

The appellees press a motion to dismiss the appeal on several grounds, the first of which is that the judgment of the State Supreme Court does not draw in question the 'validity of a statute of any State' as required by [section 344 of title 28 of the United States

Code]. This contention rests on the admitted fact that the challenged program of religious instruction was not expressly authorized by statute. But the State Supreme Court has sustained the validity of the program on the ground that the Illinois statutes granted the board authority to establish such a program. This holding is sufficient to show that the validity of an Illinois statute was drawn in question within the meaning of [section 344 of title 28 of the United States Code].[5] A second ground for the motion to dismiss is that the appellant lacks standing to maintain the action, a ground which is also without merit.[6] A third ground for the motion is that the appellant failed properly to present in the State Supreme Court her challenge that the state program violated the Federal Constitution. But in view of the express rulings of both state courts on this question, the argument cannot be successfully maintained. The motion to dismiss the appeal is denied.

Although there are disputes between the parties as to various inferences that may or may not properly be drawn from the evidence concerning the religious program, the following facts are shown by the record without dispute.[i] In 1940, interested members of the Jewish, Roman Catholic, and a few of the Protestant faiths formed a voluntary association called the Champaign Council on Religious Education. They obtained permission from the Board of Education to offer classes in religious instruction to public school pupils in grades four to nine, inclusive. Classes were made up of pupils whose parents signed printed cards requesting that their children be permitted to attend;[ii] they were held weekly, thirty minutes for the lower grades, forty-five minutes for the higher. The council employed the religious teachers at no expense to the school authorities, but

i Appellant, taking issue with the facts found by the Illinois courts, argues that the religious education program in question is invalid under the Federal Constitution for any one of the following reasons: (1) In actual practice certain Protestant groups have obtained an overshadowing advantage in the propagation of their faiths over other Protestant sects; (2) the religious education program was voluntary in name only, because, in fact, subtle pressures were brought to bear on the students to force them to participate in it, and (3) the power given the school superintendent to reject teachers selected by religious groups and the power given the local Council on Religious Education to determine which religious faiths should participate in the program was a prior censorship of religion. In view of our decision, we find it unnecessary to consider these arguments or the disputed facts upon which they depend.

ii The [State] Supreme Court described the request card system as follows:

> Admission to the classes was to be allowed only upon the express written request of parents, and then only to classes designated by the parents. [. . .] Cards were distributed to the parents of elementary students by the public school teachers requesting them to indicate whether they desired their children to receive religious education. After being filled out, the cards were returned to the teachers of religious education classes either by the public school teachers or the children.

On this subject, the trial court found that

> Those students who have obtained the written consent of their parents therefore are released by the school authorities from their secular work, and in the grade schools for a period of thirty minutes' instruction in each week during said school hours, and forty-five minutes during each week in the junior high school, receive training in religious education. [. . .] Certain cards are used for obtaining permission of parents for their children to take said religious instruction courses, and they are made available through the offices of the superintendent of schools and through the hands of principals and teachers to the pupils of the school district. Said cards are prepared at the cost of the council of religious education. The handling and distribution of said cards does not interfere with the duties or suspend the regular secular work of the employees of the defendant.

the instructors were subject to the approval and supervision of the superintendent of schools.[iii] The classes were taught in three separate religious groups by Protestant teachers,[iv] Catholic priests, and a Jewish rabbi, although, for the past several years, there have apparently been no classes instructed in the Jewish religion. Classes were conducted in the regular classrooms of the school building. Students who did not choose to take the religious instruction were not released from public school duties; they were required to leave their classrooms and go to some other place in the school building for pursuit of their secular studies. On the other hand, students who were released from secular study for the religious instructions were required to be present at the religious classes. Reports of their presence or absence were to be made to their secular teachers.[v]

The foregoing facts, without reference to others that appear in the record, show the use of tax supported property for religious instruction and the close cooperation between the school authorities and the religious council in promoting religious education. The operation of the State's compulsory education system thus assists and is integrated with the program of religious instruction carried on by separate religious sects. Pupils compelled by law to go to school for secular education are released in part from their legal duty upon the condition that they attend the religious classes. This is beyond all question a utilization of the tax-established and tax-supported public school system to aid religious groups to spread their faith. And it falls squarely under the ban of the First Amendment (made applicable to the States by the Fourteenth) as we interpreted it in *Everson v. Board of Education*. There we said:

iii The State Supreme Court said:

> The record further discloses that the teachers conducting the religious classes were not teachers in the public schools, but were subject to the approval and supervision of the superintendent.

The trial court found:

> Before any faith or other group may obtain permission from the defendant for the similar, free and equal use of rooms in the public school buildings, said faith or group must make application to the superintendent of schools of said School District Number 71, who in turn will determine whether or not it is practical for said group to teach in said school system.

The president of the local school board testified:

> The Protestants would have one group and the Catholics, and would be given a room where they would have class and we would go along with the plan of the religious people. They were all to be treated alike, with the understanding that the teachers they would bring into the school were approved by the superintendent. [. . .] The superintendent was the last word so far as the individual was concerned.

iv There were two teachers of the Protestant faith. One was a Presbyterian, and had been a foreign missionary for that church. The second testified as follows:

> I am affiliated with the Christian church. I also work in the Methodist Church, and I taught at the Presbyterian. I am married to a Lutheran.

v The director of the Champaign Council on Religious Education testified:

> If any pupil is absent, we turn in a slip just like any teacher would to the superintendent's office. The slip is a piece of paper with a number of hours in the school day and a square, and the teacher of the particular room for the particular hour records the absentees. It has their names and the grade and the section to which they belong. It is the same sheet that the geography and history teachers and all the other teachers use, and is furnished by the school.

> Neither a state nor the Federal Government can set up a church. Neither can pass laws which aid one religion, aid all religions, or prefer one religion over another.[vi] Neither can force or influence a person to go to or to remain away from church against his will, or force him to profess a belief or disbelief in any religion. No person can be punished for entertaining or professing religious beliefs or disbeliefs, for church attendance or nonattendance. No tax in any amount, large or small, can be levied to support any religious activities or institutions, whatever they may be called or whatever form they may adopt to teach or practice religion.[vii] Neither a state nor the Federal Government can, openly or secretly, participate in the affairs of any religious organizations or groups, and vice versa. In the words of Jefferson, the clause against establishment of religion by law was intended to erect 'a wall of separation between church and State.'

The majority in the *Everson* case, and the minority as shown by quotations from the dissenting views in our notes [vi] and [vii], agreed that the First Amendment's language, properly interpreted, had erected a wall of separation between Church and State. They disagreed as to the facts shown by the record and as to the proper application of the First Amendment's language to those facts.

Recognizing that the Illinois program is barred by the First and Fourteenth Amendments if we adhere to the views expressed both by the majority and the minority in the *Everson* case, counsel for the respondents challenge those views as dicta [commentary less judicially powerful], and urge that we reconsider and repudiate them. They argue that, historically, the First Amendment was intended to forbid only government preference of one religion over another, not an impartial governmental assistance of all religions. In addition, they ask that we distinguish or overrule our holding in the *Everson* case that the Fourteenth Amendment made the 'establishment of religion' clause of the First Amendment applicable as a prohibition against the States. After giving full consideration to the arguments presented, we are unable to accept either of these contentions.

To hold that a state cannot, consistently with the First and Fourteenth Amendments, utilize its public school system to aid any or all religious faiths or sects in the dissemination of their doctrines and ideals does not, as counsel urge, manifest a governmental hostility to religion or religious teachings. A manifestation of such hostility would be at war

vi The dissent, agreed to by four judges, said:

> The problem then cannot be cast in terms of legal discrimination or its absence. This would be true even though the state, in giving aid, should treat all religious instruction alike. [. . .] Again, it was the furnishing of 'contributions of money for the propagation of opinions which he disbelieves' that the fathers outlawed. That consequence and effect are not removed by multiplying to all-inclusiveness the sects for which support is exacted. The Constitution requires, not comprehensive identification of state with religion, but complete separation. (*Everson v. Board of Education*, citation: 330 U.S. 1, 59 and 60).

vii The dissenting judges said:

> In view of this history, no further proof is needed that the Amendment forbids any appropriation, large or small, from public funds to aid or support any and all religious exercises. [. . .] Legislatures are free to make, and courts to sustain, appropriations only when it can be found that, in fact, they do not aid, promote, encourage or sustain religious teaching or observances, be the amount large or small. (*Everson v. Board of Education*, citation: 330 U.S. 1, pages 41, and 52–53).

with our national tradition as embodied in the First Amendment's guaranty of the free exercise of religion. For the First Amendment rests upon the premise that both religion and government can best work to achieve their lofty aims if each is left free from the other within its respective sphere. Or, as we said in the *Everson* case, the First Amendment has erected a wall between Church and State which must be kept high and impregnable.

Here not only are the State's tax-supported public school buildings used for the dissemination of religious doctrines. The State also affords sectarian groups an invaluable aid in that it helps to provide pupils for their religious classes through use of the State's compulsory public school machinery. This is not separation of Church and State.

The cause is reversed and remanded to the State Supreme Court for proceedings not inconsistent with this opinion.

Reversed and remanded.

* * *

Importance

Vashti McCollum was an Atheist-American at a time when being an Atheist in America was far from publicly accepted. It was synonymous with anti-Americanism and communism, and was seen as an affront to the sacred norms of American culture. Religion in the public square was thoroughly accepted. It was assumed and taken-for-granted. It was tradition.

Being an Atheist was not.

Vashti and her family were immediately judged as outsiders, as dangerous. They endured death threats and violence. Their cat was lynched. In order to protect him from further harassment after his testimony in the Circuit Court trial, James was sent to live with relatives outside of Champaign, Illinois. Vashti was quickly known nationwide as 'that Atheist woman.'[7]

And this represents the first of this decision's two important outcomes.

The description of Vashti's Atheism throughout this case's judicial process provides an invaluable source not only toward better understanding the signifiers that defined that term at that time, but also for understanding the ways in which Atheists were perceived within the American context.

While the description of the Circuit Court's trial above offers some insight into this, perhaps the better example comes from John Franklin's description of her in his brief for that Court, in which he wrote:

> [S]he is an atheist [who] asserts that religious worship is a chronic disease of the imagination contracted in childhood, that religion is born of fear, ignorance and superstition, that religion is a racket advanced by unscrupulous preachers, that the Bible contains so much that is bad, so little that is good, and little or nothing that is true that it is unfit for our youth to read, that the principles and attitude of Christ are hateful and selfish, that we need to write and use a 'twentieth century bible' based upon rationalism glorifying man and science and giving an account of all religious beliefs that man has held and setting forth its own moral code of ethics, that the delinquency of youth and adults in America is attributable to economic reasons and not moral ones and that they may be solved by a twentieth century bible and by the erection of community parks and recreation centers.[8]

He then went on to describe James in a similarly sardonic manner:

> James Terry, so the record discloses, has been taught [. . .] to ridicule the belief of his fellows in the Deity and his own home training has left him with a feeling of contempt for their intellectual processes. The values that they place upon their relationship with God, he scoffs at. He is proud of his atheism, finds it fun to be an atheist – non-conformity is a position to which value has been attached in his mind.[9]

And then in his final argument, where he contended that neither had suffered the injury necessary to determine the case in their favor, he described them both as follows:

> [McCollum] has wholly failed to show any infringement of her rights. No one has impaired or interfered in any way with her freedom to be an atheist. She was one before the religious education classes were instituted. She is one now. The same is true of James Terry. No one requires her or her son to enroll in these classes. If they enter, no one tells them atheism is wrong. No one seeks to change their belief. Except as their unbelief may be dispelled by being exposed to the words of the Bible, it remains the same. Is their unbelief so shallow, so unsure, so frail, that it will not stand before acquaintanceship with the Bible? If so, they are under no compulsion to expose themselves to the light. (58) [. . .] If either [of them] has felt anything which they interpreted as social pressure, it must have been the still small voice of conscience or the result of their own proclamations of their unbelief. It was not the result of the presence of the classes in the school building, but the fact that they chose to make a parade and display of their atheism. The law cannot protect people against the social consequences of their atheism. What it can and does protect against is discrimination by the law and the government. When that duty is fulfilled, the social consequences of pursuing a course belong just as certainly to the individual as does the right in the first instance to make a choice between atheism and religion.[10]

These descriptions, from this source, are not surprising. Across all three trials, John Franklin was adamant that he was fighting to protect religion from a virulent assault, even declaring that a decision in her favor would be an endorsement of anti-religion. Because, for him, the McCollums' Atheism was abnormal and strange. It was un-American, and by means of their unwillingness to participate in the School's religious education classes, it represented a belief that conflicted with the traditions inherent in American history itself.

While his descriptions here are an excellent example that we might use to better understand how Vashti and John's Atheism was defined via an external source, in regard to the Court's decision in her favor, they also serve to point out the unique nature of Vashti's success. Not only did the result of her case forever restrict public school policies concerning religious education, it also determined, for the first time, that an Atheist-American was guaranteed the same First Amendment religious protections as her Catholic, Protestant, and Jewish neighbors. Which, in a seemingly contradictory way, meant that Atheists and religious Americans were for the first time considered equals by constitutional law. Of course, whether or not this in turn meant that Atheism itself could be interpreted as a 'religion' under the same precedence was not discussed. That, the Court would deal with in later decisions.

With respect to this decision's second level of importance, John Franklin's brief is once again quite useful; in this instance via his prediction of what would occur were the Court to rule in her favor:

> To insulate the school from all contact with or knowledge of religion is tacitly to deny that religion has any place in life. In effect, it would convert the schools into pagan and atheistic institutions much more sectarian in favoring unreligion than the present religious education classes favor any faith or sect. It seems clear that the present case is an effort to place atheists at a distinct advantage in the propagation of their unbelief over persons who espouse a religious faith. Success of this effort would fly in the face of the historical fact that we are a religious people and that the very essence of democracy is the dignity of the individual and reverence for God which religion alone teaches.[11]

Franklin's fear here, which was in many ways realized by the Court's decision, speaks as well to a larger fear concerning the broadening scope of the Court's jurisdiction, made all the more real by the paradigm that it used to determine that decision. Established by both *Cantwell v. Connecticut* (1940) and *Everson v. Board of Education* (1947), this process would become the foundation on which all religion-based case decisions would be decided from here on, with roots that reached back to the Supreme Court's first decision dealing with religion, *Reynolds v. United States* (1878). In short, in both *Cantwell* and *Everson*, the Court used the Fourteenth Amendment's Due Process Clause to expand the First Amendment's religion clauses to legal questions within the boundaries of particular states.

For example, in *Cantwell*, a statute that forbade residents of the State of Connecticut the right to religiously solicit, unless they procured a license to do so from a government official who would determine whether their beliefs were 'religious' or not, was not only found to be a violation of the Free Exercise Clause of the First Amendment, but a deprivation of the 'liberty' protected by the Due Process Clause of the Fourteenth as well. If, the Court argued, this government official decided that a religious person – in this example a Jehovah's Witness – was not acting, in his estimation, in a manner that *he* deemed religious enough, not granting that person a permit to freely exercise their religious beliefs was akin to a government censorship of religion-in-general. The Court determined that this type of regulation demanded the sort of higher federal judicial review that it could provide, especially since it would need to overrule the State Supreme Court of Connecticut. More specifically, Justice Owen J. Roberts, in his unanimous decision for the Court, remarked:

> We hold that the statute, [as] construed and applied to the appellants, deprives them of their liberty without due process of law in contravention of the Fourteenth Amendment. The fundamental concept of liberty embodied in that Amendment embraces the liberties guaranteed by the First Amendment. The First Amendment declares that Congress shall make no law respecting an establishment of religion or prohibiting the free exercise thereof. The Fourteenth Amendment has rendered the legislatures of the states as incompetent as Congress to enact such laws.[12]

Then in *Everson*, the Court faced a similar concern, only this time in regard to the First Amendment's Establishment Clause. However, where in this instance it found that a New

Jersey State Statute that authorized the reimbursement of funds provided by parents for the transportation of their children on school buses that included children who attended a private Catholic school, did not reflect an Establishment Clause violation, it nevertheless considered the issue via the application of the First Amendment through the Fourteenth. In what is perhaps one of the most famous quotations from the Court's discourse on American religion, Justice Hugo Black stated there:

> Neither a state nor the Federal Government can set up a church. Neither can pass laws which aid one religion, aid all religions, or prefer one religion over another. Neither can force or influence a person to go to or to remain away from church against his will, or force him to profess a belief or disbelief in any religion. No person can be punished for entertaining or professing religious beliefs or disbeliefs, for church attendance or nonattendance. No tax in any amount, large or small, can be levied to support any religious activities or institutions, whatever they may be called or whatever form they may adopt to teach or practice religion. Neither a state nor the Federal Government can, openly or secretly, participate in the affairs of any religious organizations or groups, and vice versa. In the words of Jefferson, the clause against establishment of religion by law was intended to erect 'a wall of separation between church and State.'[13]

What these two rulings further meant was that as a Federal Judiciary, the Supreme Court secured itself the right to overrule any state law or legislature that it deemed to be unconstitutional, particularly with respect to restrictions or endorsements of religion. *McCollum* fell into the latter category, which meant that John Franklin's leading argument that the Board of Education's religious education classes were mere expressions of religious free exercise, was re-interpreted as an erroneous and unconstitutional government endorsement. As such, where the issue in the *Everson* case allowed the Court to consider its ability to apply Establishment Clause protection to a state policy, the issue in *McCollum* gave it the opportunity to directly enact it. Or, as Justice Black concluded:

> To hold that a state cannot, consistently with the First and Fourteenth Amendments, utilize its public school system to aid any or all religious faiths or sects in the dissemination of their doctrines and ideals does not, as counsel urge, manifest a governmental hostility to religion or religious teachings. A manifestation of such hostility would be at war with our national tradition as embodied in the First Amendment's guaranty of the free exercise of religion. For the First Amendment rests upon the premise that both religion and government can best work to achieve their lofty aims if each is left free from the other within its respective sphere.[14]

In this way, Franklin's fears were even more realized than he might have originally thought. And more than that, they would continue to be realized over the next thirty years, as cases like this one continually altered the relationship between church and state in America. Once the Supreme Court ruled that it had final jurisdiction over state issues concerning religious free exercise and religious establishment, the notion of American religion itself began to change. This was especially the case as what might have once been considered 'traditional' in America, such as public school religious education, began to be replaced by a new approach that argued for a strict 'wall of separation' between these two entities.

This speaks directly to this decision's second importance. As a discursive text in this regard, it provides a valuable introduction to the exact point in which the Supreme Court expanded its jurisdictional reach. After all, here was a federal agency, the highest ranking tribunal of the Judicial Branch of the federal government, dictating what a state agency could and could not do within the borders of its own state, by overruling what that state's own highest ranking tribunal had approved as a permissible policy under its own constitution. In this way, *McCollum v. Board of Education* is not *just* about removing religious education from American public schools, or *just* about the process with which an Atheist is guaranteed equal protection by the First Amendment's Establishment Clause. It is also about the Court's broadening reach, which for some, including future Justices of the Court itself, represented a far more damaging action than the religious endorsement by the School Board in Champaign, Illinois.

It serves, then, as an excellent starting point: an ideal example of the complexities inherent in the Judiciary's description of American religion, as well as the role played by Atheist-Americans in shaping that description. Which we shall see even more broadly applied in the decisions that follow this one, with the Court's further re-interpretation of state laws endorsing religion, and especially with the further popularization of American Atheism via the words and actions of the plaintiffs and defendants involved.

Notes

1 *The Edwardsville Intelligencer*, September 15th, 1945, page 2. See also, Jay Rosenstein, Producer and Director, 'The Lord is Not on Trial Here Today,' *PBS Documentary*, first aired, October 22nd, 2010. Available online at: www.youtube.com/watch?v=EeSHLnrgaqY (Accessed 10 October 2017).
2 *The People v. Board of Education* (Illinois State Supreme Court, 1947), citation: 71 N.E.2d 161, 29.
3 Section 237. (a), (b), and (c).
4 Sections 123 and 301, Chapter 122 of the Revised Statutes of the State of Illinois, 1943.
5 See *Hamilton v. Regents of University of California* (1934), citation: 293 U.S. 245, 258.
6 See, *Coleman v. Miller* (1939), citation: 307 U.S. 433, 443, 445, and 464.
7 In the years after the Court's decision, Vashti McCollum continued her activism as an Atheist, and became a vocal representative of American Humanism, serving two terms as President of the American Humanist Association from 1962 to 1965. She signed both the second and third *Humanist Manifestos* in 1973 and 2003, and published a memoir of her experiences in 1953 titled, *One Woman's Fight*. She died in Champaign, Illinois, at the age of ninety-three, in August of 2006.
8 John Franklin, *Brief of Defendant and Intervenors*, 2.
9 Ibid., 27.
10 Ibid., 59.
11 Ibid., 94–95.
12 *Cantwell v. Connecticut* (1940), citation: 310 US 296, 303.
13 *Everson v. Board of Education* (1947), citation: 330 U.S. 1, 15–16.
14 *McCollum v. Board of Education* (1948), 211–212.

5 *Torcaso v. Watkins* (1961)

Argued: April 24th, 1961 – Decided: June 19th, 1961.

> That no religious test ought ever to be required as a qualification for any office of profit or trust in this State, other than a declaration of belief in the existence of God; nor shall the Legislature prescribe any other oath of office than the oath prescribed by this Constitution.
>
> — Article 37 of the Declaration of Rights of the Maryland State Constitution

Question before the Court: Does a state government's requirement of an individual, in order to hold public office, to declare a belief in the existence of God, violate the First Amendment?

Decision: 9–0 unanimous. Yes, such a requirement violates the First Amendment, and is thus unconstitutional.

Antecedent Case Decisions:

- COURT OF APPEALS OF MARYLAND (Maryland State Supreme Court), June 30th, 1960.

  Ruling: The Judgment of the Circuit Court for Montgomery County was affirmed, so Torcaso petitioned the Supreme Court for a writ of certiorari.

- CIRCUIT COURT FOR MONTGOMERY COUNTY, Maryland, January 1960.

  Ruling: The Court found in favor of the Defendant, Clayton Watkins.

Background

In 1959, Roy Reed Torcaso was 'duly appointed' by the Governor of the State of Maryland a notary public in and for Montgomery County, Maryland. As an administrative official who witnesses and authenticates the signing of significant transactional documents, the position of notary public is 'an office of profit or trust,' and as such it required the swearing and signing of a state oath. When Torcaso arrived at the Montgomery County Circuit Court to take up his commission, the acting clerk, Clayton Watkins, tendered the following oath:

> In the presence of Almighty God, I, Roy R. Torcaso, do solemnly promise and declare that I will support the Constitution of the United States; and that I will be faithful and bear true allegiance to the State of Maryland, and support the Constitution and Laws thereof; and that I will, to the best of my skill and judgment, diligently and faithfully without partiality or prejudice execute the office of Notary Public of The State of Maryland In and For Montgomery County according to the Constitution and Laws of this State.
>
> I, Roy R. Torcaso, do declare that I believe in the existence of God.[1]

Torcaso was an Atheist. And as an Atheist, he declined to declare a belief in the existence of God, offering instead to affirm solely the oath required of him to take up his position. Watkins rejected this offer and refused him his commission. In response, Torcaso filed suit with the Montgomery County Circuit Court, requesting a writ of mandamus, and declaring: 'the point at issue [was] not whether I believe[d] in a supreme being, but whether the state [had] a right to inquire into my beliefs.'[2]

The Montgomery County Circuit Court ruled against him, so he appealed to the Maryland State Supreme Court, which affirmed the Circuit Court's decision on June 30th, 1960.

Writing for the latter, Judge William L. Henderson argued that, though contradictory to Article 37 of the Declaration of Rights of the Constitution of the State of Maryland, which prohibited a religious test as a qualification for any 'office of profit' or 'trust' – aside from a 'declaration of belief in the existence of God' – as well as Article 1, Section 6 (later re-numbered as Section 9 in 1978) of the same, the oath and declaration tendered to Torcaso was not central to his complaint, and thus was not imperative to the Court's decision.

Instead, Judge Henderson argued, since the religious test apparent in the oath tendered to Torcaso had never been 'put into effect by the legislature,' and because it was self-executing, meaning it did not need further legislation to enforce it, it did not reflect an unconstitutional restraint on his ability to take up his commission:

> [Torcaso] is not compelled to believe or disbelieve, under threat of punishment or other compulsion. True, unless he makes the declaration of belief he cannot hold public office in Maryland, but he is not compelled to hold office.[3]

Furthermore, because Torcaso did not claim that, like the First Amendment, Article VI of the Federal Constitution – 'no religious Test shall ever be required as a Qualification to any Office or public Trust under the United States' – was applicable to his complaint via the Fourteenth Amendment, Henderson asserted that the religious test at question neither deprived him of 'due process of law,' nor of 'equal protection of the laws.' This was especially true, he maintained, regarding Torcaso's claim that as a 'non-believer' he was being both discriminated against, and being divested of his 'liberty' to disbelieve in God.

In regard to Torcaso's Atheism, and by citing a statement made by Justice William O. Douglas in his decision for *Zorach v. Clauson* (1952), Henderson declared:

> In the absence of any direct authority on the point, we find it difficult to believe that the Supreme Court will hold that a declaration of belief in the existence of God,

> required by Article 37 of our Declaration of Rights as a qualification for State office, is discriminatory and invalid. As Mr. Justice Douglas, speaking for a majority of the Court in *Zorach v. Clauson* (1952), said: 'We are a religious people whose institutions presuppose a Supreme Being.'[4] The problem here is more basic than in any of the cases cited. An oath, predicated upon a belief in God, is a regular incident of judicial proceedings. There can be no doubt that at common law an atheist was incompetent as a witness.[5]

With a sense of finality, Henderson also made clear his opinion that Atheists like Torcaso had disqualified themselves from serving as public officials, giving testimony, or serving on a jury, because of their Atheism:

> To the members of the Convention, as to the voters who adopted our Constitution, belief in God was equated with a belief in moral accountability and the sanctity of an oath. We may assume that there may be permissible differences in the individual's conception of God. But it seems clear that under our Constitution disbelief in a Supreme Being, and the denial of any moral accountability for conduct, not only renders a person incompetent to hold public office, but to give testimony, or serve as a juror. The historical record makes it clear that religious toleration, in which this State has taken pride, was never thought to encompass the ungodly.[6]

Torcaso petitioned the Supreme Court for a writ of certiorari, which it granted, and the case was argued on April 4th, 1961. On June 19th of that year it announced a unanimous 9–0 decision in his favor.

The *Torcaso* case broke new ground in at least two ways. First, it was the first case considered at this level that examined the constitutionality of a religious qualification for state public office, and thus was the first decision at this level to invalidate state constitutional provisions – such as Maryland's – that limited office-holding to individuals who believed in God. And second, it broadened the First Amendment protections expressed in previous case decisions, such as *Everson v. Board of Education* and *McCollum v. Board of Education*, in consideration of the 'free exercise' that might be found in the beliefs of 'non-believing' individuals like Roy Torcaso.

In addition to these, two other significant outcomes should be noted here as well.

First, a similar trial came before the South Carolina State Supreme Court in 1997, inspired by the Court's decision in *Torcaso*.[7] In 1992 a mathematics professor at the College of Charleston, and Atheist, Herb Silverman, purposefully applied to be a notary public, knowing that the State Constitution of South Carolina had a similar restriction against Atheists holding public office. Both Article 6, Section 2, and Article 17, Section 4 of the State Constitution stated: 'No person who denies the existence of a Supreme Being shall hold any office under this Constitution.' When submitting his application, Silverman crossed off the line 'So help me God' from his oath, and it was quickly rejected. He filed suit with the Fifth Judicial Circuit in the Court of Common Pleas, which ruled in his favor. After which, the acting Secretary of State for South Carolina, James Miles, urged the named state officials in that lawsuit to appeal the decision to the State Supreme Court, which Governor David Beasley did in 1996. In a unanimous decision, the State Supreme Court affirmed the Circuit Court's ruling, declaring the two religious provisions in the State's Constitution in violation of both the

First Amendment, as well as the prohibition on religious tests in Article VI of the United States Constitution. In his decision, Chief Justice Ernest A. Finney, Jr. cited *Torcaso v. Watkins* as crucial precedence.

And second, it should also be noted that while the states of Maryland and South Carolina have had their religious provisions deemed unenforceable by the decisions in *Torcaso* and *Silverman*, they are still present in each state's constitutions. And moreover, they are just two of the eight states that still have requirements within their constitutions demanding a declaratory oath in order to either hold public office or to testify as a witness.

These are:

Arkansas.

> No person who denies the being of a God shall hold any office in the civil departments of this State, nor be competent to testify as a witness in any Court.
>
> Article 19, Section 1 of the Constitution of the State of Arkansas, titled: 'Atheists Disqualified From Holding Office or Testifying as Witness.'

Maryland.

> That no religious test ought ever to be required as a qualification for any office of profit or trust in this State, other than a declaration of belief in the existence of God; nor shall the Legislature prescribe any other oath of office than the oath prescribed by this Constitution.
>
> Article 37 of the Declaration of Rights of the Maryland State Constitution.

Mississippi.

> No person who denies the existence of a Supreme Being shall hold any office in this state.
>
> Article 14, Section 265 of the Constitution of the State of Mississippi.

North Carolina.

> The following persons shall be disqualified for office: First, any person who shall deny the being of Almighty God. Second, with respect to any office that is filled by election by the people, any person who is not qualified to vote in an election for that office. Third, any person who has been adjudged guilty of treason or any other felony against this State or the United States, or any person who has been adjudged guilty of a felony in another state that also would be a felony if it had been committed in this State, or any person who has been adjudged guilty of corruption or malpractice in any office, or any person who has been removed by impeachment from any office, and who has not been restored to the rights of citizenship in the manner prescribed by law.
>
> Article 6, Section 8 of the State Constitution of North Carolina under the title: 'Disqualifications for Office.'

Pennsylvania.

> No person who acknowledges the being of a God and a future state of rewards and punishments shall, on account of his religious sentiments, be disqualified to hold any office or place of trust or profit under this Commonwealth.
>
> Article 1, Section 4 of the Declaration of Rights of the Constitution of the Commonwealth of Pennsylvania.

South Carolina.

> No person who denies the existence of a Supreme Being shall hold any office under this Constitution.
>
> Article 17, Section 4 of the Constitution of the State of South Carolina under the title: 'Supreme Being'; and Article 6, Section 2 of the same, under the title: 'Person Denying Existence of Supreme Being Not to Hold Office.'

Tennessee.

> No person who denies the being of God, or a future state of rewards and punishments, shall hold any office in the civil department of this state.
>
> Article 9, Section 2 of the Constitution of the State of Tennessee, under the Title 'Disqualifications.'

Texas.

> No religious test shall ever be required as a qualification to any office, or public trust, in this State; nor shall any one be excluded from holding office on account of his religious sentiments, provided he acknowledge the existence of a Supreme Being.
>
> Article 1, Section 4 of the Constitution of the State of Texas, under the title 'Religious Tests.'

* * *

Torcaso v. Watkins (1961)

Full Title

Torcaso v. Watkins, Clerk

Official Citation

367 U.S. 488
Argued: April 24, 1961
Decided: June 19, 1961

Author

Justice Hugo Black

Syllabus

Appellant was appointed by the Governor of Maryland to the office of Notary Public, but he was denied a commission because he would not declare his belief in God, as required by the Maryland Constitution. Claiming that this requirement violated his rights under the First and Fourteenth Amendments, he sued in a state court to compel issuance of his commission, but relief was denied. The State Court of Appeals affirmed, holding that the state constitutional provision is self-executing, without need for implementing legislation, and requires declaration of a belief in God as a qualification for office.

Held:

This Maryland test for public office cannot be enforced against appellant, because it unconstitutionally invades his freedom of belief and religion guaranteed by the First Amendment and protected by the Fourteenth Amendment from infringement by the States.

[*Torcaso v. Watkins, Clerk* (State Court of Appeals of Maryland, 1960), citation: 223 Md. 49, 162 A.2d 438], *reversed.*

Opinion

Article 37 of the Declaration of Rights of the Maryland Constitution provides:

> [N]o religious test ought ever to be required as a qualification for any office of profit or trust in this State, other than a declaration of belief in the existence of God.

The appellant Torcaso was appointed to the office of Notary Public by the Governor of Maryland, but was refused a commission to serve because he would not declare his belief in God. He then brought this action in a Maryland Circuit Court to compel issuance of his commission, charging that the State's requirement that he declare this belief violated 'the First and Fourteenth Amendments to the Constitution of the United States.'[i] The Circuit Court rejected these federal constitutional contentions, and the highest court of the State, the Court of Appeals, affirmed,[ii] holding that the state constitutional provision is self-executing, and requires declaration of belief in God as a qualification for office without need for implementing legislation. The case is therefore properly here on appeal under 28 U.S.C. [section] 1257(2).

There is, and can be, no dispute about the purpose or effect of the Maryland Declaration of Rights requirement before us – it sets up a religious test which was designed to, and, if valid, does, bar every person who refuses to declare a belief in God from holding a public 'office of profit or trust' in Maryland. The power and authority of the State of Maryland thus is put on the side of one particular sort of believers – those who are willing to say they believe in 'the existence of God.' It is true that there is much historical precedent for such laws. Indeed, it was largely to escape religious test oaths and declarations that a great many of the early colonists left Europe and came here hoping to worship in their own way. It soon developed, however, that many of those who had fled to escape religious test oaths turned out to be perfectly willing, when they had the power to do so, to force dissenters from their faith to take test oaths in conformity with that faith. This brought on a host of laws in the New Colonies imposing burdens and disabilities of various kinds upon varied beliefs depending largely upon what group happened to be politically strong enough to legislate in favor of its own beliefs. The effect of all this was the formal or practical 'establishment' of particular religious faiths in most of the Colonies, with consequent burdens imposed on the free exercise of the faiths of nonfavored believers.[iii]

There were, however, wise and farseeing men in the Colonies – too many to mention – who spoke out against test oaths and all the philosophy of intolerance behind them. One of these, it so happens, was George Calvert (the first Lord Baltimore), who took a most important part in the original establishment of the Colony of Maryland. He was a Catholic and had, for this reason, felt compelled by his conscience to refuse to take the Oath of Supremacy in England at the cost of resigning from high governmental office. He again refused to take that oath when it was demanded by the Council of the Colony of Virginia, and, as a result, he was denied settlement in that Colony.[iv] A recent historian

i Appellant also claimed that the State's test oath requirement violates the provision of Art. VI of the Federal Constitution that 'no religious Test shall ever be required as a Qualification to any Office or public Trust under the United States.' Because we are reversing the judgment on other grounds, we find it unnecessary to consider appellant's contention that this provision applies to state as well as federal offices.

ii 223 Md. 49, 162 A.2d 438. Appellant's alternative contention that this test violates the Maryland Constitution also was rejected by the state courts.

iii See, e.g., I Stokes, *Church and State in the United States*, 358–446. See also cases cited, note [vii] infra.

iv The letter from the Virginia Council to the King's Privy Council is quoted in Hanley, *Their Rights and Liberties* (Newman Press 1959), 65, as follows:

> According to the instructions from your Lordship and the usual course held in this place, we tendered the oaths of supremacy and allegiance to his Lordship[;] [Baltimore] and some of his followers, who making profession of the Romish Religion, utterly refused to take the same [. . .]. His Lordship then offered to take this oath, a copy whereof is included [. . .] but we could not imagine that so much latitude was left for us to decline from the prescribed form, so strictly exacted and so well justified and defended by the pen of our late sovereign, Lord King James of happy memory. [. . .] Among the many blessings and favors for which we are bound to bless God [. . .] there is none whereby it hath been

of the early period of Maryland's life has said that it was Calvert's hope and purpose to establish in Maryland a colonial government free from the religious persecutions he had known – one 'securely beyond the reach of oaths. [. . .]'[v]

When our Constitution was adopted, the desire to put the people 'securely beyond the reach' of religious test oaths brought about the inclusion in Article VI of that document of a provision that 'no religious Test shall ever be required as a Qualification to any Office or public Trust under the United States.' Article VI supports the accuracy of our observation in *Girouard v. United States*, that '[t]he test oath is abhorrent to our tradition.'[8] Not satisfied, however, with Article VI and other guarantees in the original Constitution, the First Congress proposed and the States very shortly thereafter adopted our Bill of Rights, including the First Amendment.[vi] That Amendment broke new constitutional ground in the protection it sought to afford to freedom of religion, speech, press, petition and assembly. Since prior cases in this Court have thoroughly explored and documented the history behind the First Amendment, the reasons for it, and the scope of the religious freedom it protects, we need not cover that ground again.[vii] What was said in our prior cases we think controls our decision here.

In *Cantwell v. Connecticut* (1940),[9] we said:

> The First Amendment declares that Congress shall make no law respecting an establishment of religion or prohibiting the free exercise thereof. The Fourteenth Amendment has rendered the legislatures of the states a incompetent as Congress to enact such laws. [. . .] Thus, the Amendment embraces two concepts – freedom to believe and freedom to act. The first is absolute but, in the nature of things, the second cannot be.

Later, we decided *Everson v. Board of Education* (1947),[10] and said this at pages 15 and 16:

> The 'establishment of religion' clause of the First Amendment means at least this: neither a state nor the Federal Government can set up a church. Neither can pass laws which aid one religion, aid all religions, or prefer one religion over another. Neither can force nor influence a person to go to or to remain away from church against his will or force him to profess a belief or disbelief in any religion. No person can be punished for entertaining or professing religious beliefs or disbeliefs, for

> made more happy than in the freedom of our Religion [. . .] and that no papists have been suffered to settle their abode amongst us. [. . .]

Of course, this was long before Madison's great *Memorial and Remonstrance* and the enactment of the famous Virginia Bill for Religious Liberty, discussed in our opinion in *Everson v. Board of Education*, 330 U. S. 1, 330 U. S. 11–13.

v Hanley, op. cit., supra, p. 65.

vi 'Congress shall make no law respecting an establishment of religion, or prohibiting the free exercise thereof; or abridging the freedom of speech, or of the press; or the right of the people peaceably to assemble, and to petition the Government for a redress of grievances.'

vii See, e.g., the opinions of the Court and also the concurring and dissenting opinions in *Reynolds v. United States*, 98 U. S. 145; *Davis v. Beason*, 133 U. S. 333; *Cantwell v. Connecticut*, 310 U. S. 296; *West Virginia State Bd. of Education v. Barnette*, 319 U. S. 624; *Fowler v. Rhode Island*, 345 U. S. 67; *Everson v. Board of Education*, 330 U. S. 1; *Illinois ex rel. McCollum v. Board of Education*, 333 U. S. 203; *McGowan v. Maryland*, 366 U. S. 420.

church attendance or nonattendance. No tax in any amount, large or small, can be levied to support any religious activities or institutions, whatever they may be called, or whatever form they may adopt to teach or practice religion. Neither a state nor the Federal Government can, openly or secretly, participate in the affairs of any religious organizations or groups, and vice versa. In the words of Jefferson, the clause against establishment of religion by law was intended to erect 'a wall of separation between church and State.'

While there were strong dissents in the Everson case, they did not challenge the Court's interpretation of the First Amendment's coverage as being too broad, but thought the Court was applying that interpretation too narrowly to the facts of that case. Not long afterward, in *Illinois ex rel. McCollum v. Board of Education*, we were urged to repudiate as dicta the above-quoted *Everson* interpretation of the scope of the First Amendment's coverage. We declined to do this, but instead strongly reaffirmed what had been said in *Everson*, calling attention to the fact that both the majority and the minority in *Everson* had agreed on the principles declared in this part of the *Everson* opinion. And a concurring opinion in *McCollum*, written by Mr. Justice Frankfurter and joined by the other *Everson* dissenters, said this:

> We are all agreed that the First and Fourteenth Amendments have a secular reach far more penetrating in the conduct of Government than merely to forbid an 'established church.' [. . .] We renew our conviction that we have staked the very existence of our country on the faith that complete separation between the state and religion is best for the state and best for religion.[viii]

The Maryland Court of Appeals thought, and it is argued here, that this Court's later holding and opinion in *Zorach v. Clauson*,[11] had in part repudiated the statement in the *Everson* opinion quoted above and previously reaffirmed in *McCollum*. But the Court's opinion in *Zorach* specifically stated: 'We follow the *McCollum* case.'[12] Nothing decided or written in *Zorach* lends support to the idea that the Court there intended to open up the way for government, state or federal, to restore the historically and constitutionally discredited policy of probing religious beliefs by test oaths or limiting public offices to persons who have, or perhaps more properly profess to have, a belief in some particular kind of religious concept.[ix]

viii 333 U. S. at 333 U. S. 213, 333 U. S. 232. Later, in *Zorach v. Clauson*, 343 U. S. 306, 343 U. S. 322, Mr. Justice Frankfurter stated in dissent that

> [t]he result in the *McCollum* case . . . was based on principles that received unanimous acceptance by this Court, barring only a single vote.

ix In one of his famous letters of 'a Landholder,' published in December, 1787, Oliver Ellsworth, a member of the Federal Constitutional Convention and later Chief Justice of this Court, included among his strong arguments against religious test oaths the following statement:

> In short, test laws are utterly ineffectual; they are no security at all, because men of loose principles will, by an external compliance, evade them. If they exclude any persons, it will be honest men, men of principle, who will rather suffer an injury than act contrary to the dictates of their consciences. [. . .]

Quoted in Ford, *Essays on the Constitution of the United States*, 170. See also 4 Elliott, *Debates in the Several State Conventions on the Adoption of the Federal Constitution*, 193.

We repeat and again reaffirm that neither a State nor the Federal Government can constitutionally force a person 'to profess a belief or disbelief in any religion.' Neither can constitutionally pass laws or impose requirements which aid all religions as against nonbelievers,[x] and neither can aid those religions based on a belief in the existence of God as against those religions founded on different beliefs.[xi]

In upholding the State's religious test for public office, the highest court of Maryland said:

> The petitioner is not compelled to believe or disbelieve, under threat of punishment or other compulsion. True, unless he makes the declaration of belief, he cannot hold public office in Maryland, but he is not compelled to hold office.

The fact, however, that a person is not compelled to hold public office cannot possibly be an excuse for barring him from office by state-imposed criteria forbidden by the Constitution. This was settled by our holding in *Wieman v. Updegraff*.[13] We there pointed out that, whether or not 'an abstract right to public employment exists,' Congress could not pass a law providing '[. . .] that no federal employee shall attend Mass or take any active part in missionary work.'[xii]

This Maryland religious test for public office unconstitutionally invades the appellant's freedom of belief and religion, and therefore cannot be enforced against him.

The judgment of the Court of Appeals of Maryland is accordingly reversed, and the cause is remanded for further proceedings not inconsistent with this opinion.

Reversed and remanded.

* * *

Importance

Justice Black's use of *Everson v. Board of Education* here, as well as his reference to the Court's decision in *Zorach v. Clauson*, reveals an interesting pattern relevant to the

x In discussing Article VI in the debate of the North Carolina Convention on the adoption of the Federal Constitution, James Iredell, later a Justice of this Court, said:

> [. . .] [i]t is objected that the people of America may, perhaps, choose representatives who have no religion at all, and that pagans and Mahometans may be admitted into offices. But how is it possible to exclude any set of men without taking away that principle of religious freedom which we ourselves so warmly contend for?

And another delegate pointed out that Article VI

> leaves religion on the solid foundation of its own inherent validity, without any connection with temporal authority, and no kind of oppression can take place.

4 Elliot, *op. cit., supra*, at 194, 200.

xi Among religions in this country which do not teach what would generally be considered a belief in the existence of God are Buddhism, Taoism, Ethical Culture, Secular Humanism and others. See *Washington Ethical Society v. District of Columbia*, 101 U.S. App .D.C. 371, 249 F.2d 127; *Fellowship of Humanity v. County of Alameda*, 153 Cal. App.2d 673, 315 P.2d 394; *II Encyclopaedia of the Social Sciences* 293; *4 Encyclopaedia Britannica* (1957 ed.) 325–327; 21 *id.* at 797; Archer, *Faiths Men Live By* (2d ed. revised by Purinton), 120–138, 254–313; 1961 *World Almanac* 695, 712; *Year Book of American Churches* for 1961, at 29, 47.

xii *Wieman v. Updegraff* (1952), citation: 344 U. S. 183, 191–192, quoting from *United Public Workers v. Mitchell*, 330 U. S. 75, 330 U. S. 100.

intentions of this book. Between *Everson* and this decision, the Court began to intermittently consider the place of 'non-believers' in its application of the First Amendment's two religion clauses, and these sporadic inferences reflect a shifting narrative wherein these non-believers were provided equal treatment alongside believers.

For example, in *Everson v. Board of Education*, Justice Black also argued:

> New Jersey cannot, consistently with the 'establishment of religion' clause of the First Amendment, contribute tax raised funds to the support of an institution which teaches the tenets and faith of any church. On the other hand, other language of the amendment commands that New Jersey cannot hamper its citizens in the free exercise of their own religion. Consequently, it cannot exclude individual Catholics, Lutherans, Mohammedans, Baptists, Jews, Methodists, ***Nonbelievers***, Presbyterians, or the members of any other faith, because of their faith, or lack of it, from receiving the benefits of public welfare legislation [emphasis mine].[14]

Or, as he also stated in his dissenting opinion to Justice William Douglas' decision in *Zorach v. Clauson*:

> Under our system of religious freedom, people have gone to their religious sanctuaries not because they feared the law, but because they loved their God. The choice of all has been as free as the choice of those who answered the call to worship moved only by the music of the old Sunday morning church bells. The spiritual mind of man has thus been free to believe, ***disbelieve***, or ***doubt***, without repression, great or small, by the heavy hand of government. Statutes authorizing such repression have been stricken. Before today, our judicial opinions have refrained from drawing invidious distinctions between ***those who believe in no religion*** and those who do believe. The First Amendment has lost much if the religious follower and the ***atheist*** are no longer to be judicially regarded as entitled to equal justice under law [emphases mine].[15]

Or in Justice Douglas' own dissent to Chief Justice Earl Warren's decision in *McGowan v. Maryland*:

> The First Amendment commands government to have no interest in theology or ritual; it admonishes government to be interested in allowing religious freedom to flourish – whether the result is to produce Catholics, Jews, or Protestants, or to turn the people toward the path of Buddha, or to end in a predominantly Moslem nation, or to produce in the long run ***atheists*** or ***agnostics***. On matters of this kind, government must be neutral. This freedom plainly includes ***freedom from religion***, with the right to believe, speak, write, publish and advocate ***anti-religious*** programs [emphases mine].[16]

While these references provide at least a minimal sense of clarification regarding the Court's position on the place of 'non-believers' with respect to the protections of the First Amendment, they likewise lead us toward a much more complex issue concerning the legality, and possibly even support, of 'Atheistic belief systems,' such as 'secular humanism.'

Since its first usage by Justice Black in an innocuous footnote to his decision in *Torcaso v. Watkins*, where he briefly defined 'different beliefs' beyond the existence of God, the moniker of 'secular humanism' has been used by defendants, plaintiffs, and even judges, as a target toward which they might direct arguments in favor of, and against, the equal treatment of ideologies that would constitute a 'religion of Atheism.'

Because this begins with the *Torcaso* decision, this issue is part of its legacy, and deserves a brief discussion here, beginning with Justice Black's footnote:

> [xi]. Among religions in this country which do not teach what would generally be considered a belief in the existence of God are Buddhism, Taoism, Ethical Culture, Secular Humanism and others.[17]

Justice Black based this description on the *Encyclopedia of the Social Sciences*, the *Encyclopedia Britannica*, the *1961 World Almanac*, the *Year Book of American Churches for 1961*, *Faiths Men Live By*, by John Clark Archer, and two Appeals Court case decisions that concluded the 'Ethical Culture' and 'humanism' of two non-theistic organizations qualified them for the same tax-exempt status as theistic ones.[18] And while it functioned, for this decision, as nothing more than a citation of the existence in America of non-theistic religions, and thus held no legal weight – 'dicta' – it has since come to be utilized by plaintiffs and defendants in some rather creative ways.

For example, in the case of *Edwards v. Aguillard* (1987), in which the Court passed a 7–2 decision arguing that the teaching of 'creation science' was unconstitutional because it reflected a direct attempt at advancing a particular religious agenda, the lead sponsor of the bill at question, Louisiana State Senator Bill P. Keith, defended the Balanced Treatment for Creation Science and Evolution-Science Act as a means of equalizing two religious ideologies. As Justice William J. Brennan wrote in his opinion for the Court:

> The sponsor of the Creationism Act explained during the legislative hearings that his disdain for the theory of evolution resulted from the support that evolution supplied to views contrary to his own religious beliefs. According to Senator Keith, the theory of evolution was consonant with the 'cardinal principle[s] of religious humanism, secular humanism, theological liberalism, aetheistism [sic].' The state senator repeatedly stated that scientific evidence supporting his religious views should be included in the public school curriculum to redress the fact that the theory of evolution incidentally coincided with what he characterized as religious beliefs antithetical to his own.[19]

Moreover, in his own dissenting opinion, Justice Antonin Scalia defended Senator Keith's argument here by estimating that because the theory of evolution was the central dogma of secular humanism, and since secular humanism was defined as a religion via Justice Black's footnote in *Torcaso*, the teaching of evolution violated the establishment clause of the First Amendment:

> The censorship of creation science has at least two harmful effects. First, it deprives students of knowledge of one of the two scientific explanations for the origin of life, and leads them to believe that evolution is proven fact; thus, their education suffers, and they are wrongly taught that science has proved their religious beliefs false.

> Second, it violates the Establishment Clause. The United States Supreme Court has held that secular humanism is a religion. Thus, by censoring creation science and instructing students that evolution is fact, public school teachers are now advancing religion in violation of the Establishment Clause.[20]

This line of reasoning, that secular humanism characterized an Atheist religion accepted by the Court through Justice Black's dicta description, became a larger issue the more it was used, and the more the Court allowed it without clarification. Leo Pfeffer, who defended Roy Torcaso in *Torcaso v. Watkins*, wrote in 1987 that the Court had only itself to blame for this issue, as a lack of judicial explanation meant that 'secular humanism' could substitute any legal concern, from federally accepted Atheism, to the promotion of evolution, sexual education, or any other relevant issue. He cited a number of examples where this had already occurred:

> The Supreme Court's avoidance of clarifying the meaning of secular humanism has encouraged numerous assaults by fundamentalists upon actions taken by public school teachers and administrators in the course of their responsibilities. [. . .] Among these assaults are the following: In Hillsboro, Missouri: A parents' group fearing secular humanism protested the school showing of the movie 'Romeo and Juliet.' In Maryland: Coalition of Concerned Parents on Privacy Rights distributed a letter citing the Hatch amendment as requiring parental permission for twenty four categories of classroom practice and material. (The New York Times suggests in an editorial in its 19 May 1985 issue that, strictly speaking, to ask a student to write about 'What I did on my summer vacation,' would require a letter from home.) In Mobile, Alabama: More than six hundred teachers, parents, and students sponsored a suit to enjoin the school board from using textbooks that advance humanism and that censor 'the existence, history, contribution and current role of Christianity in the United States and the World.' In Rhode Island: According to its opponents, 'excessive' funding of public education amounts to an advancement of the religion of 'Secular Humanism,' and as a matter of fairness equal funding should therefore be provided for religious schools.[21]

Of these, the suit against the School Board in Mobile, Alabama stands out the loudest, especially because of its correlation with the Supreme Court's decision in *Wallace v. Jaffree* in 1985, and that case's subsequent focus on 'secular humanism.'

A brief discussion of it is pertinent here.

* * *

In 1982, Ishmael Jaffree, a father of three and self-described 'agnostic' – who would later be named 'Freethinker of the Year' by the Freedom from Religion Foundation, as well as serve on the advisory board of African Americans for Humanism – sued the Mobile County School Board seeking a declaratory judgment and injunction toward revoking three school statutes enacted in 1978 (16-1-20), 1981 (16-1-20.1), and 1982 (16-1-20.2). The first authorized a one-minute period of silence at the start of each school day to be observed for 'meditation.' The second authorized the same period of silence, for the same duration and at the same time, adding 'or voluntary prayer.' The third amended the period of silence to accommodate a particular prayer:

16-120.2. From henceforth, any teacher or professor in any public educational institution within the state of Alabama, recognizing that the Lord God is one, at the beginning of any homeroom or any class, may pray, may lead willing students in prayer, or may lead the willing students in the following prayer to God:

'Almighty God, You alone are our God. We acknowledge You as the Creator and Supreme Judge of the world. May Your justice, Your truth, and Your peace abound this day in the hearts of our countrymen, in the counsels of our government, in the sanctity of our homes and in the classrooms of our schools in the name of our Lord. Amen.'[22]

The United States District Court for the Southern District of Alabama initially dismissed 16-1-20 on the grounds that it merely supported a period of silence for meditation, but then also argued that 16-1-20.1 and 16-1-20.2 were constitutionally permissible because, as Chief Judge Brevard Hand concluded, the establishment clause of the First Amendment did not prohibit the state of Alabama from establishing its own religion.

In 1983, the 11th Circuit Court of Appeals agreed with the District Court's interpretation of 16-1-20, but found both 16-1-20.1 and 16-1-20.2 to be unconstitutional.[23]

In April 1984, the Supreme Court unanimously affirmed the Court of Appeal's decision concerning the unconstitutionality of 16-1-20.2,[24] and in June 1985, with a 6–3 opinion, also affirmed the Court of Appeals' decision concerning 16-1-20.1, concluding: 'The addition of "or voluntary prayer" indicates that the State intended to characterize prayer as a favored practice. Such an endorsement is not consistent with the established principle that the government must pursue a course of complete neutrality toward religion.'[25] Moreover, in his decision for the Court, and in reference to both Justice Black's decision in *Everson v. Board of Education*, as well as James Madison's *Memorial and Remonstrance*,[26] Justice John Paul Stevens made the following statement:

> Just as the right to speak and the right to refrain from speaking are complementary components of a broader concept of individual freedom of mind, so also the individual's freedom to choose his own creed is the counterpart of his right to refrain from accepting the creed established by the majority. At one time, it was thought that this right merely proscribed the preference of one Christian sect over another, but would not require equal respect for the conscience of the infidel, the atheist, or the adherent of a non-Christian faith such as Islam or Judaism. But when the underlying principle has been examined in the crucible of litigation, the Court has unambiguously concluded that the individual freedom of conscience protected by the First Amendment embraces the right to select any religious faith or none at all. This conclusion derives support not only from the interest in respecting the individual's freedom of conscience, but also from the conviction that religious beliefs worthy of respect are the product of free and voluntary choice by the faithful, and from recognition of the fact that the political interest in forestalling intolerance extends beyond intolerance among Christian sects – or even intolerance among 'religions' – to encompass intolerance of the disbeliever and the uncertain.[27]

As per judicial process, the case was remanded back to the District Court from which it originated, at which point Chief Judge Hand 'reconsolidated' it, providing the opportunity for certain defendant-intervenors who were originally denied an intervening injunction in the original case, to file their own complaint. That case became *Smith v. Board of School*

Commissioners of Mobile County. These defendant-intervenors, now plaintiffs, had initially requested that if Jaffree was able to obtain his injunction against the school prayer, that it should be expanded to include 'the religions of secularism, humanism, evolution, materialism, agnosticism, atheism and others,'[28] which they argued were being fostered by the Mobile public schools and School Board through the implementation of forty-four textbooks that supported such religious beliefs.

Both the original complaints, and those in support of this new case, came from teachers and parents alike, who argued that not only were these textbooks offensive to their Christian beliefs, but that the school's use of them demanded a 're-education' process wherein the latter would, day-to-day, need to reaffirm in their children the truth of creationism.

One instructor, Douglas T. Smith, for whom the case was named, drafted a brief on behalf of his fellow plaintiffs in order to argue that the curriculum used within the school system not only inhibited Christianity and excluded the historical contributions of Christianity to the 'American way of life,' it also unconstitutionally 'advanced the religion of humanism.' As Judge Hand described:

> At least half of the original trial dealt with textbooks and, though this was not an issue on appeal, it was an issue squarely presented to the Court. One of the positions the original 624 intervenors, now plaintiffs, took was that humanism is being advanced in the textbooks. It is a religion and therefore should be excluded as have other religious beliefs. In this case the plaintiffs draw a distinction between tenets of faith and facts about religion. Tenets of faith consist of dogma, doctrine and belief and are prohibited from being advanced in the public school classroom. Facts about religion are not. The plaintiffs concede that tenets of faith, dogma and doctrine cannot be advanced in the public school room, but they believe that this restriction should be equally applied to all such. Humanism being such a religion, it should be excluded.[29]

After Judge Hand ruled in favor of the plaintiffs, demanding the School Board remove these offending texts, the 11th Circuit Court of Appeals reversed his opinion, arguing that even if 'secular humanism' were considered a religion, the plaintiffs failed to prove the offending textbooks had violated the establishment clause.[30]

Then with respect to 'secular humanism,' which Judge Hand had defined as the religious label of secularism, humanism, evolution, materialism, agnosticism, and Atheism, the Court of Appeals further concluded:

> The district court found that secular humanism constitutes a religion within the meaning of the first amendment and that the forty-four textbooks at issue in this case both advanced that religion and inhibited theistic faiths in violation of the establishment clause. The Supreme Court has never established a comprehensive test for determining the 'delicate question' of what constitutes a religious belief for purposes of the first amendment, and we need not attempt to do so in this case, for we find that, even assuming that secular humanism is a religion for purposes of the establishment clause, Appellees have failed to prove a violation of the establishment clause through the use in the Alabama public schools of the textbooks at issue in this case.[31]

Since the resolution of this case, however, this issue has appeared a few more times. In *Peloza v. Capistrano School District* (1994),[32] 'secular humanism' was used, again unsuccessfully, to argue that the teaching of the 'religion of evolution' violated the First Amendment. And in *American Humanist Association v. United States of America* (2014),[33] Justice Black's footnote became the basis for deciding in favor of a humanist – Jason Michael Holden – who argued that his First Amendment right of free exercise was being violated because, as a federal prisoner, he was not permitted the right to create a Humanist study group.

Alongside the innate terminological discussions here, within each of these examples we find as well a shared conversation about the place of Atheist-Americans and American non-believers in the broader understanding of the applicability of the First Amendment's religion clauses. A complexity that is matched equally by the inherent consequences that might exist in such applications, especially with the Court's continued re-conceptualization of the very meaning of the 'religious beliefs' deserving of the rights and protections that they grant.

Like *McCollum*, then, the decision in *Torcaso v. Watkins* propels these discussions further toward an even stronger understanding of both American Atheism, as well as its influence on American religion. An understanding that will gain even more traction with the next case decision as we return once again to an issue pertaining to religion in the public school system, and perhaps one of the most famous American Atheists of the twentieth century: Madalyn Murray O'Hair.

Notes

1 *Torcaso v. Watkins, Clerk* (Court of Appeals of Maryland, 1960), citation: 223 Md. 49.
2 Roy Torcaso quoted by Adam Bernstein, 'Roy Torcaso, 96; Defeated Md. in 1961 Religious Freedom Case,' *Washington Post*, June 21st, 2007.
3 *Torcaso v. Watkins, Clerk* (1960), 58.
4 *Zorach v. Clauson* (1952), citation: 343 U.S. 306, 313.
5 *Torcaso v. Watkins, Clerk* (1960), 58.
6 Ibid., 60.
7 *Silverman v. Campbell* (Supreme Court of South Carolina, 1997), No. 24622.
8 *Girouard v. United States* (1946), citation: 328 U.S., 61, page 69.
9 *Cantwell v. Connecticut* (1940), citation: 310 U.S. 296, 303–304.
10 *Everson v. Board of Education* (1947), citation: 330 U.S. 1, 15–16.
11 *Zorach v. Clauson* (1952), 306.
12 Ibid., 315.
13 *Wieman v. Updegraff* (1952), citation: 344 U.S. 183.
14 *Everson v. Board of Education* (1947), 16.
15 *Zorach v. Clauson*, (1952), 320.
16 *McGowan v. Maryland* (1961), citation: 366 U.S. 420, 564.
17 *Torcaso v. Watkins* (1961), Footnote 11.
18 *Washington Ethical Society v. District of Columbia* (United States Court of Appeals for the District of Columbia, 1957), citation: 249 F.2d 127; and *Fellowship of Humanity v. County of Alameda* (California Courts of Appeal, 1957), citation: 315 P.2d 394.
19 *Edwards v. Aguillard* (1987), citation: 482 U.S. 578, 592.
20 Justice Antonin Scalia, dissenting in *Edwards v. Aguillard*, 623–624.
21 Leo Pfeffer, 'The "Religion" of Secular Humanism' (*Journal of Church and State*, Vol. 29, Iss. 3, 1987, 503–504.
22 *Wallace v. Jaffree* (1985) 472 U.S. 38, Footnote 3.
23 *Jaffree v. Wallace* (11th Circuit Court of Appeals, 1983), citation: 705 F.2d 1526.
24 *Wallace v. Jaffree* (1984), citation: 466 U.S. 924.

25 *Wallace v. Jaffree* (1985), 60.
26 Accessible online at: https://founders.archives.gov/documents/Madison/01-08-02-0163.
27 *Wallace v. Jaffree* (1985), 53–54.
28 *Smith v. Board of School Commissioners of Mobile County* (U.S. District Court for the Southern District of Alabama, 1987), citation: 655 F.Supp. 939, 946.
29 Ibid.
30 *Smith v. Board of School Commissioners of Mobile County* (11th Circuit Court of Appeals, 1987), citation: 827 F.2d 684.
31 Ibid.
32 *Peloza v. Capistrano School District* (9th Circuit Court of Appeals, 1994), citation: 37 F.3d 517.
33 *American Humanist Association v. United States of America* (U.S. District Court for the District of Oregon, 2014), citation: 63 F.Supp.3d 1274.

6 *Abington v. Schempp* and *Murray v. Curlett* (1963)

Argued: February 27th–28th, 1963 – Decided: June 17th, 1963.

> It is insisted that, unless these religious exercises are permitted, a 'religion of secularism' is established in the schools. We agree, of course, that the State may not establish a 'religion of secularism' in the sense of affirmatively opposing or showing hostility to religion, thus 'preferring those who believe in no religion over those who do believe.' We do not agree, however, that this decision in any sense has that effect.
>
> — Justice Clark, decision in *Abington v. Schempp* (1963)

Question before the Court: Does a law requiring public school students to participate in religious exercises, such as reading and/or reciting passages from the Bible, as well as the recitation of the Lord's Prayer, constitute a violation of the First Amendment rights of those children and their parents?

Decision: 8–1. Yes, such laws and actions are unconstitutional.

Antecedent Case Decisions:

Abington v. Schempp was based on two companion cases, which means it was the result of two separate antecedent case decision backgrounds.

Abington v. Schempp.

- U.S. DISTRICT COURT FOR THE EASTERN DISTRICT OF PENNSYLVANIA, February 1st, 1962.

  Ruling: The Court found in favor of Edward Schempp. The School District, its officials, and the Superintendent, petitioned the Supreme Court for an appeal.

- U.S. DISTRICT COURT FOR THE EASTERN DISTRICT OF PENNSYLVANIA, June 22nd, 1961.

  Ruling: The Court granted plaintiff Schempp a motion toward a new ruling.

- UNITED STATES SUPREME COURT, October 24th, 1960.

  Ruling: The Judgment was vacated and the case was remanded upon amendment of the offending law of the General Assembly of the Commonwealth of Pennsylvania.

- U.S. DISTRICT COURT FOR THE EASTERN DISTRICT OF PENNSYLVANIA, September 16th, 1959.

  Ruling: The Court found in favor of Edward Schempp.

Murray v. Curlett

- COURT OF APPEALS OF MARYLAND (Maryland State Supreme Court), April 6th, 1962.

  Ruling: The Court affirmed the decision of the Superior Court, and Madalyn Murray petitioned the Supreme Court for a writ of certiorari.

- SUPERIOR COURT OF BALTIMORE, April 27th, 1961.

  Ruling: Judge J. Gilbert Pendergast found in favor of the School Board.

Background

As companion cases, both *Abington v. Schempp* and *Murray v. Curlett* share similar backgrounds.

Abington v. Schempp

In 1958, Edward Lewis Schempp, his wife Sydney Gerber Schempp, and their three children, Roger, Donna, and Ellory, filed suit against the School District of Abington Township, Pennsylvania, in regard to Title 24 of the Pennsylvania Statutes, section 15-1516, which required:

> At least ten verses from the Holy Bible shall be read, or caused to be read, without comment, at the opening of each public school on each school day, by the teacher in charge: Provided, That where any teacher has other teachers under and subject to direction, then the teacher exercising such authority shall read the Holy Bible, or cause it to be read, as herein directed. If any school teacher, whose duty it shall be to read the Holy Bible, or cause it to be read, shall fail or omit so to do, said school teacher shall, upon charges preferred for such failure or omission, and proof of the same, before the board of school directors of the school district, be discharged.[1]

As directed by this rule, on each school day morning, between 8:15 and 8:30, students at the Abington Senior High School would participate in 'opening exercises' during their 'homeroom' attendance. These exercises were broadcast throughout the school via an intercommunications system, were conducted by students – under teacher supervision – in the school's radio and television workshop, and consisted of the following actions: ten Bible verses of the child's choosing would be read, without commentary, followed by the Lord's Prayer; students would stand and recite the Lord's Prayer in unison to the broadcast; after which students would salute the flag, recite the Pledge of Allegiance, and then pertinent announcements would be made. If a parent did not want his or her child to participate, they could absent themselves, upon signed permission, either by leaving the classroom, or by remaining and simply not taking part.

The Schempp family were members of the Unitarian Church in Germantown, Pennsylvania, and because of their Unitarian Faith, they objected to both the Bible readings, as well as the requirement of their children to recite the Lord's Prayer.

After the U.S. District Court for the Eastern District of Pennsylvania ruled in their favor on September 16th, 1959, their case was put on hold by the Supreme Court with respect to an amendment made to Title 24 by Governor David L. Lawrence that clarified the voluntary nature of the morning exercises. In response, they re-filed their suit, directing it in this instance at the new statute, and after the District Court once again ruled in their favor on February 1st, 1962, the School Board officially appealed for a writ of certiorari, which the Supreme Court granted.

Murray v. Curlett

In April 1961, Madalyn Murray and her son, William filed suit against the Board of School Commissioners of Baltimore City requesting a writ of mandamus that would rescind and cancel the compulsory opening exercises within the public school system, as mandated by Section 6, Article VI of the Rules of the Board [of School Commissioners] as such:

> Each school, either collectively or in classes, shall be opened by the reading, without comment, of a chapter in the Holy Bible and/or the use of the Lord's Prayer. The Douay version may be used by those pupils who prefer it. Appropriate patriotic exercises should [also] be held as a part of the general opening exercise of the school or class.[2]

Just prior to their suit, and in order to ensure William could not say he was 'compelled' to participate, the State Attorney General, C. Ferdinand Sybert, passed an amendment to this rule at the request of the State Superintendent of Schools. It added:

> Any child shall be excused from participating in the opening exercises or from attending the opening exercises upon written request of his parent or guardian.[3]

In their initial complaint to the Superior Court of Baltimore, Madalyn and William contended that the rule, even amended, 'contravened' the freedom of religion granted them by the First Amendment, that it threatened their 'religious liberty,' subjected their 'freedom of conscience to the rule of the majority,' rendered their beliefs and ideals as 'sinister, alien, and suspect,' and that the amendment, though it allowed William to absent himself, nevertheless placed him at a disadvantage with respect to his fellow classmates, causing him to 'lose caste, to be regarded with aversion, and to be subjected to reproach and insult.'[4]

In response, the Board of School Commissioners demurred, meaning they filed a rejoinder that argued that the Murray's complaint had no legal basis on which to support their claim. The Superior Court agreed, and ruled in favor of the Board on April 27th, 1961. Madalyn and William appealed to the Court of Appeals of Maryland, which affirmed the lower Court's decision on April 6th, 1962.

Writing for the latter, Justice William R. Horney based his decision on the Supreme Court's ruling in *Zorach v. Clauson* (1952), which had re-interpreted *McCollum v. Board of Education* in order to permit a similar released time program. And then by arguing that William was not, as State Attorney Sybert's amendment had ensured, 'compelled' to participate in what he defined as a mere acknowledgement of America's traditional religious heritage, he concluded that the morning exercises at central focus in their complaint did not express a constitutional violation. As to whether or not this conclusion would be admissible beyond the context of the State of Maryland, however, he stated:

> Inasmuch as the Supreme Court has not yet spoken with respect to the Bible reading and Prayer recitation ceremonies at school opening exercises, we think we are bound by what we understand is the effect of *McCollum* as it is explained and expanded in *Zorach* until such time as the Court speaks further in this uncertain area.[5]

The Supreme Court resolved that uncertainty a year later when, on June 17th, 1963 it ruled, 8–1, in favor of both the Schempp family, as well as Madalyn and William.

* * *

Abington v. Schempp/Murray v. Curlett (1963)

Full Title

School District of Abington Township, Pennsylvania, et al. v. Edward Schempp, et al.; Murray, et al. v. Curlett, et al., Constituting the Board of School Commissioners of Baltimore City

Official Citation

374 U.S. 203
Argued: February 27–28, 1963
Decided: June 17, 1963*

Author

Justice Tom C. Clark

Syllabus

Because of the prohibition of the First Amendment against the enactment by Congress of any law 'respecting an establishment of religion,' which is made applicable to the States by the Fourteenth Amendment, no state law or school board may require that passages from the Bible be read or that the Lord's Prayer be recited in the public schools of a State at the beginning of each school day – even if individual students may be excused from attending or participating in such exercises upon written request of their parents.

* Together with No. 119, *Murray et al. v. Curlett et al., Constituting the Board of School Commissioners of Baltimore City*, on certiorari to the Court of Appeals of Maryland, argued February 27, 1963.

[*Edward L. Schempp et al. v. School District of Abington Township, PA., et al.* (1962), District Court, Eastern District, Pennsylvania, citation: 201 F.Supp. 815], *affirmed.*

[*Murray et al. v. Curlett et al.* (1962), Court of Appeals of Maryland, citation: 228 Md. 239, 179 A.2d 698], *reversed.*

Opinion

Once again, we are called upon to consider the scope of the provision of the First Amendment to the United States Constitution which declares that 'Congress shall make no law respecting an establishment of religion, or prohibiting the free exercise thereof [. . .].' These companion cases present the issues in the context of state action requiring that schools begin each day with readings from the Bible. While raising the basic questions under slightly different factual situations, the cases permit of joint treatment. In light of the history of the First Amendment and of our cases interpreting and applying its requirements, we hold that the practices at issue and the laws requiring them are unconstitutional under the Establishment Clause, as applied to the States through the Fourteenth Amendment.

I

The Facts in Each Case:

No. 142 [*Abington v. Schempp* (1959 and 1962)].

The Commonwealth of Pennsylvania, by law, [of Title 24 of the Pennsylvania Statutes, sections 15-1516, as amended by Public Law 1928 (Supplemented 1960)] Dec. 17, 1959, requires that

> At least ten verses from the Holy Bible shall be read, without comment, at the opening of each public school on each school day. Any child shall be excused from such Bible reading, or attending such Bible reading, upon the written request of his parent or guardian.

The Schempp family, husband and wife and two of their three children, brought suit to enjoin enforcement of the statute, contending that their rights under the Fourteenth Amendment to the Constitution of the United States are, have been, and will continue to be, violated unless this statute be declared unconstitutional as violative of these provisions of the First Amendment. They sought to enjoin the appellant school district, wherein the Schempp children attend school, and its officers and the Superintendent of Public Instruction of the Commonwealth from continuing to conduct such readings and recitation of the Lord's Prayer in the public schools of the district pursuant to the statute. A three-judge statutory District Court for the Eastern District of Pennsylvania held that the statute is violative of the Establishment Clause of the First Amendment as applied to the States by the Due Process Clause of the Fourteenth Amendment, and directed that appropriate injunctive relief issue.[i] On appeal by the District, its officials, and the Superintendent under [United States Code 28, section 1253], we noted probable jurisdiction.

The appellees Edward Lewis Schempp, his wife Sidney, and their children, Roger and Donna, are of the Unitarian faith, and are members of the Unitarian Church in Germantown, Philadelphia, Pennsylvania, where they, as well as another son, Ellory, regularly attend religious services. The latter was originally a party, but, having graduated from the school system *pendente lite* ['awaiting the litigation'], was voluntarily dismissed from the action. The other children attend the Abington Senior High School, which is a public school operated by appellant district.

On each school day at the Abington Senior High School between 8:15 and 8:30 a.m., while the pupils are attending their home rooms or advisory sections, opening exercises are conducted pursuant to the statute. The exercises are broadcast into each room in the school building through an intercommunications system, and are conducted under the supervision of a teacher by students attending the school's radio and television workshop. Selected students from this course gather each morning in the school's workshop studio for the exercises, which include readings by one of the students of 10 verses of the Holy Bible, broadcast to each room in the building. This is followed by the recitation of the Lord's Prayer, likewise over the intercommunications system, but also by the students in the various classrooms, who are asked to stand and join in repeating the prayer in unison. The exercises are closed with the flag salute and such pertinent announcements as are of interest to the students. Participation in the opening exercises, as directed by the statute, is voluntary. The student reading the verses from the Bible may select the passages and read from any version he chooses, although the only copies furnished by the school are the King James version, copies of which were circulated to each teacher by the school district. During the period in which the exercises have been conducted, the King James, the Douay, and the Revised Standard versions of the Bible have been used, as well as the Jewish Holy Scriptures. There are no prefatory statements, no questions asked or solicited, no comments or explanations made, and no interpretations given at or during the exercises. The students and parents are advised that the student may absent himself from the classroom or, should he elect to remain, not participate in the exercises.

It appears from the record that, in schools not having an intercommunications system the Bible reading and the recitation of the Lord's Prayer were conducted by the homeroom teacher,[ii] who chose the text of the verses and read them herself or had students read them in rotation or by volunteers. This was followed by a standing recitation of the Lord's Prayer, together with the Pledge of Allegiance to the Flag by the class in unison and a closing announcement of routine school items of interest.

At the first trial, Edward Schempp and the children testified as to specific religious doctrines purveyed by a literal reading of the Bible 'which were contrary to the religious beliefs which they held, and to their familial teaching.'[6] The children testified that all of the doctrines to which they referred were read to them at various times as part of the exercises. Edward Schempp testified at the second trial that he had considered having Roger and Donna excused from attendance at the exercises, but decided against it for

i The action was brought in 1958, prior to the 1959 amendment of § 15-1516 authorizing a child's nonattendance at the exercises upon parental request. The three-judge court held the statute and the practices complained of unconstitutional under both the Establishment Clause and the Free Exercise Clause. 177 F.Supp. 398. Pending appeal to this Court by the school district, the statute was so amended, and we vacated the judgment and remanded for further proceedings. 364 U. S. 298. The same three-judge court granted appellees' motion to amend the pleadings, 195 F.Supp. 518, held a hearing on the amended pleadings and rendered the judgment, 201 F.Supp. 815, from which appeal is now taken.

ii The statute, as amended, imposes no penalty upon a teacher refusing to obey its mandate. However, it remains to be seen whether one refusing could have his contract of employment terminated for 'willful violation of the school laws.' [Title 24 of the Pennsylvania Statutes (Supp. 1960), sections 11-1122].

several reasons, including his belief that the children's relationships with their teachers and classmates would be adversely affected.[iii]

Expert testimony was introduced by both appellants and appellees at the first trial, which testimony was summarized by the trial court as follows:

> Dr. Solomon Grayzel testified that there were marked differences between the Jewish Holy Scriptures and the Christian Holy Bible, the most obvious of which was the absence of the New Testament in the Jewish Holy Scriptures. Dr. Grayzel testified that portions of the New Testament were offensive to Jewish tradition, and that, from the standpoint of Jewish faith, the concept of Jesus Christ as the Son of God was 'practically blasphemous.' He cited instances in the New Testament which, assertedly, were not only sectarian in nature but tended to bring the Jews into ridicule or scorn. Dr. Grayzel gave as his expert opinion that such material from the New Testament could be explained to Jewish children in such a way as to do no harm to them. But if portions of the New Testament were read without explanation, they could be, and, in his specific experience with children, Dr. Grayzel observed, had been, psychologically harmful to the child, and had caused a divisive force within the social media of the school.
>
> Dr. Grayzel also testified that there was significant difference in attitude with regard to the respective Books of the Jewish and Christian Religions in that Judaism attaches no special significance to the reading of the Bible *per se*, and that the Jewish Holy Scriptures are source materials to be studied. But Dr. Grayzel did state that many portions of the New, as well as of the Old, Testament contained passages of great literary and moral value.
>
> Dr. Luther A. Weigle, an expert witness for the defense, testified in some detail as to the reasons for and the methods employed in developing the King James and the Revised Standard Versions of the Bible. On direct examination, Dr. Weigle stated that the Bible was nonsectarian. He later stated that the phrase 'nonsectarian' meant to him nonsectarian within the Christian faiths. Dr. Weigle stated that his definition of the Holy Bible would include the Jewish Holy Scriptures, but also stated that the 'Holy Bible' would not be complete without the New Testament. He stated that the New Testament 'conveyed the message of Christians.' In his opinion, reading of the Holy Scriptures to the exclusion of the New Testament would be a sectarian

iii The trial court summarized his testimony as follows:

> Edward Schempp, the children's father, testified that, after careful consideration, he had decided that he should not have Roger or Donna excused from attendance at these morning ceremonies. Among his reasons were the following. He said that he thought his children would be 'labeled as *odd balls' before their teachers and classmates every school day; that children, like Roger's and Donna's classmates, were liable 'to lump all particular religious difference[s] or religious objections [together] as "atheism",' and that, today, the word 'atheism' is often connected with 'atheistic communism,' and has 'very bad' connotations, such as 'un-American' or 'anti-Red,' with overtones of possible immorality. Mr. Schempp pointed out that, due to the events of the morning exercises following in rapid succession, the Bible reading, the Lord's Prayer, the Flag Salute, and the announcements, excusing his children from the Bible reading would mean that probably they would miss hearing the announcements so important to children. He testified also that, if Roger and Donna were excused from Bible reading, they would have to stand in the hall outside their 'homeroom,' and that this carried with it the imputation of punishment for bad conduct.* (*Edward L. Schempp et al. v. School District of Abington Township, PA., et al.*, citation: 201 F.Supp., page 818.)

> practice. Dr. Weigle stated that the Bible was of great moral, historical and literary value. This is conceded by all the parties, and is also the view of the court.[7]

The trial court, in striking down the practices and the statute requiring them, made specific findings of fact that the children's attendance at Abington Senior High School is compulsory, and that the practice of reading 10 verses from the Bible is also compelled by law. It also found that:

> The reading of the verses, even without comment, possesses a devotional and religious character and constitutes, in effect, a religious observance. The devotional and religious nature of the morning exercises is made all the more apparent by the fact that the Bible reading is followed immediately by a recital in unison by the pupils of the Lord's Prayer. The fact that some pupils, or, theoretically, all pupils, might be excused from attendance at the exercises does not mitigate the obligatory nature of the ceremony, for [. . .] Section 1516 [. . .] unequivocally requires the exercises to be held every school day in every school in the Commonwealth. The exercises are held in the school buildings, and perforce are conducted by and under the authority of the local school authorities, and during school sessions. Since the statute requires the reading of the 'Holy Bible,' a Christian document, the practice [. . .] prefers the Christian religion. The record demonstrates that it was the intention of [. . .] the Commonwealth [. . .] to introduce a religious ceremony into the public schools of the Commonwealth.[8]

> No. 119 [*Murray v. Curlett* (1962)].

In 1905, the Board of School Commissioners of Baltimore City adopted a rule pursuant to [Article 77, section 202 of the Annotated Code of Maryland]. The rule provided for the holding of opening exercises in the schools of the city, consisting primarily of the 'reading, without comment, of a chapter in the Holy Bible and/or the use of the Lord's Prayer.' The petitioners, Mrs. Madalyn Murray and her son, William J. Murray III, are both professed atheists. Following unsuccessful attempts to have the respondent school board rescind the rule, this suit was filed for mandamus to compel its rescission and cancellation. It was alleged that William was a student in a public school of the city, and Mrs. Murray, his mother, was a taxpayer therein; that it was the practice under the rule to have a reading on each school morning from the King James version of the Bible; that, at petitioners' insistence, the rule was amended[iv] to permit children to be excused from the exercise on request of the parent, and that William had been excused pursuant thereto; that nevertheless the rule as amended was in violation of the petitioners' rights 'to freedom of religion under the First and Fourteenth Amendments' and in violation of 'the principle of separation between church and state, contained therein. [. . .]' The

iv The rule as amended provides as follows:

> Opening Exercises. Each school, either collectively or in classes, shall be opened by the reading, without comment, of a chapter in the Holy Bible and/or the use of the Lord's Prayer. The Douay version may be used by those pupils who prefer it. Appropriate patriotic exercises should be held as a part of the general opening exercise of the school or class. Any child shall be excused from participating in the opening exercises or from attending the opening exercises upon the written request of his parent or guardian.

petition particularized the petitioners' atheistic beliefs and stated that the rule, as practiced, violated their rights 'in that it threatens their religious liberty by placing a premium on belief as against non-belief and subjects their freedom of conscience to the rule of the majority; it pronounces belief in God as the source of all moral and spiritual values, equating these values with religious values, and thereby renders sinister, alien and suspect the beliefs and ideals of your Petitioners, promoting doubt and question of their morality, good citizenship and good faith.'

The respondents demurred, and the trial court, recognizing that the demurrer admitted all facts well pleaded, sustained it without leave to amend. The Maryland Court of Appeals affirmed, the majority of four justices holding the exercise not in violation of the First and Fourteenth Amendments, with three justices dissenting.[9] We granted certiorari.

II

It is true that religion has been closely identified with our history and government. As we said in *Engel v. Vitale* (1962),

> The history of man is inseparable from the history of religion. And [. . .], since the beginning of that history, many people have devoutly believed that 'More things are wrought by prayer than this world dreams of.'[10]

In *Zorach v. Clauson* (1952),[11] we gave specific recognition to the proposition that '[w]e are a religious people whose institutions presuppose a Supreme Being.' The fact that the Founding Fathers believed devotedly that there was a God and that the unalienable rights of man were rooted in Him is clearly evidenced in their writings, from the Mayflower Compact to the Constitution itself. This background is evidenced today in our public life through the continuance in our oaths of office from the Presidency to the Alderman of the final supplication, 'So help me God.' Likewise, each House of the Congress provides through its Chaplain an opening prayer, and the sessions of this Court are declared open by the crier in a short ceremony, the final phrase of which invokes the grace of God. Again, there are such manifestations in our military forces, where those of our citizens who are under the restrictions of military service wish to engage in voluntary worship. Indeed, only last year, an official survey of the country indicated that 64% of our people have church membership, while less than 30% profess no religion whatever.[12] It can be truly said, therefore, that today, as in the beginning, our national life reflects a religious people who, in the words of Madison, are 'earnestly praying, as [. . .] in duty bound, that the Supreme Lawgiver of the Universe [. . .] guide them into every measure which may be worthy of his [blessing]. [. . .].'[13]

This is not to say, however, that religion has been so identified with our history and government that religious freedom is not likewise as strongly imbedded in our public and private life. Nothing but the most telling of personal experiences in religious persecution suffered by our forebears,[14] could have planted our belief in liberty of religious opinion any more deeply in our heritage. It is true that this liberty frequently was not realized by the colonists, but this is readily accountable by their close ties to the Mother Country.[v]

v There were established churches in at least eight of the original colonies, and various degrees of religious support in others as late as the Revolutionary War. See *Engel v. Vitale*, *supra*, at 370 U. S. 428, n. 10.

However, the views of Madison and Jefferson, preceded by Roger Williams,[vi] came to be incorporated not only in the Federal Constitution but likewise in those of most of our States. This freedom to worship was indispensable in a country whose people came from the four quarters of the earth and brought with them a diversity of religious opinion. Today authorities list 83 separate religious bodies, each with membership exceeding 50,000, existing among our people, as well as innumerable smaller groups.[15]

III

Almost a hundred years ago, in *Minor v. Board of Education of Cincinnati* (1870),[vii] Judge Alphonso Taft, father of the revered Chief Justice, in an unpublished opinion, stated the ideal of our people as to religious freedom as one of

> absolute equality before the law, of all religious opinions and sects.
> [. . .] The government is neutral, and, while protecting all, it prefers none, and it disparages none.

Before examining this 'neutral' position in which the Establishment and Free Exercise Clauses of the First Amendment place our Government, it is well that we discuss the reach of the Amendment under the cases of this Court.

First, this Court has decisively settled that the First Amendment's mandate that 'Congress shall make no law respecting an establishment of religion, or prohibiting the free exercise thereof' has been made wholly applicable to the States by the Fourteenth Amendment. Twenty-three years ago, in *Cantwell v. Connecticut* (1940),[16] this Court, through Mr. Justice Roberts, said:

> The fundamental concept of liberty embodied in that [Fourteenth] Amendment embraces the liberties guaranteed by the First Amendment. The First Amendment declares that Congress shall make no law respecting an establishment of religion or prohibiting the free exercise thereof. The Fourteenth Amendment has rendered the legislatures of the states as incompetent as Congress to enact such laws.[viii]

vi 'There goes many a ship to sea, with many hundred souls in one ship, whose weal and woe is common, and is a true picture of a commonwealth, or human combination, or society. It hath fallen out sometimes that both Papists and Protestants, Jews and Turks, may be embarked in one ship; upon which supposal, I affirm that all the liberty of conscience I ever pleaded for turns upon these two hinges, that none of the Papists, Protestants, Jews, or Turks be forced to come to the ship's prayers or worship, nor compelled from their own particular prayers or worship, if they practice any.'

vii Superior Court of Cincinnati, February, 1870. The opinion is not reported, but is published under the title *The Bible in the Common Schools* (Cincinnati: Robert Clarke & Co. 1870). Judge Taft's views, expressed in dissent, prevailed on appeal. See *Board of Educational of Cincinnati v. Minor*, 23 Ohio St. 211, 253 (1872), in which the Ohio Supreme Court held that:

> The great bulk of human affairs and human interests is left by any free government to individual enterprise and individual action. Religion is eminently one of these interests, lying outside the true and legitimate province of government.

viii Application to the States of other clauses of the First Amendment obtained even before *Cantwell*. Almost 40 years ago, in the opinion of the Court in *Gitlow v. New York* (1925), citation: 268 U. S., pages 652 and 666, Mr. Justice Sanford said:

In a series of cases since *Cantwell*, the Court has repeatedly reaffirmed that doctrine, and we do so now. *Murdock v. Pennsylvania* (1943);[17] *Everson v. Board of Education* (1947);[18] *Illinois ex rel. McCollum v. Board of Education* (1948);[19] *Zorach v. Clauson* (1952);[20] *McGowan v. Maryland* (1961);[21] *Torcaso v. Watkins* (1961);[22] and *Engel v. Vitale* (1962).[23]

Second, this Court has rejected unequivocally the contention that the Establishment Clause forbids only governmental preference of one religion over another. Almost 20 years ago in *Everson*, the Court said that '[n]either a state nor the Federal Government can set up a church. Neither can pass laws which aid one religion, aid all religions, or prefer one religion over another.'[24]

And Mr. Justice Jackson, dissenting, agreed:

> There is no answer to the proposition [. . .] that the effect of the religious freedom Amendment to our Constitution was to take every form of propagation of religion out of the realm of things which could directly or indirectly be made public business, and thereby be supported in whole or in part at taxpayers' expense. [. . .] This freedom was first in the Bill of Rights because it was first in the forefathers' minds; it was set forth in absolute terms, and its strength is its rigidity.[25]

Further, Mr. Justice Rutledge, joined by Justices Frankfurter, Jackson and Burton, declared:

> The [First] Amendment's purpose was not to strike merely at the official establishment of a single sect, creed or religion, outlawing only a formal relation such as had prevailed in England and some of the colonies. Necessarily, it was to uproot all such relationships. But the object was broader than separating church and state in this narrow sense. It was to create a complete and permanent separation of the spheres of religious activity and civil authority by comprehensively forbidding every form of public aid or support for religion.[26]

The same conclusion has been firmly maintained ever since that time, see *Illinois ex rel. McCollum*, pages 210–211; *McGowan v. Maryland*, pages 442–443; *Torcaso v. Watkins*, pages 492–493, and 495, and we reaffirm it now.

While none of the parties to either of these cases has questioned these basic conclusions of the Court, both of which have been long established, recognized, and consistently reaffirmed, others continue to question their history, logic and efficacy. Such contentions, in the light of the consistent interpretation in cases of this Court, seem entirely untenable, and of value only as academic exercises.

IV

The interrelationship of the Establishment and the Free Exercise Clauses was first touched upon by Mr. Justice Roberts for the Court in *Cantwell v. Connecticut*, pages 303–304, where it was said that their 'inhibition of legislation' had

> For present purposes, we may and do assume that freedom of speech and of the press – which are protected by the First Amendment from abridgment by Congress – are among the fundamental personal rights and 'liberties' protected by the due process clause of the Fourteenth Amendment from impairment by the States.

> a double aspect. On the one hand, it forestalls compulsion by law of the acceptance of any creed or the practice of any form of worship. Freedom of conscience and freedom to adhere to such religious organization or form of worship as the individual may choose cannot be restricted by law. On the other hand, it safeguards the free exercise of the chosen form of religion. Thus, the Amendment embraces two concepts – freedom to believe and freedom to act. The first is absolute but, in the nature of things, the second cannot be.

A half dozen years later in *Everson v. Board of Education*, pages 14–15, this Court, through Mr. Justice Black, stated that the 'scope of the First Amendment [. . .] was designed forever to suppress' the establishment of religion or the prohibition of the free exercise thereof. In short, the Court held that the Amendment

> requires the state to be a neutral in its relations with groups of religious believers and nonbelievers; it does not require the state to be their adversary. State power is no more to be used so as to handicap religions than it is to favor them.[27]

And Mr. Justice Jackson, in dissent, declared that public schools are organized

> on the premise that secular education can be isolated from all religious teaching so that the school can inculcate all needed temporal knowledge and also maintain a strict and lofty neutrality as to religion. The assumption is that, after the individual has been instructed in worldly wisdom, he will be better fitted to choose his religion.[28]

Moreover, all of the four dissenters, speaking through Mr. Justice Rutledge, agreed that

> Our constitutional policy [. . .] does not deny the value or the necessity for religious training, teaching or observance. Rather, it secures their free exercise. But, to that end, it does deny that the state can undertake or sustain them in any form or degree. For this reason, the sphere of religious activity, as distinguished from the secular intellectual liberties, has been given the two-fold protection, and, as the state cannot forbid, neither can it perform or aid in performing, the religious function. The dual prohibition makes that function altogether private.[29]

Only one year later, the Court was asked to reconsider and repudiate the doctrine of these cases in *McCollum v. Board of Education*. It was argued that,

> historically, the First Amendment was intended to forbid only government preference of one religion over another. [. . .] In addition, they ask that we distinguish or overrule our holding in the *Everson* case that the Fourteenth Amendment made the 'establishment of religion' clause of the First Amendment applicable as a prohibition against the States.[30]

The Court, with Mr. Justice Reed alone dissenting, was unable to 'accept either of these contentions.'[31] Mr. Justice Frankfurter, joined by Justices Jackson, Rutledge and Burton, wrote a very comprehensive and scholarly concurrence in which he said that '[s]eparation is a requirement to abstain from fusing functions of Government and of religious sects, not merely to treat them all equally.'[32]

Continuing, he stated that:

> the Constitution [. . .] prohibited the Government common to all from becoming embroiled, however innocently, in the destructive religious conflicts of which the history of even this country records some dark pages.[33]

In 1952, in *Zorach v. Clauson*, Mr. Justice Douglas, for the Court, reiterated:

> There cannot be the slightest doubt that the First Amendment reflects the philosophy that Church and State should be separated. And, so far as interference with the 'free exercise' of religion and an 'establishment' of religion are concerned, the separation must be complete and unequivocal. The First Amendment, within the scope of its coverage, permits no exception; the prohibition is absolute. The First Amendment, however, does not say that, in every and all respects, there shall be a separation of Church and State. Rather, it studiously defines the manner, the specific ways, in which there shall be no concert or union or dependency one on the other. That is the common sense of the matter.[34]

And then, in 1961, in *McGowan v. Maryland* and in *Torcaso v. Watkins*, each of these cases was discussed and approved. Chief Justice Warren, in *McGowan*, for a unanimous Court on this point, said:

> But the First Amendment, in its final form, did not simply bar a congressional enactment *establishing a church*; it forbade all laws *respecting an establishment of religion* [emphasis in original]. Thus, this Court has given the Amendment a 'broad interpretation [. . .] in the light of its history and the evils it was designed forever to suppress.'[35]

And Mr. Justice Black, for the Court, in *Torcaso*, without dissent but with Justices Frankfurter and Harlan concurring in the result, used this language:

> We repeat and again reaffirm that neither a State nor the Federal Government can constitutionally force a person 'to profess a belief or disbelief in any religion.' Neither can constitutionally pass laws or impose requirements which aid all religions as against nonbelievers, and neither can aid those religions based on a belief in the existence of God as against those religions founded on different beliefs.[36]

Finally, in *Engel v. Vitale*, only last year, these principles were so universally recognized that the Court, without the citation of a single case and over the sole dissent of Mr. Justice Stewart, reaffirmed them. The Court found the 22-word prayer used in 'New York's program of daily classroom invocation of God's blessings as prescribed in the Regents' prayer [. . .] [to be] a religious activity.'[37] It held that 'it is no part of the business of government to compose official prayers for any group of the American people to recite as a part of a religious program carried on by government.'[38]

In discussing the reach of the Establishment and Free Exercise Clauses of the First Amendment, the Court said:

> Although these two clauses may in certain instances overlap, they forbid two quite different kinds of governmental encroachment upon religious freedom. The Establishment Clause, unlike the Free Exercise Clause, does not depend upon any showing of direct governmental compulsion, and is violated by the enactment of laws which establish an official religion, whether those laws operate directly to coerce nonobserving individuals or not. This is not to say, of course, that laws officially prescribing a particular form of religious worship do not involve coercion of such individuals. When the power, prestige and financial support of government is placed behind a particular religious belief, the indirect coercive pressure upon religious minorities to conform to the prevailing officially approved religion is plain.[39]

And, in further elaboration, the Court found that the 'first and most immediate purpose [of the Establishment Clause] rested on the belief that a union of government and religion tends to destroy government and to degrade religion.'[40] When government, the Court said, allies itself with one particular form of religion, the inevitable result is that it incurs 'the hatred, disrespect and even contempt of those who held contrary beliefs.'[41]

V

The wholesome 'neutrality' of which this Court's cases speak thus stems from a recognition of the teachings of history that powerful sects or groups might bring about a fusion of governmental and religious functions or a concert or dependency of one upon the other to the end that official support of the State or Federal Government would be placed behind the tenets of one or of all orthodoxies. This the Establishment Clause prohibits. And a further reason for neutrality is found in the Free Exercise Clause, which recognizes the value of religious training, teaching and observance and, more particularly, the right of every person to freely choose his own course with reference thereto, free of any compulsion from the state. This the Free Exercise Clause guarantees. Thus, as we have seen, the two clauses may overlap. As we have indicated, the Establishment Clause has been directly considered by this Court eight times in the past score of years and, with only one Justice dissenting on the point, it has consistently held that the clause withdrew all legislative power respecting religious belief or the expression thereof. The test may be stated as follows: what are the purpose and the primary effect of the enactment? If either is the advancement or inhibition of religion, then the enactment exceeds the scope of legislative power as circumscribed by the Constitution. That is to say that, to withstand the strictures of the Establishment Clause, there must be a secular legislative purpose and a primary effect that neither advances nor inhibits religion. The Free Exercise Clause, likewise considered many times here, withdraws from legislative power, state and federal, the exertion of any restraint on the free exercise of religion. Its purpose is to secure religious liberty in the individual by prohibiting any invasions thereof by civil authority. Hence, it is necessary in a free exercise case for one to show the coercive effect of the enactment as it operates against him in the practice of his religion. The distinction between the two clauses is apparent – a violation of the Free Exercise Clause is predicated on coercion, while the Establishment Clause violation need not be so attended.

Applying the Establishment Clause principles to the cases at bar, we find that the States are requiring the selection and reading at the opening of the school day of verses from the Holy Bible and the recitation of the Lord's Prayer by the students in unison. These exercises are prescribed as part of the curricular activities of students who are required by law to attend school. They are held in the school buildings under the supervision and with the participation of teachers employed in those schools. None of these factors, other than compulsory school attendance, was present in the program upheld in *Zorach v. Clauson*. The trial court in No. 142 [*Abington v. Schempp* (1959 and 1962)] has found that such an opening exercise is a religious ceremony, and was intended by the State to be so. We agree with the trial court's finding as to the religious character of the exercises. Given that finding, the exercises and the law requiring them are in violation of the Establishment Clause.

There is no such specific finding as to the religious character of the exercises in No. 119 [*Murray v. Curlett* (1962)], and the State contends (as does the State in No. 142) that the program is an effort to extend its benefits to all public school children without regard to their religious belief. Included within its secular purposes, it says, are the promotion of moral values, the contradiction to the materialistic trends of our times, the perpetuation of our institutions and the teaching of literature. The case came up on demurrer, of course, to a petition which alleged that the uniform practice under the rule had been to read from the King James version of the Bible, and that the exercise was sectarian. The short answer, therefore, is that the religious character of the exercise was admitted by the State. But even if its purpose is not strictly religious, it is sought to be accomplished through readings, without comment, from the Bible. Surely the place of the Bible as an instrument of religion cannot be gainsaid, and the State's recognition of the pervading religious character of the ceremony is evident from the rule's specific permission of the alternative use of the Catholic Douay version, as well as the recent amendment permitting nonattendance at the exercises. None of these factors is consistent with the contention that the Bible is here used either as an instrument for nonreligious moral inspiration or as a reference for the teaching of secular subjects.

The conclusion follows that, in both cases, the laws require religious exercises, and such exercises are being conducted in direct violation of the rights of the appellees and petitioners.[ix] Nor are these required exercises mitigated by the fact that individual students may absent themselves upon parental request, for that fact furnishes no defense to a claim of unconstitutionality under the Establishment Clause. Further, it is no defense to urge that the religious practices here may be relatively minor encroachments on the First Amendment. The breach of neutrality that is today a trickling stream may all too soon become a raging torrent and, in the words of Madison, 'it is proper to take alarm at the first experiment on our liberties.'[42]

It is insisted that, unless these religious exercises are permitted, a 'religion of secularism' is established in the schools. We agree, of course, that the State may not establish a 'religion of secularism' in the sense of affirmatively opposing or showing hostility to

ix It goes without saying that the laws and practices involved here can be challenged only by persons having standing to complain. But the requirements for standing to challenge state action under the Establishment Clause, unlike those relating to the Free Exercise Clause, do not include proof that particular religious freedoms are infringed. *McGowan v. Maryland*, *supra*, at 366 U. S. 429–430. The parties here are school children and their parents, who are directly affected by the laws and practices against which their complaints are directed. These interests surely suffice to give the parties standing to complain. See *Engel v. Vitale*, *supra*. Cf. *McCollum v. Board of Education*, *supra*; *Everson v. Board of Education*, *supra*. Compare *Doremus v. Board of Education*, 342 U. S. 429 (1952), which involved the same substantive issues presented here. The appeal was there dismissed upon the graduation of the school child involved and because of the appellants' failure to establish standing as taxpayers.

religion, thus 'preferring those who believe in no religion over those who do believe.'[43] We do not agree, however, that this decision in any sense has that effect. In addition, it might well be said that one's education is not complete without a study of comparative religion or the history of religion and its relationship to the advancement of civilization. It certainly may be said that the Bible is worthy of study for its literary and historic qualities. Nothing we have said here indicates that such study of the Bible or of religion, when presented objectively as part of a secular program of education, may not be effected consistently with the First Amendment. But the exercises here do not fall into those categories. They are religious exercises, required by the States in violation of the command of the First Amendment that the Government maintain strict neutrality, neither aiding nor opposing religion.

Finally, we cannot accept that the concept of neutrality, which does not permit a State to require a religious exercise even with the consent of the majority of those affected, collides with the majority's right to free exercise of religion.[x] While the Free Exercise Clause clearly prohibits the use of state action to deny the rights of free exercise to *anyone*, it has never meant that a majority could use the machinery of the State to practice its beliefs [emphasis in original]. Such a contention was effectively answered by Mr. Justice Jackson for the Court in *West Virginia Board of Education v. Barnette* (1943):

> The very purpose of a Bill of Rights was to withdraw certain subjects from the vicissitudes of political controversy, to place them beyond the reach of majorities and officials, and to establish them as legal principles to be applied by the courts. One's right to [. . .] freedom of worship [. . .] and other fundamental rights may not be submitted to vote; they depend on the outcome of no elections.[44]

The place of religion in our society is an exalted one, achieved through a long tradition of reliance on the home, the church and the inviolable citadel of the individual heart and mind. We have come to recognize through bitter experience that it is not within the power of government to invade that citadel, whether its purpose or effect be to aid or oppose, to advance or retard. In the relationship between man and religion, the State is firmly committed to a position of neutrality. Though the application of that rule requires interpretation of a delicate sort, the rule itself is clearly and concisely stated in the words of the First Amendment. Applying that rule to the facts of these cases, we affirm the judgment in No. 142 [*Abington v. Schempp* (1959 and 1962)].

In No. 119 [*Murray v. Curlett* (1962)], the judgment is reversed, and the cause remanded to the Maryland Court of Appeals for further proceedings consistent with this opinion.

It is so ordered.

* * *

x We are not, of course, presented with, and therefore do not pass upon, a situation such as military service, where the Government regulates the temporal and geographic environment of individuals to a point that, unless it permits voluntary religious services to be conducted with the use of government facilities, military personnel would be unable to engage in the practice of their faiths.

Importance

The importance of the Court's decision in *Abington v. Shempp* can be measured in two ways.

First, in the influence it imposed on future case decisions concerning violations of the religion clauses of the First Amendment, and in particular in how the Court came to 'test' such violations. And second, in how it further directed the Court's perception of American Atheism.

As it continued to hear cases dealing with the First Amendment, the Court quickly began developing an interrogative pattern. In each case it would ask certain questions, and in the twenty-three years between *McCollum* and *Abington*, those questions were honed down to a particular formula, a 'test' that it could apply in order to more expediently reach a conclusion. As it pertained to its opinion in *Abington v. Schempp*, Justice Clark described this as such:

> The test may be stated as follows: what are the purpose and the primary effect of the enactment? If either is the advancement or inhibition of religion, then the enactment exceeds the scope of legislative power as circumscribed by the Constitution. That is to say that, to withstand the strictures of the Establishment Clause, there must be a secular legislative purpose and a primary effect that neither advances nor inhibits religion.[45]

In an exhaustive concurrence to Justice Clark's decision, Justice William J. Brennan reiterated and complemented this test, by adding:

> I believe that the line we must draw between the permissible and the impermissible is one which accords with history and faithfully reflects the understanding of the Founding Fathers. It is a line which the Court has consistently sought to mark in its decisions expounding the religious guarantees of the First Amendment. What the Framers meant to foreclose, and what our decisions under the Establishment Clause have forbidden, are those involvements of religious with secular institutions which (a) serve the essentially religious activities of religious institutions; (b) employ the organs of government for essentially religious purposes; or (c) use essentially religious means to serve governmental ends where secular means would suffice.[46]

Seven years later, and after finding too many deficiencies in this 'Schempp Test,' the Supreme Court's process culminated in a more precise one, composed by Chief Justice Warren E. Burger, in his decision for the Court in *Lemon v. Kurtzman* (1971).

The issue at focus in *Lemon* dealt with two state statutes, the 1969 Salary Supplement Act in Rhode Island, and the 1968 Nonpublic Elementary and Secondary Education Act in Pennsylvania, both of which the Court ruled as unconstitutional representations of an 'excessive entanglement' between church and state. And Chief Justice Burger reached this conclusion in two ways, based on Justice Byron R. White's decision in *Board of Education v. Allen* (1968),[47] and his own in *Walz v. Tax Commission of the City of New York* (1970).[48] First, he simplified the Court's position by arguing that only through a sense of interpretive plasticity could it achieve any form of constitutional neutrality, especially in adherence to a 'general principle' that stated: 'we will not tolerate either governmentally established religion or governmental interference with religion.'[49] And second, he utilized a colonial understanding of 'religious establishment' to better define such a violation in terms of 'sponsorship, financial support, and active involvement of the sovereign in religious activity.'[50]

As all of this pertained to the issues concerning the Court in its consideration of the Constitutional violations assessed in *Lemon v. Kurtzman*, he applied elements from each into a three-pronged test:

> In the absence of precisely stated constitutional prohibitions, we must draw lines with reference to the three main evils against which the Establishment Clause was intended to afford protection: 'sponsorship, financial support, and active involvement of the sovereign in religious activity.' Every analysis in this area must begin with consideration of the cumulative criteria developed by the Court over many years. Three such tests may be gleaned from our cases. First, the statute must have a secular legislative purpose; second, its principal or primary effect must be one that neither advances nor inhibits religion; finally, the statute must not foster 'an excessive government entanglement with religion.'[51]

Of course, this 'Lemon Test' did not simply render every case decision since its inception more easily determined, and in fact, it has come under immense scrutiny over the years by a number of Justices arguing that it still reflects a deficient and rigid understanding of the Court's role in interpreting the First Amendment. For instance, in his concurrent opinion to Justice White's decision in *Lamb's Chapel v. Center Moriches Union Free School District* (1993), Justice Antonin Scalia described it as 'some ghoul in a late night horror movie that repeatedly sits up in its grave and shuffles abroad, after being repeatedly killed and buried.'[52] Nevertheless, it is still applied by tribunals throughout the federal judicial system, even as recently as the Fourth Circuit Court of Appeals' continuance of an injunction against President Donald Trump's contentious executive order banning immigration from majority-Muslim countries.[53]

It has, as well, been amended from time to time. For example, in her concurrence to Chief Justice Warren E. Burger's decision in *Lynch v. Donnelly* (1984), Justice Sandra Day O'Connor 'clarified' how she felt the Lemon Test should be re-written to better reflect an 'endorsement test.' In a case dealing with the City of Pawtucket, Rhode Island's placement of a 'nativity scene' alongside other holiday decorations within a shopping center, in which the Court found such inclusion to be constitutionally permissible, she remarked:

> The Establishment Clause prohibits government from making adherence to a religion relevant in any way to a person's standing in the political community. Government can run afoul of that prohibition in two principal ways. One is excessive entanglement with religious institutions, which may interfere with the independence of the institutions, give the institutions access to government or governmental powers not fully shared by nonadherents of the religion, and foster the creation of political constituencies defined along religious lines. The second and more direct infringement is government endorsement or disapproval of religion. Endorsement sends a message to nonadherents that they are outsiders, not full members of the political community, and an accompanying message to adherents that they are insiders, favored members of the political community. Disapproval sends the opposite message. See generally *Abington School District v. Schempp* (1963). Our prior cases have used the three-part

> test articulated in *Lemon v. Kurtzman* (1971), as a guide to detecting these two forms of unconstitutional government action. It has never been entirely clear, however, how the three parts of the test relate to the principles enshrined in the Establishment Clause. Focusing on institutional entanglement and on endorsement or disapproval of religion clarifies the Lemon test as an analytical device.[54]

As well, in Justice Anthony Kennedy's decision for the Court in *Lee v. Weisman* (1992), he proclaimed the Lemon Test to be completely unnecessary, replacing it instead with a 'coercion test.' The case dealt with another example of the unconstitutionality of a prayer given prior to a public school ceremony, and in citing *Lynch v. Donnelly*, he remarked:

> This Court need not revisit the questions of the definition and scope of the principles governing the extent of permitted accommodation by the State for its citizens' religious beliefs and practices, for the controlling precedents as they relate to prayer and religious exercise in primary and secondary public schools compel the holding here. Thus, the Court will not reconsider its decision in *Lemon v. Kurtzman*. The principle that government may accommodate the free exercise of religion does not supersede the fundamental limitations imposed by the Establishment Clause, which guarantees at a minimum that a government may not coerce anyone to support or participate in religion or its exercise, or otherwise act in a way which 'establishes a [state] religion or religious faith, or tends to do so' (*Lynch v. Donnelly*, 678).[55]

Nonetheless, whatever faults the Court may have eventually found with the Lemon Test, it was still used to decide every Establishment Clause issue from 1971 to 1984, with the only exception being *Marsh v. Chambers* in 1983. That it began here in the Court's decision in *Abington v. Schempp* further solidifies that decision's essential importance in the wider discourse of its narrative concerning American religion.

And in a related manner, its secondary importance derives from its influence on American Atheism.

Not only was the decision in *Abington v. Schempp* another example of the Court's secularization of a 'traditional' relationship between church and state, it also gave a voice to the widening public perception of American Atheism that, through the aggressive crusades of Madalyn Murray O'Hair, became quite boisterous and emphatic. And because her influence on the discourse of American Atheism is so distinct, both within and beyond the boundaries of this book's examination, she deserves a brief discussion.

* * *

Madalyn Murray saw the Supreme Court's ruling in her favor as the start of a great crusade:

> We are Atheists. As such, we are foes of any and all religions. We want the Bible out of school because we do not accept it as being either holy or an accurate historical document. We want the Lord's Prayer out of school because we doubt the historicity of Jesus Christ and also we do not believe in the efficacy of prayer. [. . .] We want this clear: we are foes of religion. We are using what means are available to us, legally, to pursue our object: the fight against religion. This case is one aspect of that fight only.[56]

For the next thirty years she waged that crusade on many fronts, pursuing further lawsuits, speaking publicly, and publishing widely. She was loud and garish and represented a more combative form of Atheism than that characterized by Vashti McCollum. She also drew constant criticism and disapproval, from both Christians and fellow Atheists. As an example of the latter, consider this condemnation from Vitali Negri, who in 1964 wrote of her in *The American Rationalist*:

> Madalyn Murray has brought more discord to adherents of the free thought movement, more bad publicity in the press, more hatred by the public at large toward free thinkers, rationalists, secularists and humanists than have all the combined theologians from the beginning of man's fight for freedom. As a public representative of atheism, Madalyn Murray's general abnormal behavior has branded all atheists in the eyes of their antagonists as extremists, vulgarists, opportunists and law breakers.[57]

Nevertheless, her commitment never faltered.

In 1963 she founded the Society of Separationists, an organization dedicated to the promotion of religious inquiry, ethics without religion, and the study of art and science, that also functioned as an activist group committed to the advocacy, 'in all lawful ways,' of the 'complete separation of church and state and the establishment and maintenance of a thoroughly secular system of education available to all.'[58]

That organization became American Atheists, centered in Austin, Texas. The first issue of the organization's newsletter, also called *American Atheists*, was published in July 1963. It was originally titled, *The Free Humanist*, but not wanting to associate with humanism, Madalyn changed the name.[59]

The organization also broadcast a radio series, and in 1977 shifted this to a television program, called the *American Atheist Forum*. It created an American Atheist Speakers' Bureau, and oversaw the creation and maintenance of American Atheists chapters throughout the United States. It built a library devoted to Atheist materials as well as a museum. It created a program called 'Dial-an-Atheist,' a messaging system that offered information on the organization's operations. And it created an international outreach program called United World Atheists.[60]

Aside from these, she also organized the Freethought Society of America, Inc. and a legal-action group: Other Americans, Inc.

During the 1960s and 1970s, Madalyn was perhaps America's most famous Atheist. She appeared on radio and television programs, and toured college campuses, giving lectures and angering audiences. She used obscenities to describe religion and openly insulted religious people. She spoke out against the war in Vietnam. She attacked Roman Catholicism, which received a heavy share of her criticism, particularly in her campaigns in support of birth control and abortion. She declared herself a 'militant feminist,' and repeatedly denied being a communist. She relentlessly campaigned for funding.

She persistently filed lawsuits, not necessarily in an effort to win, but instead to further the cause of publicly decrying any entanglement between church and state. For example, she sued NASA, President Nixon, the Department of the Treasury, and the Department of the Interior, losing in each attempt.[61]

Aside from her judicial activism, her life also invited scandal and controversy.

After a physical altercation with police on June 20th, 1964, she and her son William were arrested for assault, after which they, along with her mother, her other son Jon, and William's pregnant wife, Susan, fled to Hawaii, and then Mexico, when her request to have the charges dropped was denied. She was arrested again in Mexico (on separate charges) on September 24th, 1965, and expelled to Texas. One month later the Baltimore Criminal Court dropped all the charges against her, but she remained in Texas for the rest of her life.

In August 1995, she, her son Jon Garth, and her granddaughter, Robin (daughter of William and Susan) disappeared from the offices of American Atheists in Austin, Texas. They were considered missing, possibly on the run from the IRS, until 2001, when David Roland Waters led authorities to their charred remains in Camp Woods, Texas. Waters had kidnapped the O'Hairs with the assistance of Danny Fry, Gary Karr, and Gerald Lee 'Chico' Osborne, extorted from them $600,000, and murdered them. Their bodies were dismembered in a storage unit in North Austin, where they were kept until Waters moved them to a ranch in Camp Woods, where he burned and buried their remains. Danny Fry had also been murdered by the group, in 1995, and his remains were burned and buried amongst theirs.[62]

About her life and her activism, much has been written,[63] but more importantly, Madalyn wrote a lot about herself, and her Atheism as she perceived it.[64] As discourse, this represents an excellent source, both for American Atheism in general, as well as for the Atheism considered within the context of this book.

Consider, for example, these two samples from *Life Magazine* and *Playboy*, published during and shortly after the Supreme Court's decision in *Abington v. Schempp*.[65]

'Letter to Life Magazine,' *Life*, April 12th, 1963:

> The atheist's position (I am that Maryland atheist you mentioned) is one arrived at after considerable study, cogitation and inner search. It is a position which is founded in science, in reason and in love for fellow man rather than in a love for God. We find the Bible to be nauseating, historically inaccurate, replete with the ravings of madmen. We find God to be sadistic, brutal, and a representation of hatred, vengeance. We find the Lord's Prayer to be that muttered by worms groveling for meager existence in a traumatic, paranoid world. This is not appropriate untouchable dicta to be forced on adult or child. The business of the public schools, where attendance is compulsory, is to prepare children to face the problems on earth, not to prepare for heaven – which is a delusional dream of the unsophisticated minds of the ill-educated clergy. Fortunately, we atheists can seek legal remedy through our Constitution, which was written by deists (not Christians) who had *enough* of religion and wanted to grow toward freedom from it, not enslavement in it [emphasis in original].[66]

'Playboy Interview,' *Playboy Magazine*, October 1965.

> Because religion is a crutch, and only the crippled need crutches. I can get around perfectly well on my own two feet, and so can everyone else with a backbone and a grain of common sense. [. . .] Perhaps this sort of claptrap was good for the Stone Age, when people actually believed that if they prayed for rain they would get it. But we're a grown-up world now, and it's time to put away childish things. But people don't, because most of them don't even know what atheism is. It's not a negation of anything. You don't have to negate what no one can prove exists. No, atheism is a very positive affirmation of man's ability to think for himself, to do for himself, to find answers to his own problems. I'm thrilled to feel that I can rely on myself totally and absolutely; that my children are being brought up so that when they meet a

> problem they can't cop out by foisting it off on God. Madalyn Murray's going to solve her own problems, and nobody's going to intervene. It's about time the world got up off its knees and looked at itself in the mirror and said: 'Well, we are men. Let's start acting like it.'[67]

These simple passages provide extraordinary examples of American Atheism as described by an American Atheist, in her own words. And in that way, the value that this discourse offers us is as undeniable as Madalyn's role in altering American religion via the Court's decision in her favor in *Abington v. Schempp*. After all, not only did this decision provide the precursors for the Lemon Test, it once more re-calibrated the relationship between church and state by secularizing yet another 'traditionally permissible' endorsement of religion. An ideological transformation that would change even further with respect to the very definition of the concept 'religious belief' in the case decision that follows it here: *Welsh v. United States.*

Notes

1 *Schempp v. School District of Abington Township, Pa.* (U.S. District Court for the Eastern District of Pennsylvania, 1959), citation: 177 F.Supp. 398, Footnote 3.
2 As cited in *Murray v. Curlett* (Court of Appeals of Maryland, 1962), citation: 179 A.2d 698, 228 Md. 239, 242–243.
3 Ibid.
4 Ibid.
5 *Murray v. Curlett* (Court of Appeals of Maryland, 1962), 247–250.
6 *Schempp v. School District of Abington Township, Pa.* (U.S. District Court for the Eastern District of Pennsylvania, 1959), 398 and 400.
7 Ibid., 398, and 401–402.
8 *Schempp v. School District of Abington Township, Pa.* (U.S. District Court for the Eastern District of Pennsylvania, 1962), 819.
9 *Murray v. Curlett* (Court of Appeals of Maryland, 1962).
10 *Engel v. Vitale* (1962), citation: 370 U.S. 421 and 434.
11 *Zorach v. Clauson* (1952), citation: 343 U.S. 306 and 313.
12 'Statistical Abstract of the United States.' Bureau of the Census, U.S. Department of Commerce, (83rd ed., 1962), 48 and 46.
13 *Memorial and Remonstrance Against Religious Assessments*, quoted in *Everson v. Board of Education* (1947), 71–72.
14 See *Everson v. Board of Education* (1947), 8–11.
15 Bureau of the Census, 46–47.
16 *Cantwell v. Connecticut* (1940), citation: 310 U.S. 296, 296 and 303.
17 *Murdock v. Pennsylvania* (1943), citation: 319 U.S. 105 and 108.
18 *Everson v. Board of Education* (1947).
19 *McCollum v. Board of Education* (1948), citation: 333 U.S. 203, 210–211.
20 *Zorach v. Clauson* (1952).
21 *McGowan v. Maryland* (1961), citation: 366 U.S. 420.
22 *Torcaso v. Watkins* (1961), 488.
23 *Engel v. Vitale* (1962), 421.
24 *Everson v. Board of Education* (1947), 15.
25 Ibid., 26.
26 Ibid., 31–32.
27 Ibid., 18.
28 Ibid., 23–24.
29 Ibid., 52.
30 *McCollum v. Board of Education* (1948), 211.
31 Ibid.

32 Ibid., 227.
33 Ibid., 228.
34 *Zorach v. Clauson* (1952), 312.
35 *McGowan v. Maryland* (1961), 441–442.
36 *Torcaso v. Watkins* (1961), 495.
37 *Engel v. Vitale* (1962), 424.
38 Ibid., 425.
39 Ibid., 430–431.
40 Ibid., 431.
41 Ibid.
42 *Memorial and Remonstrance Against Religious Assessments*, quoted in *Everson v. Board of* Education, as discussed above, 65.
43 See *Zorach v. Clauson* (1952), 314.
44 *West Virginia Board of Education v. Barnette* (1943), citation: 319 U.S. 624 and 638.
45 *Abington v. Schempp* (1963), 223.
46 Justice Brennan, concurring, *Abington v. Schempp*, 294–295.
47 *Board of Education v. Allen* (1968), citation: 392 U.S. 236, 242.
48 *Walz v. Tax Commission of the City of New York* (1970), citation: 397 U.S. 664, 669.
49 Ibid.
50 Ibid., 668.
51 Citing *Board of Education v. Allen* (1968) and *Walz v. Tax Commission of the City of New York* (1970) in *Lemon v. Kurtzman* (1971), 612–613.
52 *Lamb's Chapel v. Center Moriches Union Free School District* (1993), citation: 508 U.S. 384, 398.
53 *International Refugee Assistance Project v. Trump* (Fourth Circuit Court of Appeals, 2017), citation: No. 17-135.
54 Sandra Day O'Connor, concurrence in *Lynch v. Donnelly* (1983), citation: 465 U.S. 668, 688–689.
55 *Lee v. Weisman* (1992), citation: 505 U.S. 577.
56 *Murray Newsletter*, re-quoted in Madalyn Murray O'Hair, *An Atheist Epic: Bill Murray, the Bible, and the Baltimore Board of Education* (Austin: American Atheist Press, 1970), 272–273.
57 Vitali Negri, quoted by Brian F. Le Beau, *The Atheist: Madalyn Murray O'Hair* (New York: New York University Press, 2003), 101.
58 Madalyn Murray, quoted by Le Beau, *The Atheist*, 134.
59 Le Beau, *The Atheist*, 135.
60 Ibid., 280.
61 Respectively: *O'Hair v. Paine* (5th Circuit Court of Appeals, 1970), citation: 432 F.2d 66; *O'Hair v. Nixon, et al.*, Civil Action No. 410-73 (1973); *O'Hair v. Blumenthal* (U.S. District Court for the Western District of Texas, 1978), citation: 462 F. Supp. 19; *O'Hair v. Andrus* (Court of Appeals for the District of Columbia Circuit, 1979), citation: 613 F.2d 931.
62 Le Beau, *The Atheist*, 319.
63 See Le Beau, *The Atheist*, as well as Ann Rowe Seaman, *America's Most Hated Woman: The Life and Gruesome Death of Madalyn Murray O'Hair* (New York: Continuum, 2005).
64 See also her memoir, collected and provided by Baylor University's Oral History Project: http://digitalcollections.baylor.edu/cdm/compoundobject/collection/buioh/id/1433/rec/6 (Accessed August 10th, 2017).
65 See also, Brian Liston, 'Mrs. Murray's War on God,' *The Saturday Evening Post*, July 11th, 1964; and Bynum Shaw, 'Nevertheless, God Probably Loves Mrs. Murray,' *Esquire*, October 1964.
66 Madalyn Murray, 'Letter to Life Magazine' (*Life Magazine*, 12 April 1963), 63.
67 'Playboy Interview' (*Playboy Magazine*, October 1965).

7 *Welsh v. United States* (1970)

Argued: January 20th, 1970 – Decided: June 15th, 1970.

> Hence, consistent with Tillich's expansive definition of religion, the Court chose to construe the notion of 'an individual's relation to a Supreme Being' in terms which would permit even an avowed atheist protection of 'religious' exemption from military service if the individual's beliefs were 'ultimately' held, i.e., functioned in a parallel fashion to those practiced by orthodox believers.
>
> — James McBride, 'Paul Tillich and the Supreme Court' (*Journal of Church and State*, Vol. 30, No. 2, 1988), 258

Question before the Court: Does an individual who proclaims neither any religious affiliation, nor belief in God, qualify for conscientious objector status, regardless of the requirement of such affiliation or belief to grant such qualification?

Decision: 5–3 plurality opinion. Yes, an individual does indeed qualify, if the conviction they use to justify their opposition to war represents a sincere and meaningful belief 'parallel to that filled by God.'

Antecedent Case Decisions:

- NINTH CIRCUIT COURT OF APPEALS, September 23rd, 1968.

  Ruling: In a 2–1 decision, the Court affirmed Welsh's conviction, arguing that there was no religious basis within Welsh's claim for conscientious objector status.

- UNITED STATES DISTRICT COURT, June 1st, 1966.

  Ruling: Welsh was convicted for refusing to submit to induction in the Armed Forces in violation of Title 50 of the United States Code, section 462(a), which oversaw the offenses and penalties for such acts.

Background

On June 1st, 1966, Elliot Ashton Welsh II was convicted and sentenced to three years imprisonment for refusing to submit to his induction into the Armed Forces. Welsh had registered with his local draft board on February 2nd, 1960, and was classified 1-A status, designating him available for unrestricted military service. He was ordered to report for a physical examination, which he passed, in March of 1964. In April of that year he submitted a Selective Service System special request (Form 150) for conscientious objector status. On that form, he amended the statement that read 'I am, by reason of my religious training and belief, conscientiously opposed to participation in war in any form' to 'I am, by reason of ~~my religious training and~~ belief, conscientiously opposed to participation in war in any form,' crossing out the words 'my religious training and.' In the box on the form next to the question, 'Do you believe in a Supreme Being,' he wrote 'No.' His request was approved and his classification was changed to 1-A-O, conscientious objector available for noncombatant military service.

On May 25th, 1964 he sent a letter to his local draft board requesting an amendment to his SSS Form 150, asking to be newly classified to 1-O, complete conscientious objector status to all military service.

He appeared before his draft board on June 9th, and the following day was informed that he was still classified as 1-A-O. He appealed to the Draft Appeal board, which in July 1964, determined that he should neither be classified as 1-O, nor any other lower classification.

On November 15th, 1965, Welsh's file was re-submitted, with a new classification that returned him to 1-A status. He was ordered to report for induction on December 8th, which he did, but when called to step forward for induction, he refused. He was convicted, in a short bench trial, in June of 1966.

Welsh appealed his conviction to the Ninth Circuit Court of Appeals, relying heavily on *United States v. Seeger*, which the Supreme Court had decided a year earlier.

In a 2–1 decision, that Court affirmed his conviction in 1968.

He appealed his case to the Supreme Court in 1969, and oral arguments were heard on January 20th, 1970. In a 5–3 plurality opinion – which meant that though a majority of the Justices agreed with one another about how the Court should rule, they did not collectively agree on the reasons why – the Court reversed his conviction and granted him complete objector status on June 15th. However, because that decision was 'controlled' by *United States v. Seeger*, a quick overview of that case is essential here before continuing.

* * *

Prior to the 1960s, the United States Government had long recognized the importance of permitting individuals the right to object to military service based on their religious convictions. Initially, this was regulated on a state-to-state basis, and varied accordingly. For example, chapter 1, section VIII of the 1776 Constitution of the Commonwealth of Pennsylvania, under the title, 'Declaration of the Rights of the Inhabitants of the State of Pennsylvania,' stated: 'Nor can any man who is conscientiously scrupulous of bearing arms, be justly compelled thereto.'[1] These sorts of permissions broadened to a national level during the Civil War, as the notion of military conscription became a necessity. As such, the 1864 Draft Act federally extended exemptions to compulsory military enlistment to conscientious objectors whose religious beliefs prohibited them from taking up and bearing arms.

During the First World War, the Draft Act of 1917 likewise extended these same exemptions nationwide, clarifying however that objectors would need to prove their personal affiliation to a 'well recognized religious sect or organization [then] organized and existing and whose existing creed or principles [forbade] its members to participate in war in any form.'[2]

With the adoption of the Selective Training and Service Act in 1940, which had initially required all American men between the ages of twenty-one and thirty-six to register with their local draft boards, those applying for objector exemptions no longer needed to belong to a specific pacifist religious group. Instead, they could prove their moral opposition to war via their personal 'religious training and belief.' This ensured that the tradition in which those excused from the Armed Services 'who believed that they owed an obligation, superior to that due the state, of not participating in war in any form,'[3] would be maintained, while simultaneously acknowledging the broad religious beliefs of the American men being conscripted into that military service. This emendation was altered once more in 1948 in order to clarify what was meant by 'religious training and belief,' which was thereafter defined as: 'an individual's belief in a relation to a Supreme Being involving duties superior to those arising from any human relation, but [not including] essentially political, sociological, or philosophical views or a merely personal moral code.'[4]

This provision defined the basis of Section 6(j) of the Universal Military Training and Service Act:

> Nothing contained in this title shall be construed to require any person to be subject to combatant training and service in the Armed Forces of the United States who, by reason of religious training and belief, is conscientiously opposed to participation in war in any form. Religious training and belief in this connection means an individual's belief in a relation to a Supreme Being involving duties superior to those arising from any human relation, but does not include essentially political, sociological, or philosophical views or a merely personal moral code.[5]

When evaluated by the Supreme Court in *United States v. Seeger*, this language became the central focus of Justice Tom C. Clark's decision, specifically in how the phrase 'religious training and belief' was used to reject the conscientious objector applications of three men who, like Welsh, had based their objections on 'moral codes,' rather than on more conventional religious beliefs.

Daniel Andrew Seeger – for whom the case was named – stated in his form that his opposition to war was based on a 'belief in and devotion to goodness and virtue for their own sakes,' and a 'religious faith' in a 'purely ethical creed,' citing the works of individuals such as Plato, Aristotle, and Baruch Spinoza as philosophical support. With respect to his declaration in a belief in the existence of God, he preferred to leave the question 'open,' and rather than answer 'yes' or 'no'; he argued that his 'ethical belief' and 'intellectual and moral integrity' existed 'without belief in God, except in the remotest sense.' And this 'skepticism or disbelief in the existence of God,' he contended, did not necessarily mean a 'lack of faith in anything whatsoever.'[6] His request was denied, but his conviction was eventually reversed by the 2nd Circuit Court of Appeals in 1964.[7]

Arno Sascha Jakobson's request differed slightly from Seeger's, particularly in that he willingly expressed a belief in a 'Supreme Being,' who he also identified as the 'Creator of Man,' the 'Supreme Reality,' and that entity ultimately responsible for the existence of man. He also further described his 'religious and social thinking' as based on these beliefs, so that his opposition to war stemmed largely from his conviction that, as 'partly akin to the Supreme Reality' no man ought to 'ever willfully sacrifice another man's life as a means to any other end.'[8] His request was denied, however, because his justification for objector status was seen as a personal moral code, and because the Draft Board did not find his claim to be sincere. Like Seeger, though, the 2nd Circuit Court of Appeals also reversed his conviction.[9]

Forest Britt Peter was convicted in the Northern District of California; however, unlike Seeger and Jakobson, the 9th Circuit Court of Appeals affirmed that conviction in 1963.[10] On his initial form he stated that he was not a member of any organized religious sect or church, and later circumvented the question as to his belief in the existence of a 'Supreme Being' by reasoning that his answer depended on the different definitions of such a term. He further contended that because his worldview was based on reading and meditating on 'our democratic American culture, with its values derived from the western religious and philosophical tradition,' for the purposes of his request, this might be appropriately construed as a 'belief' in a Supreme Being or God, but that 'these just do not happen to be the words I use.'[11]

The 'crux of the problem' with each man's rejection, Justice Clark argued, was that they were determined by the imprecise language of Section 6(j)'s requirement that conscientious objection be founded upon a distinct 'religious training and belief,' that was itself dependent on an equally distinct association to a 'Supreme Being.' Both concepts, he said, were inherently difficult to define, especially as the latter was nothing more than an emendation of Chief Justice Charles Evans Hughes' definition of religion in his dissenting opinion in *United States v. Macintosh* (1931): 'The essence of religion is belief in a relation to God involving duties superior to those arising from any human relation.'[12] This made simply trading 'God' for 'Supreme Being' even more difficult when Section 6(j) was meant to accommodate the 'vast panoply of beliefs' in America. Rather than concern itself with interpreting, comparing, or even defining an individual's religious convictions in relation to this complex and growing diversity, he proposed a simple test that the federal government might use instead:

> Does the claimed belief occupy the same place in the life of the objector as an orthodox belief in God holds in the life of one clearly qualified for exemption?[13]

Of course, though this indeed simplified the process, it in turn generated a secondary issue, particularly in regard to its effect on the greater theological discussion inherent in its wording. By turning toward the 'essence' of what constituted in a person's religious beliefs that which looked like the sort of conviction once applicable, Justice Clark had veered into a more complex conversation about the 'essence' of God, specifically through his use of two renowned Protestant theologians of the time. And while his treatment of Bishop John A.T. Robinson's discourse on God's 'location' with respect to humanity was pragmatic in framing his rationale, it was his use of Paul Tillich's notion of 'ultimate concern' that has had the most lasting effect on the Court's interpretation of what constitutes a 'sincerely held religious belief.'

> We are reminded once more of Dr. Tillich's thoughts: 'And if that word [God] has not much meaning for you, translate it, and speak of the depths of your life, of the source of your being, or your ultimate concern, *of what you take seriously without any reservation*. Perhaps, in order to do so, you must forget everything traditional that you have learned about God' [emphasis in original].[14]

In the context of the religious convictions of Seeger, Jakobson, and Peter, this re-interpretation of 'Supreme Being' worked well. And Justice Clark's conclusion granting them objector status reflects that. In the context of the similar question in *Welsh v. United States* a few years later, however, this same re-interpretation presented a new set of issues, namely how the 'ultimate concern' of a person openly agnostic or Atheistic in his world-view might further extend the notion of 'religious training and belief' into a philosophical realm it had not before explored. Or, as Justice William O. Douglas clarified in a footnote to his own concurring opinion in *Seeger*: 'If he was an atheist, quite different problems would be presented.'[15]

* * *

Welsh v. United States (1970)

Full Title

Welsh v. United States

Official Citation

398 U.S. 333
Argued: January 20, 1970
Decided: June 15, 1970

Author

Justice Hugo Black

Syllabus

Petitioner was convicted of refusing to submit to induction into the Armed Forces despite his claim for conscientious objector status under [section] 6(j) of the Universal Military Training and Service Act. That provision exempts from military service persons who by reason of 'religious training and belief' are conscientiously opposed to war in any form, that term being defined in the Act as 'belief in a relation to a Supreme Being involving duties superior to those arising from any human relation' but not including 'essentially political, sociological, or philosophical views or a merely personal code.' In his exemption application, petitioner stated that he could not affirm or deny belief in a 'Supreme Being,' and struck the words 'my religious training and' from the form. He affirmed that he held deep conscientious scruples against participating in wars where people were killed. The Court of Appeals, while noting that petitioner's 'beliefs are held with the strength of more traditional religious convictions,' concluded that those beliefs were not sufficiently 'religious' to meet the terms of [section] 6(j), and affirmed the conviction. Petitioner contends that the Act violates the First Amendment prohibition of establishment of religion, and that his conviction should be set aside on the basis of *United States v. Seeger* (1965),[16] which held that the test of religious belief under [section] 6(j) is whether it is a sincere and meaningful belief occupying in the life of its possessor a place parallel to that filled by the God of those admittedly qualified for the exemption.

Held:

The judgment is reversed.

[*Elliott Ashton Welsh, II, Appellant, v. United States of America, Appellee* (1969), Ninth Circuit Court of Appeals, citation: 404 F.2d 1078], *reversed.*

Mr. Justice Black, joined by Mr. Justice Douglas, Mr. Justice Brennan, and Mr. Justice Marshall, concluded that:

This case is controlled by *United States v. Seeger, supra*, to which it is factually similar.

Under *Seeger*, [section] 6(j) is not limited to those whose opposition to war is prompted by orthodox or parochial religious beliefs. A registrant's conscientious objection to all war is 'religious' within the meaning of [section] 6(j) if this opposition stems from the registrant's moral, ethical, or religious beliefs about what is right and wrong and these beliefs are held with the strength of traditional religious convictions. In view of the broad scope of the word 'religious,' a registrant's characterization of his beliefs as 'nonreligious' is not a reliable guide to those administering the exemption.

Mr. Justice Harlan concluded that:

1. The language of [section] 6(j) cannot be construed (as it was in *United States v. Seeger, supra*, and as it is in the prevailing opinion) to exempt from military service all individuals who in good faith oppose all war, it being clear from both the legislative history and textual analysis of that provision that Congress used the words 'by reason of religious training and belief' to limit religion to its theistic sense, and to confine it to formal, organized worship or shared beliefs by a recognizable and cohesive group.

2. The question of the constitutionality of [section] 6(j) cannot be avoided by a construction of that provision that is contrary to its intended meaning.

3. Section 6(j) contravenes the Establishment Clause of the First Amendment by exempting those whose conscientious objection claims are founded on a theistic belief, while not exempting those whose claims are based on a secular belief. To comport with that clause, an exemption must be 'neutral' and include those whose belief emanates from a purely moral, ethical, or philosophical source.

4. In view of the broad discretion conferred by the Act's severability clause and the longstanding policy of exempting religious conscientious objectors, the Court, rather than nullifying the exemption entirely, should extend its coverage to those like petitioner who have been unconstitutionally excluded from its coverage.

Mr. Justice Black announced the judgment of the Court and delivered an opinion in which Mr. Justice Douglas, Mr. Justice Brennan, and Mr. Justice Marshall join.

Opinion

The petitioner, Elliott Ashton Welsh II, was convicted by a United States District Judge of refusing to submit to induction into the Armed Forces in violation of [Title] 50 [of the United States Code, Appendix] [section] 462(a),[17] and was, on June 1, 1966, sentenced to imprisonment for three years. One of petitioner's defenses to the prosecution was that [section] 6(j) of the Universal Military Training and Service Act exempted him from combat and noncombat service because he was 'by reason of religious training and belief [. . .] conscientiously opposed to participation in war in any form.'[i] After finding that there was no religious basis for petitioner's conscientious objector claim, the Court of Appeals, Judge Hamley dissenting, affirmed the conviction. We granted certiorari chiefly to review the contention that Welsh's conviction should be set aside on the basis of this Court's decision in *United States v. Seeger*. For the reasons to be stated, and without passing upon the constitutional arguments that have been raised, we vote to reverse this conviction because of its fundamental inconsistency with *United States v. Seeger, supra*.

The controlling facts in this case are strikingly similar to those in *Seeger*. Both Seeger and Welsh were brought up in religious homes and attended church in their childhood, but in neither case was this church one which taught its members not to engage in war at any time for any reason. Neither Seeger nor Welsh continued his childhood religious ties into his young manhood, and neither belonged to any religious group or adhered to the teachings of any organized religion during the period of his involvement with the Selective Service System. At the time of registration for the draft, neither had yet come to accept pacifist principles. Their views on war developed only in subsequent years, but, when their ideas did fully mature, both made application to their local draft boards for conscientious objector exemptions from military service under [section] 6(j) of the Universal Military Training and Service Act. That section then provided, in part:

> Nothing contained in this title shall be construed to require any person to be subject to combatant training and service in the armed forces of the United States who, by reason of religious training and belief, is conscientiously opposed to participation in war in any form. Religious training and belief in this connection means an individual's belief in a relation to a Supreme Being involving duties superior to those arising from any human relation, but does not include essentially political, sociological, or philosophical views or a merely personal moral code.[ii]

In filling out their exemption applications, both Seeger and Welsh were unable to sign the statement that, as printed in the Selective Service form, stated, 'I am, by reason of my religious training and belief, conscientiously opposed to participation in war in any form.' Seeger could sign only after striking the words 'training and' and putting quotation marks around the word 'religious.' Welsh could sign only after striking the words 'my religious training and.' On those same applications, neither could definitely affirm or deny that he believed in a 'Supreme Being,' both stating that they preferred to leave the question open.[iii] But both Seeger and Welsh affirmed on those applications that they held deep conscientious scruples against taking part in wars where people were killed. Both strongly believed that killing in war was wrong, unethical, and immoral, and their

i 162 Stat. 612. See also 50 U.S.C.App. [section] 456(j). The pertinent provision as it read during the period relevant to this case is set out *infra* at 398 U. S. 336.

ii 62 Stat. 612. An amendment to the Act in 1967, subsequent to the Court's decision in the *Seeger* case, deleted the reference to 'Supreme Being' but continued to provide that 'religious training and belief' does not include 'essentially political, sociological, or philosophical views, or a merely personal moral code.' 1 Stat. 104, 50 U.S.C.App. [section] 456(j) (1964 ed., Supp. IV).

iii In his original application in April, 1964, Welsh stated that he did not believe in a Supreme Being, but, in a letter to his local board in June, 1965, he requested that his original answer be stricken and the question left open. App. 29.

consciences forbade them to take part in such an evil practice. Their objection to participating in war in any form could not be said to come from a 'still, small voice of conscience'; rather, for them, that voice was so loud and insistent that both men preferred to go to jail rather than serve in the Armed Forces. There was never any question about the sincerity and depth of Seeger's convictions as a conscientious objector, and the same is true of Welsh. In this regard the Court of Appeals noted, '[t]he government concedes that [Welsh's] beliefs are held with the strength of more traditional religious convictions.'[18] But, in both cases, the Selective Service System concluded that the beliefs of these men were in some sense insufficiently 'religious' to qualify them for conscientious objector exemptions under the terms of [section] 6(j). Seeger's conscientious objector claim was denied 'solely because it was not based upon a belief in a relation to a "Supreme Being," as required by [section] 6(j) of the Act,'[19] while Welsh was denied the exemption because his Appeal Board and the Department of Justice hearing officer 'could find no religious basis for the registrant's beliefs, opinions and convictions.'[20] Both Seeger and Welsh subsequently refused to submit to induction into the military, and both were convicted of that offense.

In *Seeger*, the Court was confronted, first, with the problem that [section] 6(j) defined 'religious training and belief' in terms of a 'belief in a relation to a Supreme Being [. . .]' a definition that arguably gave a preference to those who believed in a conventional God, as opposed to those who did not. Noting the 'vast panoply of beliefs' prevalent in our country, the Court construed the congressional intent as being in 'keeping with its long-established policy of not picking and choosing among religious beliefs,'[21] and accordingly interpreted 'the meaning of religious training and belief so as to embrace *all* religions. [. . .]'[22] But, having decided that all religious conscientious objectors were entitled to the exemption, we faced the more serious problem of determining which beliefs were 'religious' within the meaning of the statute. This question was particularly difficult in the case of Seeger himself. Seeger stated that his was a 'belief in and devotion to goodness and virtue for their own sakes, and a religious faith in a purely ethical creed.'[23] In a letter to his draft board, he wrote:

> My decision arises from what I believe to be considerations of validity from the standpoint of the welfare of humanity and the preservation of the democratic values which we in the United States are struggling to maintain. I have concluded that war, from the practical standpoint, is futile and self-defeating, and that, from the more important moral standpoint, it is unethical.[24]

On the basis of these and similar assertions, the Government argued that Seeger's conscientious objection to war was not 'religious,' but stemmed from 'essentially political, sociological, or philosophical views, or a merely personal moral code.'

In resolving the question whether Seeger and the other registrants in that case qualified for the exemption, the Court stated that '[the] task is to decide whether the beliefs professed by a registrant are sincerely held and whether they are, *in his own scheme of things*, religious.'[25] The reference to the registrant's 'own scheme of things' was intended to indicate that the central consideration in determining whether the registrant's beliefs are religious is whether these beliefs play the role of a religion and function as a religion in the registrant's life. The Court's principal statement of its test for determining whether a conscientious objector's beliefs are religious within the meaning of [section] 6(j) was as follows:

> The test might be stated in these words: a sincere and meaningful belief which occupies in the life of its possessor a place parallel to that filled by the God of those admittedly qualifying for the exemption comes within the statutory definition.[26]

The Court made it clear that these sincere and meaningful beliefs that prompt the registrant's objection to all wars need not be confined in either source or content to traditional or parochial concepts of religion. It held that [section] 6(j) 'does not distinguish between externally and internally derived beliefs,'[27] and also held that 'intensely personal' convictions which some might find 'incomprehensible' or 'incorrect' come within the meaning of 'religious belief' in the Act.[28] What is necessary under *Seeger* for a registrant's conscientious objection to all war to be 'religious' within the meaning of [section] 6(j) is that this opposition to war stem from the registrant's moral, ethical, or religious beliefs about what is right and wrong and that these beliefs be held with the strength of traditional religious convictions. Most of the great religions of today and of the past have embodied the idea of a Supreme Being or a Supreme Reality – a God – who communicates to man in some way a consciousness of what is right and should be done, of what is wrong and therefore should be shunned. If an individual deeply and sincerely holds beliefs that are purely ethical or moral in source and content, but that nevertheless impose upon him a duty of conscience to refrain from participating in any war at any time, those beliefs certainly occupy in the life of that individual 'a place parallel to that filled by [. . .] God' in traditionally religious persons. Because his beliefs function as a religion in his life, such an individual is as much entitled to a 'religious' conscientious objector exemption under [section] 6(j) as is someone who derives his conscientious opposition to war from traditional religious convictions.

Applying this standard to Seeger himself, the Court noted the 'compulsion to goodness' that shaped his total opposition to war, the undisputed sincerity with which he held his views, and the fact that Seeger had 'decried the tremendous "spiritual" price man must pay for his willingness to destroy human life.'[29] The Court concluded:

> We think it clear that the beliefs which prompted his objection occupy the same place in his life as the belief in a traditional deity holds in the lives of his friends, the Quakers.[30]

Accordingly, the Court found that Seeger should be granted conscientious objector status.

In the case before us, the Government seeks to distinguish our holding in *Seeger* on basically two grounds, both of which were relied upon by the Court of Appeals in affirming Welsh's conviction. First, it is stressed that Welsh was far more insistent and explicit than Seeger in denying that his views were religious. For example, in filling out their conscientious objector applications, Seeger put quotation marks around the word 'religious,' but Welsh struck the word 'religious' entirely, and later characterized his beliefs as having been formed 'by reading in the fields of history and sociology.'[31] The Court of Appeals found that Welsh had 'denied that his objection to war was premised on religious belief,' and concluded that '[t]he Appeal Board was entitled to take him at his word.'[32] We think this attempt to distinguish *Seeger* fails for the reason that it places undue emphasis on the registrant's interpretation of his own beliefs. The Court's statement in *Seeger* that a registrant's characterization of his own belief as 'religious' should carry great weight,[33] does not imply that his declaration that his views are nonreligious should be treated similarly. When a registrant states that his objections to war are 'religious,' that information is highly relevant to the question of the function his beliefs have in his life. But very few registrants are fully aware of the broad scope of the word 'religious' as used in [section] 6(j), and accordingly a registrant's statement that his beliefs are nonreligious is a highly unreliable guide for those charged with administering the exemption. Welsh himself presents a case in point. Although he originally characterized his beliefs as nonreligious, he later, upon reflection, wrote a long and thoughtful letter to his Appeal Board in which he declared that his beliefs were 'certainly religious in the ethical sense of the word.' He explained:

> I believe I mentioned taking of life as not being, for me, a religious wrong. Again, I assumed Mr. [Brady (the Department of Justice hearing officer)] was using the word 'religious' in the conventional sense, and, in order to be perfectly honest, did not characterize my belief as 'religious.'[34]

The Government also seeks to distinguish *Seeger* on the ground that Welsh's views, unlike Seeger's, were 'essentially political, sociological, or philosophical views, or a merely personal moral code.' As previously noted, the Government made the same argument about Seeger, and not without reason, for Seeger's views had a substantial political dimension.[35] In this case, Welsh's conscientious objection to war was undeniably based in part on his perception of world politics. In a letter to his local board, he wrote:

> I can only act according to what I am and what I see. And I see that the military complex wastes both human and material resources, that it fosters disregard for (what I consider a paramount concern) human needs and ends; I see that the means we employ to 'defend' our 'way of life' profoundly change that way of life. I see that, in our failure to recognize the political, social, and economic realities of the world, we, as a nation, fail our responsibility as a nation.[36]

We certainly do not think that [section] 6(j)'s exclusion of those persons with 'essentially political, sociological, or philosophical views or a merely personal moral code' should be read to exclude those who hold strong beliefs about our domestic and foreign affairs or even those whose conscientious objection to participation in all wars is founded to a substantial extent upon considerations of public policy. The two groups of registrants that obviously do fall within these exclusions from the exemption are those whose beliefs are not deeply held and those whose objection to war does not rest at all upon moral, ethical, or religious principle, but instead rests solely upon considerations of policy, pragmatism, or expediency. In applying [section] 6(j)'s exclusion of those whose views are 'essentially political, sociological, or philosophical' or of those who have a 'merely personal moral code,' it should be remembered that these exclusions are definitional, and do not therefore restrict the category of persons who are conscientious objectors by 'religious training and belief.' Once the Selective Service System has taken the first step and determined under the standards set out here and in *Seeger* that the registrant is a 'religious' conscientious objector, it follows that his views cannot be 'essentially political, sociological, or philosophical.' Nor can they be a 'merely personal moral code.'[37]

Welsh stated that he 'believe[d] the taking of life – anyone's life – to be morally wrong.'[38] In his original conscientious objector application, he wrote the following:

> I believe that human life is valuable in and of itself; in its living; therefore, I will not injure or kill another human being. This belief (and the corresponding 'duty' to abstain from violence toward another person) is not 'superior to those arising from any human relation.' On the contrary: it is essential to every human relation. I cannot, therefore, conscientiously comply with the Government's insistence that I assume duties which I feel are immoral and totally repugnant.[39]

Welsh elaborated his beliefs in later communications with Selective Service officials. On the basis of these beliefs and the conclusion of the Court of Appeals that he held them 'with the strength of more traditional religious convictions,'[40] we think Welsh was clearly entitled to a conscientious objector exemption. Section 6(j) requires no more. That section exempts from military service all those whose consciences, spurred by deeply held moral, ethical, or religious beliefs, would give them no rest or peace if they allowed themselves to become a part of an instrument of war.

The judgment is *Reversed*.

* * *

Importance

Welsh v. United States was a test of two things: whether the decision in *Seeger* could be applied to an individual even less devoted to more orthodox religious beliefs, and whether the Court's use of Tillich's notion of 'ultimate concern' could equally be applied to that same person, when their belief system represented a 'nonreligious' or even 'Atheistic' conviction. As such, perhaps its leading importance has to do with the Court's further re-conceptualization of 'religion' in order to rule in Welsh's favor, and the implications this would have on later decisions, as well as on the very meaning of 'American religion' itself.

* * *

Though Justice Black neither cited Tillich, nor used the phrase 'ultimate concern,' its influence is nonetheless reflected within his defense of taking both Seeger and Welsh 'at their word.' That is, by allowing them the opportunity to 'speak for themselves,' and then by basing his decision on whether or not what they described as their 'religious beliefs' were religious on nothing more than whether those things reflected, in their minds, the sort of convictions expressed by more 'orthodox' individuals, he expanded the notion of 'ultimate concern' into a guiding paradigm:

> The reference to the registrant's 'own scheme of things' was intended to indicate that the central consideration in determining whether the registrant's beliefs are religious is whether these beliefs play the role of a religion and function as a religion in the registrant's life. The Court's principal statement of its test for determining whether a conscientious objector's beliefs are religious within the meaning of [section] 6(j) was as follows: 'The test might be stated in these words: a sincere and meaningful belief which occupies in the life of its possessor a place parallel to that filled by the God of those admittedly qualifying for the exemption comes within the statutory definition.' The Court made it clear that these sincere and meaningful beliefs that prompt the registrant's objection to all wars need not be confined in either source or content to traditional or parochial concepts of religion.[41]

Moreover, by basing his decision on Welsh's 'own scheme of things,' rather than on some pre-determined understanding of what constituted a proper 'religious belief,' he likewise removed the compulsion of approaching any such issue with an established definition of religion. This permitted him the opportunity to fully justify the Court's decision in siding with Welsh, regardless of the fact that his 'religious convictions' seemed antithetical to those demanded by the language in section 6(j) of the Universal Military Training and Service Act:

> If an individual deeply and sincerely holds beliefs that are purely ethical or moral in source and content, but that nevertheless impose upon him a duty of conscience to refrain from participating in any war at any time, those beliefs certainly occupy in the life of that individual 'a place parallel to that filled by [. . .] God' in traditionally religious persons. Because his beliefs function as a religion in his life, such an individual is as much entitled to a 'religious' conscientious objector exemption under [section] 6(j) as is someone who derives his conscientious opposition to war from traditional religious convictions.[42]

Justice Black's broadening of Tillich's 'ultimate concern' here with respect to Welsh's 'religious convictions' signifies a shift in the Court's analytical process toward a more phenomenological approach to American religion. That is, where First Amendment violations were once decided by means of a pre-determined filter that, if nothing else, saw 'religion' as constituting some sort of theistic belief system, with the *Welsh* decision that filter was replaced with a methodology by which 'religion' would only be determined via each individual's 'own scheme of things.'

Of course, this is not without its faults. And here's a relatable example.

In the academic field of religious studies, the phenomenological method has, indeed, assisted in dealing with the myriad ways in which individuals express, and thus define, their 'religions.' As well, it has made the job of the scholar or student that much easier in better determining what might constitute their subject's 'religion,' which has proven to be, and will likely continue to be, an ambiguous infliction. One principal example of the phenomenological method was provided in Ninian Smart's *Dimensions of the Sacred*, first published in 1996. Smart was one of the leading pioneers in the development of religious studies as an academic discipline, and his *Dimensions* introduced a methodology by which 'religion' was more easily determined through seven dimensions – later expanded to eight – that one might use to better approach, understand, and delineate the term: the doctrinal or philosophical, the ritualistic, the mythic or narrative, the experiential or emotional, the ethical or legal, the social, the material or artistic, and the political. When combined, these dimensions represented religion.

Then again, merely listing religious dimensions is only one part of the process. The primary value of examining religion phenomenologically is perhaps best found in the empathetic approach that it extols in general.

In his definition of the term, Smart described phenomenology as the 'attempt through informed empathy to present others' experiences and beliefs from their points of view,' which also involved the 'suspension of one's own values,' which he referred to in the Greek as, 'epoche.'[43] And in many ways this is quite reflective of the Court's use of Tillich's 'ultimate concern' in both *Seeger* and *Welsh*, though perhaps more so in the latter, with Justice Black's acceptance of Welsh's 'own scheme of things' as a valid enough religious conviction in comparison to more 'established' ones.

And here is where this decision becomes essential to the discussion herein of the Court's discourse on American Atheism. Though he did not describe himself as such, and even though his legal representative, J.B. Tietz, began his oral argument before the Court by denying it,[44] Elliot Welsh was, if nothing else, an Atheist-leaning agnostic, whose 'religious convictions' were based solely on what we might perceive as entirely secular, non-religious, or politically motivated sources.[45] And yet, at least in the context of his qualification for conscientious objector status, they were deemed 'sacred' or 'religious' enough to grant him his exemption, simply because he said they were. Because, as the Court decided, they represented for him his 'ultimate concern.'

What sort of consequences, we might then ask, does the Court's acceptance of that which he found personally sacred – this 'judicial epoche' – have on its wider consideration of Atheism within the category of American religion? Certainly with respect to this decision it simply means that his beliefs were enough to grant him the same exemptions as someone who, by means of their religious affiliation, held synonymous ones.

Out of that context, though, and in light of the Court's broader use of Tillich's 'ultimate concern,' we might additionally ask: does this mean that with respect to their shared moral or ethical values, that Atheist-Americans might be considered 'religious' alongside their Christian-American, Jewish-American, Muslim-American, or Buddhist-American brothers and sisters? Which is a question with even deeper consequences when we translate the Court's consideration of Welsh's case into a Free Exercise question. After all, through his objector request he was, in essence, asking to have his secular beliefs accepted as equally sacred as those that traditionally qualified. Which means he was asking to freely exercise those secular beliefs religiously. And in this way, we are faced with perhaps even more compound questions, such as: what would other Atheist free exercises look like? Or, perhaps better asked, what would an Atheist church look like? Or Atheist prayer? Or ritual? Or doctrine? Or any of Smart's other dimensions? In addressing these questions, would the 'secular nature' of the beliefs of Atheists somehow become religion? Would just about *any belief*, so long as it was held sacred, become religion?

These sorts of questions have been the foci of phenomenological scholars of religion for years. And they will continue to direct the discussion herein, especially as the Court's open and unconventional treatment of Atheism in these last four decisions gives way to a more politically conservative one in the final three, leading to additional complex inquiries about Atheism's place within the panoply of beliefs in America, particularly in proportion to the Court's permissibility of more 'traditional' ideas regarding the separation of church and state.

Notes

1 The Constitution of the Commonwealth of Pennsylvania, 1776: www.duq.edu/academics/gumberg-library/pa-constitution/texts-of-the-constitution/1776. (Accessed September 21st, 2017.)
2 Draft Act of 1917 cited in *United States v. Seeger* (1965), citation: 380 U.S. 163, 171.
3 *United States v. Seeger* (1965), 172.
4 Cited in *United States v. Seeger* (1965), 172.
5 Section 6(j) of the Universal Military Training and Service Act, 1951: https://babel.hathitrust.org/cgi/pt?id=mdp.39015070529220;view=1up;seq=33. (Accessed September 21st, 2017.)
6 Daniel Seeger, quoted in *United States v. Seeger* (1965), 166–167.
7 *United States v. Seeger* (2nd Circuit Court of Appeals, 1964), citation: 326 F.2d 846.
8 Sascha Jakobson, quoted in *United States v. Seeger* (1965), 167–168.
9 *United States v. Jakobson* (2nd Circuit Court of Appeals, 1963), citation: 325 F.2d 409.

10 *Peter v. United States* (9th Circuit Court of Appeals, 1963), citation: 324 F.2d 173.
11 Forest Britt Peter, quoted in *United States v. Seeger* (1965), 169.
12 Justice Hughes dissenting in *United States v. Macintosh* (1931), citation: 283 U.S. 605, 634.
13 Ibid., 184.
14 Justice Clark, quoting Paul Tillich, *The Shaking of the Foundations* (New York: C. Scribner's Sons, 1948), 57.
15 Justice Douglas concurring, *United States v. Seeger* (1965), footnote 2/2.
16 *United States v. Seeger* (1965), citation: 380 U.S. 163.
17 Under Title 50 (War And National Defense) of the Military Selective Service Act, Section 462, a (Offenses and Penalties) [June 24th, 1948].
18 *Welsh v. United States* (1969), citation: 404 F.2d 1078, 1081.
19 *United States v. Seeger* (1965), 167.
20 App. 52. In Justice Black's opinion, citations to the text of Welsh's initial application are written as 'App.' They will continue in this style in this transcription.
21 *United States v. Seeger* (1965), 175.
22 Ibid., 165 [emphasis added].
23 Ibid., 166.
24 *United States, v. Seeger* (2nd Circuit Court of Appeals, 1964), 848.
25 *United States v. Seeger* (1965), 185 [emphasis added].
26 Ibid., 176.
27 Ibid., 186.
28 Ibid., 184–185.
29 Ibid., 186–187.
30 Ibid., 187.
31 App. 22.
32 *Welsh v. United States* (9th Circuit Court of Appeals, 1969), 1082.
33 *United States v. Seeger* (1965), 184.
34 App. 44.
35 See this decision above, 338–339.
36 App. 30.
37 See *United States v. Seeger* (1965), 186.
38 App. 44.
39 App. 10.
40 *Welsh v. United States* (9th Circuit Court of Appeals, 1969), 1081.
41 *Welsh v. United States* (1970), 339–340.
42 Ibid.
43 Ninian Smart, *Dimensions of the Sacred: An Anatomy of the World's Beliefs* (Berkeley: University of California Press, 1996), xxiii.
44 Tietz began by stating, definitively: 'he is not an atheist.' J.B. Tietz, *Oral Argument before the Supreme Court*, January 20th, 1970 (accessible via www.oyez.org/cases/1969/76).
45 Further evidence in support of this designation, from outside the context of this one case decision, can be found in a similar lawsuit that he initially filed with the U.S. District Court for the Northern District of Illinois in 1990, against the Boy Scouts of America. His son, Mark, had expressed interest in joining the Cub Scouts (Tiger Cubs), but because of his age, he needed an adult partner, so both he and his father attempted to join. When their application was denied because neither could 'recognize an obligation to God' because, as their original complaint stated, neither 'firmly believe[d] in a Supreme Being (God),' Welsh filed suit against the organization. And though the case concluded three years later with a decision by the Seventh Circuit Court of Appeals in favor of the Boy Scouts, it nevertheless re-affirmed that his 'religious convictions' were not religious in the conventional sense of the term. See *Welsh v. Boy Scouts of America* (U.S. District Court for the Northern District of Illinois, 1990), citation: 742 F.Supp. 1413; and *Welsh v. Boy Scout of America* (7th Circuit Court of Appeals, 1993), citation: 993 F.2d 1267.

8 *Elk Grove v. Newdow* (2004)

Argued: March 24th, 2004 – Decided: June 14th, 2004.

> Finally, we have noted that government cannot be completely prohibited from recognizing in its public actions the religious beliefs and practices of the American people as an aspect of our national history and culture. While I remain uncertain about these questions, I would suggest that such practices as the designation of 'In God We Trust' as our national motto, or the references to God contained in the Pledge of Allegiance to the flag can best be understood, in Dean Rostow's apt phrase, as a form of 'ceremonial deism,' protected from Establishment Clause scrutiny chiefly because they have lost through rote repetition any significant religious content.
>
> — Justice Brennan, dissenting opinion in *Lynch v. Donnelly* (1984)

Questions before the Court: 1. As a parent who does not maintain sufficient custody of his child, does Michael Newdow have standing to sue on her behalf? 2. Does the requirement of reciting the Pledge of Allegiance in a public school violate the Establishment Clause of the First Amendment when that Pledge includes the phrase 'under God'?

Decision: 8–0 Unanimous. No, Newdow did not have standing. The question of the Pledge's constitutionality was not considered in the decision for the Court.

Antecedent Case Decisions:

- NINTH CIRCUIT COURT OF APPEALS (Newdow III), February 28th, 2003.

  Ruling: A requested en banc review of the initial Appeals Court decision was denied, and the original order was amended to omit the initial decision's discussion of whether or not Newdow had standing to sue. The Elk Grove Unified School District petitioned for a writ of certiorari, which was granted by the Supreme Court.

- NINTH CIRCUIT COURT OF APPEALS (Newdow II), December 4th, 2002.

  Ruling: After Sandra Banning, the mother of Newdow's daughter, filed a motion for leave to intervene, requesting the case dismissed, the Court reconsidered Newdow's standing and declared that, though Banning held 'exclusive legal custody' over their daughter, he still maintained the right to sue on her behalf as a 'non-custodial parent.'

- NINTH CIRCUIT COURT OF APPEALS (Newdow I), June 26th, 2002.

  Ruling: The three-judge panel unanimously agreed that Newdow had standing to sue. In a 2–1 decision, it also declared the inclusion of 'under God' in the Pledge as unconstitutional.

- UNITED STATES DISTRICT COURT FOR THE EASTERN DISTRICT OF CALIFORNIA, July 21st, 2000.

  Ruling: A Magistrate Judge concluded that the Pledge of Allegiance did not violate the Establishment Clause of the First Amendment, and the District Court dismissed Newdow's complaint.

Background

Article 2, Section 52720, of the California Education Code, under the title 'Patriotic Exercises and Instruction,' states:

> In every public elementary school each day during the school year at the beginning of the first regularly scheduled class or activity period at which the majority of the pupils of the school normally begin the schoolday, there shall be conducted appropriate patriotic exercises. The giving of the Pledge of Allegiance to the Flag of the United States of America shall satisfy the requirements of this section.

Title 4, Chapter 1, section 4 of the United States Code defines the Pledge of Allegiance and the manner of its delivery as:

> The Pledge of Allegiance to the Flag: 'I pledge allegiance to the Flag of the United States of America, and to the Republic for which it stands, one Nation under God, indivisible, with liberty and justice for all,' should be rendered by standing at attention facing the flag with the right hand over the heart. When not in uniform men should remove any non-religious headdress with their right hand and hold it at the left shoulder, the hand being over the heart. Persons in uniform should remain silent, face the flag, and render the military salute. Members of the Armed Forces not in uniform and veterans may render the military salute in the manner provided for persons in uniform.

In its decision in *West Virginia State Board of Education v. Barnette* (1943), the Supreme Court ruled that the compulsory requirement of public school teachers and students to salute the flag and recite the Pledge of Allegiance represented a violation of the First Amendment, thereafter prohibiting such resolutions nationwide. Justice Robert H. Jackson, writing for the Court, justified the Court's argument by stating:

> If there is any fixed star in our constitutional constellation, it is that no official, high or petty, can prescribe what shall be orthodox in politics, nationalism, religion, or other matters of opinion, or force citizens to confess by word or act their faith therein. If there are any circumstances which permit an exception, they do not now occur to us.[1]

The Pledge itself has changed twice since Francis Bellamy first introduced it in the September 1892 issue of *The Youth's Companion*. It was initially created to coincide with the formation of Columbus Day as a national holiday, with President Benjamin Harrison declaring by Presidential Proclamation that same year:

> Let the national flag float over every schoolhouse in the country and the exercises be such as shall impress upon our youth the patriotic duties of American citizenship.[2]

The original Bellamy Pledge stated:

> I pledge allegiance to my Flag and the Republic for which it stands, one nation, indivisible, with liberty and justice for all.

In July 1923, the National Flag Conference, meeting for the first time in Washington, D.C., officially amended the Pledge to replace 'my Flag' with 'to the Flag of the United States.' A year later, it added 'of America':

> I pledge allegiance to the Flag of the United States of America and to the Republic for which it stands, one nation, indivisible, with liberty and justice for all.

Also in 1923, the National Flag Conference created the United States Flag Code, which was formally adopted by the United States Congress in 1942.

On June 14th, 1954, 'Flag Day,' President Dwight D. Eisenhower signed into law a Joint Resolution to officially add the phrase 'under God' into the Pledge.

Part of the necessity, President Eisenhower felt, of including these words was due to the cultural differences between the United States and the Soviet Union, which he saw as demarcated by a line that separated American religious devotion from Soviet Materialism. At the Bill signing ceremony, he remarked:

> From this day forward, the millions of our school children will daily proclaim in every city and town, every village and rural school house, the dedication of our nation and our people to the Almighty. To anyone who truly loves America, nothing could be more inspiring than to contemplate this rededication of our youth, on each school morning, to our country's true meaning. Especially is this meaningful as we regard today's world. Over the globe, mankind has been cruelly torn by violence and brutality and, by the millions, deadened in mind and soul by a materialistic philosophy of life. Man everywhere is appalled by the prospect of atomic war. In this somber setting, this law and its effects today have profound meaning. In this way we are reaffirming the transcendence of religious faith in America's heritage and future; in this way we shall constantly strengthen those spiritual weapons which forever will be our country's most powerful resource, in peace or in war.[3]

Since this addition, the Pledge of Allegiance has been the focus of numerous judicial conflicts.

Eleven years after President Eisenhower added the words 'under God,' and after fleeing to Hawaii in 1964 to escape conviction for assaulting five Baltimore police officers,

Madalyn Murray filed suit in the Federal District Court in Honolulu against the Lincoln Elementary School where her son, Jon Garth had begun attending, specifically naming the Superintendent, Burl Yarberry, and the School's Principal, Faith C. Ai. Murray's claim stated that the 1954 amendment to the U.S. Flag Code to include 'under God' was an unconstitutional violation of the First Amendment, and that her son's participation in reciting the Pledge each morning was akin to religious indoctrination. A State Deputy Attorney dismissed the case, arguing that Madalyn's accusation did not warrant a trial for three reasons: it did not represent a federal issue, the Superintendent and Principal named in her suit were not responsible for drafting the offending rules concerning the school's morning patriotic exercises and instructions, and there was no rule in practice that required students to participate – as established in *West Virginia State Board of Education v. Barnette* (1943).[4]

Four years after that, in *Smith v. Denny* (1968), the U.S. District Court for the Eastern District of California upheld the constitutionality of the pledge and its recitation at Enterprise High School in Redding, California. Writing for the Court, Chief Judge Thomas Jamison MacBride argued that the claim made by the plaintiff, Richard E. Smith, did not substantiate a 'constitutional question.'[5]

In 1992, the 7th Circuit Court of Appeals rendered a similar decision in favor of Community Consolidated School District 21, of Wheeling Township, Illinois. That suit was brought forth by Robert Ian Sherman, on his own behalf, as well as on behalf of his son, Richard Harry Sherman, and when initially heard by the U.S. District Court for the Northern District of Illinois, they were joined in their complaint by Madalyn Murray's Society of Separationists. The Court of Appeals came to its conclusion by addressing this question: 'Must ceremonial references in civic life to a deity be understood as prayer, or support for all monotheistic religions, to the exclusion of atheists and those who worship multiple gods?' It concluded that no, these references should not, and declared the Pledge a symbol that, like the motto, 'in God we trust,' had lost whatever sectarian or religious meaning it might have once had by means of 'rote repetition.'[6]

This was the legislative and judicial foundation on which Michael Newdow built his own case in March of 2000, when he filed suit in the U.S. District Court for the Eastern District of California against the United States Congress, the President of the United States, the State of California, and the Elk Grove Unified School District and its acting superintendent. Newdow's daughter was enrolled in a Kindergarten within the Elk Grove school system, and as an Atheist, he felt her recitation of the Pledge each morning was a violation not only of the Establishment Clause, but of his right as a parent to raise her as an Atheist as well. He requested a writ of mandamus and an injunction against the School District's implementation of the California Education Code's policy on patriotic exercises, which in turn demanded that both the President of the United States 'alter,' 'modify,' or 'remove' the offending language in the Pledge, as well as ordered the United States Congress to follow in kind with its own legislation. He filed on his daughter's behalf, as her 'next friend,' given her young age.

The District Court turned the case over to a Magistrate Judge, a judicial official elected by the District Judges within a particular District to assist with Court proceedings, who dismissed Newdow's claim concerning the Pledge's constitutionality. The District Court adopted that verdict, and officially dismissed Newdow's complaint on July 21st, 2000.

He then appealed to the 9th Circuit Court of Appeals.

That Court rendered three opinions, the first on June 26th, 2002, the second on December 4th, 2002, and the third on February 28th, 2003.

In the first, it found in favor of Newdow, unanimously in regard to his right to sue on behalf of his daughter, and 2–1 that the 1954 Act amending the Flag Code and the School District's policy that endorsed it, were unconstitutional. Writing for Court, Judge Alfred Goodwin used the Lemon Test, as well as Justice O'Connor's 'endorsement test' and Justice Kennedy's 'coercion test,' to do so. He also, however, clarified that the President was not an 'appropriate defendant in an action challenging the constitutionality of a federal statute,' and that a Federal Court, such as it, did not have the jurisdiction to 'issue orders directing Congress to enact or amend legislation.'[7]

In its second decision on December 4th, 2002, it reconsidered Newdow's standing in light of new information concerning his custodial rights over his daughter. Shortly after its decision earlier that year, Sandra Banning, the mother of Newdow's daughter, filed a motion for leave to intervene, challenging Newdow's standing, and providing as evidence a February 6th, 2002 California Superior Court Order granting her 'sole legal custody' of their child. Judge Goodwin, who drafted all three Appeals Court decisions, argued that while Banning was awarded sole custody of their daughter, which also granted her ultimate decision-making power in 'non-emergency' concerns, this did not 'strip' Newdow of his parental rights concerning her education, general welfare, and his right to 'inspect' his daughter's school and medical records. However, he did specify that because of the Superior Court's order, Newdow could not 'disrupt' Banning's choice of school for their daughter, nor could he name her in a lawsuit against her (Banning's) wishes. This did not mean, though, that he was restricted in protecting his own constitutional interests regarding his daughter's perception of them, which, because of the Pledge's unconstitutionality, was being challenged daily.

> The pledge to a nation 'under God,' with its imprimatur of governmental sanction, provides the message to Newdow's young daughter not only that non-believers, or believers in non-Judeo-Christian religions, are outsiders, but more specifically that her *father's* beliefs are those of an outsider, and necessarily inferior to what she is exposed to in the classroom. Just as the foundational principle of the Freedom of Speech Clause in the First Amendment tolerates unpopular and even despised ideas, so does the principle underlying the Establishment Clause protect unpopular and despised minorities from government sponsored religious orthodoxy tied to government services. Accordingly, we affirm Newdow's standing to challenge on Establishment Clause grounds the [Elk Grove Unified School District]'s practice of requiring his daughter to attend daily recitations of the 1954 version of the Pledge of Allegiance [emphasis in original].[8]

With its third decision, on February 28th, 2003, the Court of Appeals amended its initial one to remove as moot its discussion of Newdow's standing as 'next friend,' and denied a rehearing of that initial decision, so as to preserve its verdict that the Pledge was unconstitutional. The Elk Grove School District petitioned for a writ of certiorari, which the Supreme Court granted.

Oral arguments were heard on March 24th, 2004, and the Court's unanimous decision in favor of the School District was announced on June 14th of that year.

* * *

Before proceeding to the case decision itself, it should be noted here that in 2005, Michael Newdow filed an almost identical suit to his original one. In this instance, however, he was joined by three other parents, who filed anonymously. He also attempted to circumvent the custody issues that beset his first attempt by citing in this occasion direct personal injury. Not only did he now own property in the cities of Sacramento and Elk Grove – which meant that the taxes he paid on those properties were used to fund his daughter's school – he also attended classes with her, as well as school board meetings, at which the Pledge was recited.

Once again, his claim was dismissed for lack of standing.[9] However, the U.S. District Court for the Eastern District of California nonetheless considered the complaint on behalf of the unnamed parents, and in Senior District Judge Lawrence K. Karlton's decision for the Court he ruled that, in its current form, the language of the Pledge indeed made its recitation a violation of the Establishment Clause.[10]

The Rio Linda Union School District appealed to the 9th Circuit Court of Appeals, which in a 2–1 decision reversed the District Court's ruling. In an exhaustive review of Newdow's previous case history, the Supreme Court's decision in *Elk Grove v. Newdow*, a litany of judicial precedence, and the concurring opinions of Chief Justice Rehnquist and Justice O'Connor, Judge Carlos T. Bea, writing for the Court, concluded:

> The Pledge of Allegiance serves to unite our vast nation through the proud recitation of some of the ideals upon which our Republic was founded and for which we continue to strive: one Nation under God – the Founding Fathers' belief that the people of this nation are endowed by their Creator with certain inalienable rights; indivisible – although we have individual states, they are united in one Republic; with liberty – the government cannot take away the people's inalienable rights; and justice for all – everyone in America is entitled to 'equal justice under the law' (as is inscribed above the main entrance to our Supreme Court). Millions of people daily recite these words when pledging allegiance to the United States of America.[11]

This was not, however, the final word on this issue. Between 2007 and 2015, at least five similar lawsuits were filed in the states of Virginia,[12] Texas,[13] New Hampshire,[14] Massachusetts,[15] and New Jersey,[16] all featuring complaints about the Pledge's constitutionality. And while each of these cases shared the same objections to the Pledge as those expressed by Newdow, they also shared in his defeat, as each instance was decided in favor of the schools and school boards against which they were filed, with analogous arguments defending the Pledge's theistic language as a permissible representation of America's religious heritage.

* * *

Elk Grove v. Newdow (2004)

Full Title

Elk Grove Unified School District et al. v. Michael A. Newdow et al.

Official Citation

542 U.S. 1
Argued: March 24, 2004
Decided: June 14, 2004

Author

Justice John Paul Stevens

Syllabus

Petitioner school district requires each elementary school class to recite daily the Pledge of Allegiance. Respondent Newdow's daughter participates in this exercise. Newdow, an atheist, filed suit alleging that, because the Pledge contains the words 'under God,' it constitutes religious indoctrination of his child in violation of the Establishment and Free Exercise Clauses. He also alleged that he had standing to sue on his own behalf and on behalf of his daughter as 'next friend.' The Magistrate Judge concluded that the Pledge is constitutional, and the District Court agreed and dismissed the complaint. The Ninth Circuit reversed, holding that Newdow has standing as a parent to challenge a practice that interferes with his right to direct his daughter's religious education, and that the school district's policy violates the Establishment Clause. Sandra Banning, the child's mother, then filed a motion to intervene or dismiss, declaring, *inter alia*, that she had exclusive legal custody under a state-court order and that, as her daughter's sole legal custodian, she felt it was not in the child's interest to be a party to Newdow's suit. Concluding that Banning's sole legal custody did not deprive Newdow, as a noncustodial parent, of Article III standing to object to unconstitutional government action affecting his child, the Ninth Circuit held that, under California law, Newdow retains the right to expose his child to his particular religious views even if they contradict her mother's, as well as the right to seek redress for an alleged injury to his own parental interests.

Held

Because California law deprives Newdow of the right to sue as next friend [on behalf of his daughter], he lacks prudential standing to challenge the school district's policy in federal court. The standing requirement derives from the constitutional and prudential limits to the powers of an unelected, unrepresentative judiciary.[17] The Court's prudential standing jurisprudence encompasses, *inter alia*, 'the general prohibition on a litigant's raising another person's legal rights,'[18] and the Court generally declines to intervene in domestic relations, a traditional subject of state law.[19] The extent of the standing problem raised by the domestic relations issues in this case was not apparent until Banning filed her motion to intervene or dismiss, declaring that the family court order gave her '*sole* legal custody' and authorized her to 'exercise legal control' over her daughter. Newdow's argument that he nevertheless retains an unrestricted right to inculcate in his daughter his beliefs fails because his rights cannot be viewed in isolation. This case also concerns Banning's rights under the custody orders and, most important, their daughter's interests upon finding herself at the center of a highly public debate. Newdow's standing derives entirely from his relationship with his daughter, but he lacks the right to litigate as her next friend. Their interests are not parallel and, indeed, are potentially in conflict. Newdow's parental status is defined by state law, and this Court customarily defers to the state-law interpretations of the regional federal court.[20] Here, the Ninth Circuit relied on intermediate state appellate cases recognizing the right of each parent, whether custodial or noncustodial, to impart to the child his or her religious perspective. Nothing that either Banning or the school board has done, however, impairs Newdow's right to instruct his daughter in his religious views. Instead, he requests the more ambitious relief of forestalling his daughter's exposure to religious ideas endorsed by her mother, who wields a form of veto power, and to use his parental status to challenge the influences to which his daughter may be exposed in school when he and Banning disagree. The California cases simply do not stand for the proposition that Newdow has a right to reach outside the private parent–child sphere to dictate to others what they may and may not say to his child respecting religion. A next friend surely could exercise such a right, but the family court's order has deprived Newdow of that status.

[*Newdow v. U.S. Congress* (2002), Ninth Circuit Court of Appeals, citation: 328 F.3d 466], reversed.

Opinion

Justice [John Paul] Stevens delivered the opinion of the Court.

Each day elementary school teachers in the Elk Grove Unified School District (School District) lead their classes in a group recitation of the Pledge of Allegiance. Respondent, Michael A. Newdow, is an atheist whose daughter participates in that daily exercise. Because the Pledge contains the words 'under God,' he views the School District's policy as a religious indoctrination of his child that violates the First Amendment. A divided panel of the Court of Appeals for the Ninth Circuit agreed with Newdow. In light of the obvious importance of that decision, we granted certiorari to review the First Amendment issue and, preliminarily, the question whether Newdow has standing to invoke the jurisdiction of the federal courts. We conclude that Newdow lacks standing and therefore reverse the Court of Appeals' decision.

I

'The very purpose of a national flag is to serve as a symbol of our country,'[21] and of its proud traditions 'of freedom, of equal opportunity, of religious tolerance, and of good will for other peoples who share our aspirations.'[22] As its history illustrates, the Pledge of Allegiance evolved as a common public acknowledgement of the ideals that our flag symbolizes. Its recitation is a patriotic exercise designed to foster national unity and pride in those principles.

The Pledge of Allegiance was initially conceived more than a century ago. As part of the nationwide interest in commemorating the 400th anniversary of Christopher

Columbus' discovery of America, a widely circulated national magazine for youth proposed in 1892 that pupils recite the following affirmation: 'I pledge allegiance to my Flag and the Republic for which it stands: one Nation indivisible, with Liberty and Justice for all.'[i] In the 1920's, the National Flag Conferences replaced the phrase 'my Flag' with 'the flag of the United States of America.'

In 1942, in the midst of World War II, Congress adopted, and the President signed, a Joint Resolution codifying a detailed set of 'rules and customs pertaining to the display and use of the flag of the United States of America.' Section 7 of this codification provided in full:

> That the pledge of allegiance to the flag, 'I pledge allegiance to the flag of the United States of America and to the Republic for which it stands, one Nation indivisible, with liberty and justice for all,' be rendered by standing with the right hand over the heart; extending the right hand, palm upward, toward the flag at the words 'to the flag' and holding this position until the end, when the hand drops to the side. However, civilians will always show full respect to the flag when the pledge is given by merely standing at attention, men removing the headdress. Persons in uniform shall render the military salute.[23]

This resolution, which marked the first appearance of the Pledge of Allegiance in positive law, confirmed the importance of the flag as a symbol of our Nation's indivisibility and commitment to the concept of liberty.

Congress revisited the Pledge of Allegiance 12 years later when it amended the text to add the words 'under God.'[24] The House Report that accompanied the legislation observed that, '[f]rom the time of our earliest history our peoples and our institutions have reflected the traditional concept that our Nation was founded on a fundamental belief in God.'[25] The resulting text is the Pledge as we know it today: 'I pledge allegiance to the Flag of the United States of America, and to the Republic for which it stands, one Nation under God, indivisible, with liberty and justice for all.'[26]

II

Under California law, 'every public elementary school' must begin each day with 'appropriate patriotic exercises.'[27] The statute provides that '[t]he giving of the Pledge of Allegiance to the Flag of the United States of America shall satisfy' this requirement.[28] The Elk Grove Unified School District has implemented the state law by requiring that '[e]ach elementary school class recite the pledge of allegiance to the flag once each day.'[ii] Consistent with our case law, the School District permits students who object on religious grounds to abstain from the recitation.[29]

i John Wilbur Baer, *The Pledge of Allegiance: A Centennial History, 1892–1992* (Annapolis: Free State Press, Inc., 1992), 3 (internal quotation marks omitted). At the time, the phrase 'one Nation indivisible' had special meaning because the question whether a State could secede from the Union had been intensely debated and was unresolved prior to the Civil War. See James G. Randall, *Constitutional Problems Under Lincoln* (Urbana: University of Illinois Press, 1964), 12–24. See also William H. Rehnquist, *Centennial Crisis: The Disputed Election of 1876* (New York: Alfred P. Knopf, 2004), 182.

ii Elk Grove Unified School District's Policy AR 6115, App. to Brief for United States as Respondent Supporting Petitioners 2a.

In March 2000, Newdow filed suit in the United States District Court for the Eastern District of California against the United States Congress, the President of the United States, the State of California, and the Elk Grove Unified School District and its superintendent.[iii] [30] At the time of filing, Newdow's daughter was enrolled in kindergarten in the Elk Grove Unified School District and participated in the daily recitation of the Pledge. Styled as a mandamus action, the complaint explains that Newdow is an atheist who was ordained more than 20 years ago in a ministry that 'espouses the religious philosophy that the true and eternal bonds of righteousness and virtue stem from reason rather than mythology.'[31] The complaint seeks a declaration that the 1954 Act's addition of the words 'under God' violated the Establishment and Free Exercise Clauses of the United States Constitution,[iv] as well as an injunction against the School District's policy requiring daily recitation of the Pledge.[32] It alleges that Newdow has standing to sue on his own behalf and on behalf of his daughter as 'next friend.'[33]

The case was referred to a Magistrate Judge, whose brief findings and recommendation concluded, 'the Pledge does not violate the Establishment Clause.'[34] The District Court adopted that recommendation and dismissed the complaint on July 21, 2000.[35] The Court of Appeals reversed and issued three separate decisions discussing the merits and Newdow's standing.

In its first opinion the appeals court unanimously held that Newdow has standing 'as a parent to challenge a practice that interferes with his right to direct the religious education of his daughter.'[36] That holding sustained Newdow's standing to challenge not only the policy of the School District, where his daughter still is enrolled, but also the 1954 Act of Congress that had amended the Pledge, because his 'injury in fact' was 'fairly traceable' to its enactment.[37] On the merits, over the dissent of one judge, the court held that both the 1954 Act and the School District's policy violate the Establishment Clause of the First Amendment.[38]

After the Court of Appeals' initial opinion was announced, Sandra Banning, the mother of Newdow's daughter, filed a motion for leave to intervene, or alternatively to dismiss the complaint.[39] She declared that although she and Newdow shared 'physical custody' of their daughter, a state-court order granted her 'exclusive legal custody' of the child, 'including the sole right to represent [the daughter's] legal interests and make all decision[s] about her education' and welfare.[40] Banning further stated that her daughter is a Christian who believes in God and has no objection either to reciting or hearing others recite the Pledge of Allegiance, or to its reference to God.[41] Banning expressed the belief that her daughter would be harmed if the litigation were permitted to proceed, because others might incorrectly perceive the child as sharing her father's atheist views.[42] Banning accordingly concluded, as her daughter's sole legal custodian, that it was not in the child's interest to be a party to Newdow's lawsuit.[43] On September 25, 2002, the

ii Newdow also named as defendants the Sacramento Unified School District and its superintendent on the chance that his daughter might one day attend school in that district. App. 48. The Court of Appeals held that Newdow lacks standing to challenge that district's policy because his daughter is not currently a student there. *Newdow* v. *U.S. Congress*, 328 F.3d 466, 485 (CA9 2003) *(Newdow III)*. Newdow has not challenged that ruling.

iv The First Amendment provides in relevant part that 'Congress shall make no law respecting an establishment of religion, or prohibiting the free exercise thereof.' U.S. Const., Amdt. 1. The Religion Clauses apply to the States by incorporation into the Fourteenth Amendment. See *Cantwell* v. *Connecticut* (1940), citation: 310 U.S. 296, 303.

California Superior Court entered an order enjoining Newdow from including his daughter as an unnamed party or suing as her 'next friend.' That order did not purport to answer the question of Newdow's Article III standing.[44]

In a second published opinion, the Court of Appeals reconsidered Newdow's standing in light of Banning's motion. The court noted that Newdow no longer claimed to represent his daughter, but unanimously concluded that 'the grant of sole legal custody to Banning' did not deprive Newdow, 'as a noncustodial parent, of Article III standing to object to unconstitutional government action affecting his child.'[45] The court held that under California law Newdow retains the right to expose his child to his particular religious views even if those views contradict the mother's, and that Banning's objections as sole legal custodian do not defeat Newdow's right to seek redress for an alleged injury to his own parental interests.[46]

On February 28, 2003, the Court of Appeals issued an order amending its first opinion and denying rehearing en banc.[47] The amended opinion omitted the initial opinion's discussion of Newdow's standing to challenge the 1954 Act and declined to determine whether Newdow was entitled to declaratory relief regarding the constitutionality of that Act.[48] Nine judges dissented from the denial of en banc review.[49] We granted the School District's petition for a writ of certiorari to consider two questions: (1) whether Newdow has standing as a noncustodial parent to challenge the School District's policy, and (2) if so, whether the policy offends the First Amendment.

III

In every federal case, the party bringing the suit must establish standing to prosecute the action. 'In essence the question of standing is whether the litigant is entitled to have the court decide the merits of the dispute or of particular issues.'[50] The standing requirement is born partly of 'an idea, which is more than an intuition but less than a rigorous and explicit theory, about the constitutional and prudential limits to the powers of an unelected, unrepresentative judiciary in our kind of government.'[51]

The command to guard jealously and exercise rarely our power to make constitutional pronouncements requires strictest adherence when matters of great national significance are at stake. Even in cases concededly within our jurisdiction under Article III, we abide by 'a series of rules under which [we have] avoided passing upon a large part of all the constitutional questions pressed upon [us] for decision.'[52] Always we must balance 'the heavy obligation to exercise jurisdiction,'[53] against the 'deeply rooted' commitment 'not to pass on questions of constitutionality' unless adjudication of the constitutional issue is necessary.[54]

Consistent with these principles, our standing jurisprudence contains two strands: Article III standing, which enforces the Constitution's case or controversy requirement;[55] and prudential standing, which embodies 'judicially self-imposed limits on the exercise of federal jurisdiction.'[56] The Article III limitations are familiar: The plaintiff must show that the conduct of which he complains has caused him to suffer an 'injury in fact' that a favorable judgment will redress.[57] Although we have not exhaustively defined the prudential dimensions of the standing doctrine, we have explained that prudential standing encompasses 'the general prohibition on a litigant's raising another person's legal rights, the rule barring adjudication of generalized grievances more appropriately addressed in the representative branches, and the requirement that a plaintiff's complaint fall within the zone of interests protected by the law invoked.'[58] 'Without such limitations – closely related to Art. III concerns but essentially matters of judicial self-governance –

the courts would be called upon to decide abstract questions of wide public significance even though other governmental institutions may be more competent to address the questions and even though judicial intervention may be unnecessary to protect individual rights.'[59]

One of the principal areas in which this Court has customarily declined to intervene is the realm of domestic relations. Long ago we observed that '[t]he whole subject of the domestic relations of husband and wife, parent and child, belongs to the laws of the States and not to the laws of the United States.'[60] So strong is our deference to state law in this area that we have recognized a 'domestic relations exception' that 'divests the federal courts of power to issue divorce, alimony, and child custody decrees.'[61] We have also acknowledged that it might be appropriate for the federal courts to decline to hear a case involving 'elements of the domestic relationship,'[62] even when divorce, alimony, or child custody is not strictly at issue:

> This would be so when a case presents 'difficult questions of state law bearing on policy problems of substantial public import whose importance transcends the result in the case then at bar.' Such might well be the case if a federal suit were filed prior to effectuation of a divorce, alimony, or child custody decree, and the suit depended on a determination of the status of the parties.[63]

Thus, while rare instances arise in which it is necessary to answer a substantial federal question that transcends or exists apart from the family law issue,[64] in general it is appropriate for the federal courts to leave delicate issues of domestic relations to the state courts.[v]

As explained briefly above, the extent of the standing problem raised by the domestic relations issues in this case was not apparent until August 5, 2002, when Banning filed her motion for leave to intervene or dismiss the complaint following the Court of Appeals' initial decision. At that time, the child's custody was governed by a February 6, 2002, order of the California Superior Court. That order provided that Banning had '*sole* legal custody as to the rights and responsibilities to make decisions relating to the health, education and welfare of' her daughter.[65] The order stated that the two parents should 'consult with one another on substantial decisions relating to' the child's 'psychological and educational needs,' but it authorized Banning to 'exercise legal control' if the parents could not reach 'mutual agreement.'[66]

That family court order was the controlling document at the time of the Court of Appeals' standing decision. After the Court of Appeals ruled, however, the Superior Court held another conference regarding the child's custody. At a hearing on September

v Our holding does not rest, as The Chief Justice suggests, see *post*, at 2–5, on either the domestic relations exception or the abstention doctrine. Rather, our prudential standing analysis is informed by the variety of contexts in which federal courts decline to intervene because, as *Ankenbrandt v. Richards* (1992), citation: 504 U.S. 689, contemplated, the suit 'depend[s] on a determination of the status of the parties,' ibid., at 706. We deemed it appropriate to review the dispute in *Palmore* because it 'raise[d] important federal concerns arising from the Constitution's commitment to eradicating discrimination based on race.' 466 U.S., at 432. In this case, by contrast, the disputed family law rights are entwined inextricably with the threshold standing inquiry. The Chief Justice in this respect, see *post*, at 3, misses our point: The *merits* question undoubtedly transcends the domestic relations issue, but the *standing* question surely does not.

11, 2003, the Superior Court announced that the parents have 'joint legal custody,' but that Banning 'makes the final decisions if the two [. . .] disagree.'[vi] [67]

Newdow contends that despite Banning's final authority, he retains 'an unrestricted right to inculcate in his daughter – free from governmental interference – the atheistic beliefs he finds persuasive.'[68] The difficulty with that argument is that Newdow's rights, as in many cases touching upon family relations, cannot be viewed in isolation. This case concerns not merely Newdow's interest in inculcating his child with his views on religion, but also the rights of the child's mother as a parent generally and under the Superior Court orders specifically. And most important, it implicates the interests of a young child who finds herself at the center of a highly public debate over her custody, the propriety of a widespread national ritual, and the meaning of our Constitution.

The interests of the affected persons in this case are in many respects antagonistic. Of course, legal disharmony in family relations is not uncommon, and in many instances that disharmony poses no bar to federal-court adjudication of proper federal questions. What makes this case different is that Newdow's standing derives entirely from his relationship with his daughter, but he lacks the right to litigate as her next friend. In marked contrast to our case law on *jus tertii* [the rights of a third party][69] the interests of this parent and this child are not parallel and, indeed, are potentially in conflict.[vii]

Newdow's parental status is defined by California's domestic relations law. Our custom on questions of state law ordinarily is to defer to the interpretation of the Court of Appeals for the Circuit in which the State is located.[70] In this case, the Court of Appeals, which possesses greater familiarity with California law, concluded that state law vests in Newdow a cognizable right to influence his daughter's religious upbringing.[71] The court based its ruling on two intermediate state appellate cases holding that 'while the custodial parent undoubtedly has the right to make ultimate decisions concerning the child's religious upbringing, a court will not enjoin the noncustodial parent from discussing religion with the child or involving the child in his or her religious activities in the absence of a showing that the child will be thereby harmed.'[72] Animated by a conception of 'family privacy' that includes 'not simply a policy of minimum state intervention but also

vi The court confirmed that position in a written order issued January 9, 2004: 'The parties will have joint legal custody defined as follows: Ms. Banning will continue to make the final decisions as to the minor's health, education, and welfare if the two parties cannot mutually agree. The parties are required to consult with each other on substantial decisions relating to the health, education and welfare of the minor child, including [. . .] psychological and educational needs of the minor. If mutual agreement is not reached in these areas, then Ms. Banning may exercise legal control of the minor that is not specifically prohibited or is inconsistent with the physical custody.' App. to Reply Brief for United States as Respondent Supporting Petitioners 12a. Despite the use of the term 'joint legal custody' – which is defined by California statute, see Cal. Fam. Code Ann. §3003 (West 1994) – we see no meaningful distinction for present purposes between the custody order issued February 6, 2002, and the one issued January 9, 2004. Under either order, Newdow has the right to consult on issues relating to the child's education, but Banning possesses what we understand amounts to a tiebreaking vote.

vii 'There are good and sufficient reasons for th[e] prudential limitation on standing when rights of third parties are implicated – the avoidance of the adjudication of rights which those not before the Court may not wish to assert, and the assurance that the most effective advocate of the rights at issue is present to champion them.' *Duke Power Co. v. Carolina Environmental Study Group, Inc.* (1978), citation: 438 U.S. 59, 80. Banning tells us that her daughter has no objection to the Pledge, and we are mindful in cases such as this that 'children themselves have constitutionally protectible interests.' *Wisconsin v. Yoder* (1972), citation: 406 U.S. 205, 243 (Douglas, J., dissenting). In a fundamental respect, '[i]t is the future of the student, not the future of the parents,' that is at stake. Ibid., 245.

a presumption of parental autonomy,'[73] the state cases create a zone of private authority within which each parent, whether custodial or noncustodial, remains free to impart to the child his or her religious perspective.

Nothing that either Banning or the School Board has done, however, impairs Newdow's right to instruct his daughter in his religious views. Instead, Newdow requests relief that is more ambitious than that sought in *Mentry* and *Murga*. He wishes to forestall his daughter's exposure to religious ideas that her mother, who wields a form of veto power, endorses, and to use his parental status to challenge the influences to which his daughter may be exposed in school when he and Banning disagree. The California cases simply do not stand for the proposition that Newdow has a right to dictate to others what they may and may not say to his child respecting religion. *Mentry* and *Murga* are concerned with protecting 'the fragile, complex interpersonal bonds between child and parent,'[74] and with permitting divorced parents to expose their children to the 'diversity of religious experiences [that] is itself a sound stimulant for a child.'[75] The cases speak not at all to the problem of a parent seeking to reach outside the private parent–child sphere to restrain the acts of a third party. A next friend surely could exercise such a right, but the Superior Court's order has deprived Newdow of that status.

In our view, it is improper for the federal courts to entertain a claim by a plaintiff whose standing to sue is founded on family law rights that are in dispute when prosecution of the lawsuit may have an adverse effect on the person who is the source of the plaintiff's claimed standing. When hard questions of domestic relations are sure to affect the outcome, the prudent course is for the federal court to stay its hand rather than reach out to resolve a weighty question of federal constitutional law. There is a vast difference between Newdow's right to communicate with his child – which both California law and the First Amendment recognize – and his claimed right to shield his daughter from influences to which she is exposed in school despite the terms of the custody order. We conclude that, having been deprived under California law of the right to sue as next friend, Newdow lacks prudential standing to bring this suit in federal court.[viii]

The judgment of the Court of Appeals is reversed.

It is so ordered.

*Justice Scalia took no part in the consideration or decision of this case.

* * *

Importance

Aside from the slight exception of *Marsh v. Chambers* in 1983, which was overruled by *Greece v. Galloway* in 2014 (to be discussed later), between *Welsh v. United States* and

viii Newdow's complaint and brief cite several additional bases for standing: that Newdow 'at times has himself attended – and will in the future attend – class with his daughter,' App. 49, [paragraph] 80; that he 'has considered teaching elementary school students in [the School District],' Ibid., at 65, [paragraph] 120; that he 'has attended and will continue to attend' school board meetings at which the Pledge is 'routinely recited,' Ibid., at 52, [paragraph] 85; and that the School District uses his tax dollars to implement its Pledge policy, Ibid., at 62–65. Even if these arguments suffice to establish Article III standing, they do not respond to our prudential concerns. As for taxpayer standing, Newdow does not reside in or pay taxes to the School District; he alleges that he pays taxes to the District only 'indirectly' through his child support payments to Banning. Brief for Respondent Newdow 49, n. 70. That allegation does not amount to the 'direct dollars-and-cents injury' that our strict taxpayer-standing doctrine requires. *Doremus v. Board of Ed. of Hawthorne* (1952), citation: 342 U.S. 429, 434

Elk Grove v. Newdow there was a thirty-four year gap in the Supreme Court's consideration of American Atheism.

This is not to say, of course, that there were no judicial proceedings in inferior Courts involving Atheist-Americans. There were, in fact, at least seven instances, from 1980 to 2004, dealing with the constitutionality of Christmas carols in public schools,[76] a state-wide holiday for Good Friday in Wisconsin, and Christmas Day nationwide,[77] a statue of Jesus Christ in a public park,[78] federal funds provided to a Christian-based rehabilitation facility,[79] the distribution of Bibles in public schools in Tennessee,[80] and the granting of 'tax exempt' status to the Ethical Society of Austin, Texas, regardless of it being a non-theistic organization.[81]

While these case decisions reflect a broadening judicial interpretation of American Atheism, their differing outcomes likewise represent the discordant means with which the American Judiciary at large has ruled in regard to the separation of church and state. A disharmony that in equal measure mirrors the ideological shift that took place within the Supreme Court between the late 1980s and the early 2000s, as suggested by the narrative differences between its language in *McCollum v. Board of Education*, *Torcaso v. Watkins*, *Abington v. Schempp*, and *Welsh v. United States*, and that which complemented *Elk Grove v. Newdow*.

And this is perhaps best exemplified by two of the three concurrent opinions submitted alongside Justice Steven's decision in the latter, and their shared willingness to discuss, and argue in favor of, the Pledge's constitutionality.

The first was drafted by Chief Justice William H. Rehnquist, who perfectly encapsulated the more conservative narrative adopted by the Court during his tenureship with this sentence: 'our national culture allows public recognition of our Nation's religious history and character.'[82] By this reasoning, his concurrence presented a short and simple argument, namely that the history and character of the United States allowed breaches in the 'wall of separation' erected by earlier Court decisions – such as *McCollum v. Board of Education* – with respect to the cultural benefits found in certain affiliations between church and state, like that found in the Pledge of Allegiance. As further supportive evidence he cited similar breaches, such as the invocations of and to 'God' in the language of Presidential Inaugural Addresses and speeches, as well as the words of the national motto: In God We Trust. These theistic influences on America's 'civic culture,' he concluded, were so ingrained within American history that removing a part of them, such as the phrase 'under God,' would do more harm than good. With respect to Newdow's complaint, then, he firmly stated:

> There is no doubt that [Newdow] is sincere in his atheism and rejection of a belief in God. But the mere fact that he disagrees with this part of the Pledge does not give him a veto power over the decision of the public schools that willing participants should pledge allegiance to the flag in the manner prescribed by Congress. There may be others who disagree, not with the phrase 'under God,' but with the phrase 'with liberty and justice for all.' But surely that would not give such objectors the right to veto the holding of such a ceremony by those willing to participate. Only if it can be said that the phrase 'under God' somehow tends to the establishment of a religion in violation of the First Amendment can respondent's claim succeed, where one based on objections to 'with liberty and justice for all' fails. Our cases have broadly interpreted this phrase, but none have gone anywhere near as far as the decision of the Court of Appeals in this case. The recital, in a patriotic ceremony

pledging allegiance to the flag and to the Nation, of the descriptive phrase 'under God' cannot possibly lead to the establishment of a religion, or anything like it.

The second concurrence was drafted by Justice Sandra Day O'Connor, in which she defended the use of these types of 'facially religious references' as products of 'ceremonial deism,' a concept borrowed from Justice William Brennan's dissent in *Lynch v. Donnelly* (1984). In his original conception, Justice Brennan used the notion of ceremonial deism to argue that a nativity scene, placed within an otherwise secular Christmas display by the City of Pawtucket, Rhode Island, represented an endorsement of Christianity because, unlike the Christmas Tree or Santa Village, it was 'more sectarian than those references to God that we accept in ceremonial phrases or in other contexts that assure neutrality.' That is, where the nativity scene clearly represented a religious symbol, historical references to 'God,' such as those found in Presidential speeches and the national motto, had become secularized by their repetitive embeddedness into the American culture.[83] In this same way, Justice O'Connor argued, the phrase 'under God' in the Pledge was equally as 'embedded' into the patriotic aspect of reciting it, and thus no longer represented religious language. Any 'reasonable observer,' she further remarked, would understand this transition, were they aware and accepting of America's religious origins and background. As such, she concluded:

> Michael Newdow's challenge to petitioner school district's policy is a well-intentioned one, but his distaste for the reference to 'one Nation under God,' however sincere, cannot be the yardstick of our Establishment Clause inquiry. Certain ceremonial references to God and religion in our Nation are the inevitable consequence of the religious history that gave birth to our founding principles of liberty. It would be ironic indeed if this Court were to wield our constitutional commitment to religious freedom so as to sever our ties to the traditions developed to honor it.

When combined with the Court's decision against Newdow in order to ensure the Federal Judiciary did not infringe upon the State of California's family law procedures, these two concurrences are equal indicators of its narrative's larger political shift from liberal to conservative, which deserves some attention here.

* * *

By 2004, every Justice who sat for *Welsh v. United States* had been replaced. Seven Presidents had been elected to office, and twelve Justices had been appointed and confirmed. Two women sat on the bench for the first time: Justice Sandra Day O'Connor and Justice Ruth Bader Ginsburg. Thurgood Marshall, the Court's first African-American Justice, was replaced by Clarence Thomas, its second.

And this physical transformation represented an ideological one as well.

Of the eight Justices who sat for the *Newdow* case – Justice Antonin Scalia, upon request from Michael Newdow, took no part in the decision – six were appointed by Republican Presidents. Chief Justice William Rehnquist was appointed to the Court by Richard Nixon in 1971, and then made Chief Justice by Ronald Reagan in 1986. John Paul Stevens was appointed by Gerald Ford in 1975. Sandra Day O'Connor and Anthony Kennedy were appointed by Ronald Reagan in 1981 and 1988, respectively. And David Souter and Clarence Thomas were appointed by George H.W. Bush in 1990 and 1991.

Ruth Bader Ginsburg and Stephen Breyer, the two liberals on the Court, were both appointed by Bill Clinton, in 1993 and 1994.

Understandably, this conservative majority dictated the Court's essential narrative.

But the narrative of the Court is not just set by the political affiliation or personal philosophies of the Justices themselves, but by the Chief Justice as well, who serves as the Chief Administrative Official of the Federal Judiciary by officiating the oral arguments before the Court, administering the Oath of Office for the President, overseeing Presidential impeachment proceedings in the Senate, as well as the process by which cases are chosen for judicial review. He (there has yet to be a female Chief Justice) thus functions as the final arbiter in shaping the Court's narrative.

For example, the Court that sat for *McCollum v. Board of Education* in 1948 was supervised by Chief Justice Fred Vinson, the last Chief Justice appointed, and subsequently confirmed, by a Democratic President: Harry Truman. Moreover, the Court itself was entirely made up of Justices appointed by Franklin Roosevelt, aside from Justice Harold Burton, who was likewise appointed by Harry Truman. As such, the political narrative of the Vinson Court was predominately liberal, as each member was an advocate of Roosevelt's New Deal principles. Perhaps the most evidentiary example was its decision in *Everson v. Board of Education* (1947), which expanded the incorporation of the First Amendment (Establishment Clause) to the states via the Fourteenth, as initiated in *Cantwell v. Connecticut* (1940). As for the philosophies of the Justices themselves, Justice Felix Frankfurter, though a staunch supporter of judicial restraint (limiting the power of the Court), helped found the American Civil Liberties Union, while Justices Hugo Black and William O. Douglas were notable civil rights activists. Justice Frank Murphy, a civil rights activist in his own right, famously wrote in his dissent in *Korematsu v. United States* (1944), the 6–3 decision that permitted the expulsion of Japanese-Americans from areas on the West coast (leading to Japanese internment camps), that such an action was 'racist,' using the term for the first time in a Supreme Court decision.[84]

Both *Torcaso v. Watkins* (1961) and *Abington v. Schempp* (1963) were decided by the Warren Court, Chief Justice Earl Warren having been nominated by President Eisenhower and confirmed in 1953. The Warren Court expanded the liberal narrative of the Vinson Court by a great measure. In the sixteen years (1953–1969) in which Earl Warren served as Chief Justice it passed decisions that fundamentally altered the American landscape, complementing many political actions such as the Civil Rights and Voting Rights Acts of 1964 and 1965, with opinions that addressed issues such as race (*Brown v. Board of Education* in 1954 and *Loving v. Virginia* in 1967), self-incrimination (*Miranda v. Arizona* in 1964), and religious disestablishment (*Engel v. Vitale* in 1962). This last example, alongside *McCollum v. Board of Education* and *Abington v. Schempp*, further established a precedence that systematically removed religion from the public school system, making way for later decisions such as *Wallace v. Jaffree* (1985), *Lee v. Weisman* (1992), and *Santa Fe Independent School District v. Doe* (2000).

When *Welsh v. United States* was decided in 1970, the Warren Court had shifted to the Burger Court, with Warren Burger's appointment to Chief Justice by Richard Nixon in 1969. It was here where, between 1969 and 1986, the Court's political narrative began a slow shift toward the right. Justices Hugo Black and John Marshal Harlan both died in 1971, and after a second (unsuccessful) impeachment attempt by then Congressman Gerald Ford, Justice William O. Douglas, a Roosevelt appointee notorious for his liberal views on, among other things, the Vietnam War and environmentalism – arguing in *Sierra Club v. Morton* (1972) that 'inanimate objects' such as trees should have standing to sue in court – resigned in 1975. Richard Nixon replaced Black and Harlan with Justices Lewis Powell and William Rehnquist, and Gerald Ford appointed John Paul Stevens as Douglas' replacement in December 1975. When Justice Potter Stewart retired in 1981, Ronald Reagan replaced him with Sandra Day O'Connor.

Each of these new appointees were chosen for the Court because of their conservatism, though not all expressed such ideologies, and some, like Justice Stevens, even shifted to the liberal side. Others, Like Justices O'Connor and Powell, became 'swing' votes, able to shift ideologically depending on the issue at hand. This occasional lack of ideological uniformity brought with it an interesting inconsistency, as the Court periodically struggled to solidify a coherent narrative. For example, though it passed more liberal decisions such as *Lemon v. Kurtzman* (1971) and *Roe v. Wade* (1973), it also passed more conservative ones such as *Miller v. California* (1973), which declared that 'obscene materials,' such as pornography, were not protected as free speech, augmenting two previous obscenity decisions in *Roth v. United States* (1957) and *Memoirs v. Massachusetts* (1966). And in 1976 (alongside *Jurek v. Texas*, *Roberts v. Louisiana*, *Proffitt v. Florida*, and *Woodson v. North Carolina*) it affirmed the Georgia Supreme Court's ruling in *Gregg v. Georgia* that the death penalty, when carefully used, did not violate the Eighth Amendment's restriction on 'cruel and unusual punishment.' The Burger Court also famously ruled unanimously in *United States v. Nixon* (1974), declaring that the President's 'executive privilege' did not preclude him from submitting tapes and documents subpoenaed by a Grand Jury investigation of the Watergate Scandal. On behalf of the due process of law, Nixon was forced to submit the requested tapes, and he resigned sixteen days later.

The First Amendment religion decisions announced by the Burger Court shared this transitional quality. For example, while in *Wisconsin v. Yoder* (1972), *Stone v. Graham* (1980), and *Bob Jones University v. the United States* (1983), it respectively protected the religious rights of Amish Americans from compulsory public education, removed copies of the Ten Commandments from public school classrooms in Kentucky, and revoked the tax-exempt status of a private Christian college because of its promotion of racial discrimination, it also deemed constitutionally permissible the opening prayer policy of the Nebraska State Legislature in *Marsh v. Chambers* (1983). A year later, it likewise found permissible the inclusion of a nativity scene in a city-sponsored Christmas display in *Lynch v. Donnelly* (1984), because it was placed alongside other, secular, imagery. But then, in 1985, it used the Lemon Test to argue that an Alabama state law which permitted public school teachers the right to lead their students in prayer services on school grounds (*Wallace v. Jaffrey*), and the use of state funds in New York to assist students from low-income families at parochial (private) schools (*Aguilar v. Felton*), were both unconstitutional violations of the First Amendment.

This seemingly inconsistent approach continued under the tenureship of Chief Justice William Rehnquist after Chief Justice Burger retired in 1986. For example, it again used the Lemon Test in 1987 to declare as unconstitutional a Louisiana law that required the teaching of 'creation science' alongside evolution because it failed all three prongs (*Edwards v. Aguillard*), while in 1989 it decided, 5–4, that a city-sponsored Christmas display similar to that in *Lynch v. Donnelly* clearly represented a violation of the Establishment Clause because it used the phrase 'Glory to God for the birth of Jesus Christ' (*County of Allegheny v. American Civil Liberties Union*).

In the 1990s, however, its decisions began to shift toward a slow, but by no means clearly consistent, permissibility of previously impermissible religious Free Exercise. For example, where it ruled in *Lee v. Weisman* (1992) and *Santa Fe Independent School*

District v. Doe (2000) that school prayer, either given at the start of a school ceremony, or when initiated and led by students, was unconstitutionally impermissible, it nevertheless argued in 1993 that religious organizations were granted the Free Exercise right to use public school property after school hours (*Lamb's Chapel v. Center Moriches Union Free School District*), and that a public school district could not deny a deaf student a state-funded sign language interpreter, even if that student chose to attend a Catholic school (*Zobrest v. Catalina Foothills School District*). As well, where in 1990 it argued that two individuals who were fired from their jobs at an Oregon-based drug rehabilitation center did not qualify for unemployment benefits, regardless of their being terminated for ingesting peyote as part of a religious ceremony (*Employment Division v. Smith*), it defended in 1993 the religious Free Exercise of members of the Church of the Lukumi Babalu Aye, whose ritualized use of animal sacrifice had been prohibited by an ordinance passed by the city of Hialeah, Florida (*Church of the Lukumi Babalu Aye v. City of Hialeah*). Moreover, the Court likewise began associating the Free Exercise clause of the First Amendment with its Free Speech one, arguing in both *Capitol Square Review & Advisory Board v. Pinette* (1995) and *Good News Club v. Milford Central School* (2001) that not approving a local chapter of the Ku Klux Klan the right to display a cross within the 'public forum' section of the state-house plaza in Columbus, Ohio during the Christmas season, and denying access to public school property after school hours to a Christian organization for the purposes of reciting Bible verses, singing hymns, and participating in group prayer, were both Free Speech violations.

One additional common element that arose from these decisions was the manner with which the Court ideologically 'split' between 5–4 votes, such as it did in *Lynch v. Donnelly* (1984), *County of Allegheny v. American Civil Liberties Union* (1989), *Lee v. Weisman* (1992), and *Zobrest v. Catalina Foothills School District* (1993), as well as the 'landmark' case decisions in *Planned Parenthood v. Casey* (1992), *United States v. Lopez* (1995), *United States v. Morrison* (2000), and *Grutter v. Bollinger* (2003). This tendency to split took on a distinct political quality in 2000 when the Court ruled, 5–4, that given the time constraint, no constitutionally valid recount could be made in the State of Florida during the Presidential election, which in essence assured a win for the Republican candidate, George W. Bush, drawing criticisms of political favoritism as the split itself was dictated by the personal political beliefs of the Justices themselves, with Chief Justice Rehnquist and Justices O'Connor, Scalia, Kennedy, and Thomas on one side, and Stevens, Souter, Ginsburg, and Breyer on the other.

* * *

As it was announced just prior to Chief Justice Rehnquist's death in 2005, the Court's decision in *Elk Grove v. Newdow* functions as both a solid introduction to the narrative shift that occurred between his and Chief Justice Burger's tenureships in the decades following *Welsh v. United States*, as well as how that narrative initiated, and continued to support, a growing 'soft endorsement' of religion in America. In this way, it is also unique when compared to the first four decisions presented and discussed herein. Because Newdow's Atheism, and thus his First Amendment rights as such, were minimally discussed, as a discursive text it functions less with respect to the Court's perception of Atheism, and more as an example of that Atheism's influence on its perception of American religion. After all, as a case brought by an Atheist claiming a First Amendment injury, the Court's response – albeit via the concurrences of Chief Justice Rehnquist and Justice

O'Connor – by defining that which he deemed unconstitutional as entirely permissible because of 'ceremonial deism' says a great deal about the influence that Newdow's Atheism had in inspiring that response in the first place. The consequences of which we will see play out in very intriguing ways within the discourses of the next two decisions, and their continued weakening of the wall separating church and state in the name of history and tradition.

Notes

1 *West Virginia State Board of Education v. Barnette* (1943), citation: 319 U.S. 624, 643.
2 Benjamin Harrison: 'Proclamation 335 – 400th Anniversary of the Discovery of America by Columbus,' July 21st, 1892. Accessible at: www.presidency.ucsb.edu/ws/?pid=71118.
3 Dwight D. Eisenhower: 'Statement by the President Upon Signing Bill To Include the Words "Under God" in the Pledge to the Flag.' June 14th, 1954. Online by Gerhard Peters and John T. Woolley, The American Presidency Project. www.presidency.ucsb.edu/ws/?pid=9920.
4 'State Answers Suit by Madalyn Murray,' *Honolulu Star-Bulletin*, October 6th, 1964. Available in 'Madalyn Murray O'Hair,' *Federal Bureau of Investigation and Freedom of Information Act Report*: https://archive.org/stream/MadalynMurrayOHair/Madalyn%20Murray%20OHair%2001_djvu.txt
5 *Smith v. Denny* (U.S District Court for the Eastern District of California, 1968), citation: 280 F.Supp. 651.
6 *Sherman v. Community Consolidated School District 21* (7th Circuit Court of Appeals, 1992), citation: 980 F.2d 437.
7 *Newdow v. U.S. Congress* (9th Circuit Court of Appeals, 2002) (*Newdow I*), citation: 292 F.3d 597, paragraphs 7–8.
8 *Newdow v. U.S. Congress* (9th Circuit Court of Appeals, 2002) (*Newdow II*), citation: 313 F.3d 500, paragraph 19.
9 See footnote viii in *Elk Grove v. Newdow*.
10 *Newdow v. Congress* (U.S. District Court of California, Eastern District, 2005), citation: 383 F.Supp.2d 1229.
11 *Newdow v. Rio Linda School District* (9th Circuit Court of Appeals, 2010), citation: 597 F.3d 1007, 1012.
12 *Myers v. Loudoun County School Board* (U.S. District Court for the Eastern District of Virginia, 2007), citation: 500 F.Supp.2d 539.
13 *Croft v. Perry* (5th Circuit Court of Appeals, 2010), citation: 624 F.3d 157.
14 *Freedom from Religion Foundation v. Hanover School District* (1st Circuit Court of Appeals, 2010), No. 09-2473.
15 *Doe v. Acton–Boxborough Regional School District* (Supreme Judicial Court of Massachusetts, Middlesex), citation: SJC–11317.
16 *American Humanist Association v. Matawan-Aberdeen Regional School District* (Superior Court of New Jersey, 2015), No. 1317-14.
17 For example, see *Allen* v. *Wright* (1984), citation: 468 U.S. 737, 750.
18 See *Allen v. Wright*, 751.
19 See *In re Burrus* (1890), citation: 136 U.S. 586, 593–594.
20 See *Bishop* v. *Wood* (1976), citation: 426 U.S. 341, 346–347.
21 *Texas v. Johnson* (1989), citation: 491 U.S. 397, 405.
22 *Texas v. Johnson* (1989), 437 (Justice Stevens, dissenting).
23 Chapter 435, Statute 56, Section 1, 1942, 377 and 380.
24 *Act of June 14*, chapter 297, Statute 68, 1954, 249.
25 *House of Representatives Report No. 1693*, 83rd Congress, 2nd Session, 1954, 2.
26 *United States Code*, Section 4.
27 *California Education Code*, Annotated, Section 52720 (West 1989).
28 Ibid.
29 See *West Virginia Board of Education v. Barnette* (1943).
30 App. 24.
31 Ibid., 42, paragraph 53.

32 Ibid., 42.
33 Ibid.
34 Ibid., 79.
35 Application to Petition for Certificate 97.
36 *Newdow I*, 602.
37 Ibid. 603–605.
38 Ibid., 612.
39 App. 82.
40 Ibid., 82, paragraphs 2–3.
41 Ibid., 83, paragraph 4.
42 Ibid., 85, paragraph 10.
43 Ibid., 86.
44 *Newdow II*, 502.
45 Ibid., 502–503.
46 Ibid., 504–505.
47 *Newdow v. U.S. Congress* (9th Circuit Court of Appeals, 2003), citation: 328 F.3d 466, 468 (*Newdow III*).
48 Ibid., 490.
49 Ibid., 471, 482.
50 *Warth v. Seldin* (1975), citation: 422 U.S. 490, 498.
51 *Allen v. Wright* (1984), 750 (quoting *Vander Jagt v. O'Neill* (CADC 1983)), citation: 699 F.2d 1166, 1178–1179 (Judge Bork, concurring).
52 *Ashwander v. TVA* (1936), citation: 297 U.S. 288, 346 (Justice Brandeis, concurring).
53 *Colorado River Water Conservation Dist. v. United* States (1976), citation: 424 U.S. 800, 820.
54 *Spector Motor Service, Inc. v. McLaughlin* (1944), 323 U.S. 101, 105. See also *Rescue Army v. Municipal Court of Los* Angeles (1947), citation: 331 U.S. 549, 568–575.
55 See *Lujan v. Defenders of Wildlife* (1992), citation: 504 U.S. 555, 559–562.
56 See *Allen v. Wright* (1984), 751.
57 See *Lujan v. Defenders of Wildlife* (1992), 560–561.
58 *Allen v. Wright* (1984), 751. See also *Secretary of State of Md. v. Joseph H. Munson Co.* (1984), citation: 467 U.S. 947, 955–956.
59 *Warth v. Seldin* (1975), 500.
60 *In re Burrus* (1890), 593–594 (1890). See also *Mansell v. Mansell* (1989), citation: 490 U.S. 581, 587 ('[D]omestic relations are preeminently matters of state law'); *Moore v. Sims* (1979), citation: 442 U.S. 415, 435 ('Family relations are a traditional area of state concern').
61 *Ankenbrandt v. Richards* (1992), citation: 504 U.S. 689, 703.
62 Ibid., 705.
63 Ibid., 705–706 (quoting *Colorado River Water Conservation Dist. v. United* States (1976), 814).
64 See, for example, *Palmore v. Sidoti* (1984), citation: 466 U.S. 429, 432–434.
65 *Newdow II*, 502 [emphasis in original].
66 Ibid.
67 App. 127–128.
68 Ibid., 48, paragraph 78.
69 See, for example, *Singleton v. Wulff* (1976), citation: 428 U.S. 106, 113–118 (plurality opinion).
70 See *Bishop v. Wood* (1976), citation: 426 U.S. 341, 346–347.
71 *Newdow II*, 504–505.
72 *In re Marriage of Murga* (1980), citation: 103 Cal. App. 3d 498, 505, 163 Cal. Rptr. 79, 82. See also *In re Marriage of Mentry* (1983), citation: 142 Cal. App. 3d 260, 268–270, 190 Cal. Rptr. 843, 849–850 (relying on *Murga* to invalidate portion of restraining order barring noncustodial father from engaging children in religious activity or discussion without custodial parent's consent).
73 *In re Marriage of Mentry* (1983), 142 Cal. App. 3d, at 267–268, 190 Cal. Rptr., 848.
74 Ibid., 267, 190 Cal. Rptr., 848.
75 Ibid., 265, 190 Cal. Rptr., 847 (citation omitted).
76 *Florey v. Sioux Falls School District 49-5* (8th Circuit Court of Appeals, 1980), citation: 619 F.2d 1311.

77 *Freedom From Religion Foundation v. Thompson* (U.S. District Court for the Western District of Wisconsin, 1996), citation: 920 F. Supp. 969; and *Ganulin v. United States* (U.S. District Court for the Southern District of Ohio, 1999), citation: 71 F.Supp.2d 824, respectively.
78 *Freedom From Religion Foundation v. City of Marshfield* (7th Circuit Court of Appeals, 2000), citation: 203 F.3d 487.
79 *Freedom From Religion Foundation v. McCallum* (7th Circuit Court of Appeals, 2003), citation: 324 F.3d 880.
80 *Doe v. Porter* (6th Circuit Court of Appeals, 2004), citation: 370 F.3d 558.
81 *Strayhorn v. Ethical Society of Austin* (Texas Court of Appeals, Third District, 2004), Docket No. 03-02-00066-CV.
82 Chief Justice William Rehnquist, concurrent opinion in *Elk Grove v. Newdow* (2004).
83 Justice William Brennan dissenting in *Lynch v. Donnelly* (1984).
84 *Korematsu v. United States* (1944), citation: 323 US 214, 233.

9 *Hein v. Freedom From Religion Foundation, Inc.* (2007)

Argued: February 28th, 2007 – Decided: June 25th, 2007.

> Respondents set out a parade of horribles that they claim could occur if [*Flast v. Cohen* (1968)] is not extended to discretionary Executive Branch expenditures. For example, they say, a federal agency could use its discretionary funds to build a house of worship or to hire clergy of one denomination and send them out to spread their faith. Or an agency could use its funds to make bulk purchases of Stars of David, crucifixes, or depictions of the star and crescent for use in its offices or for distribution to the employees or the general public. Of course, none of these things has happened, even though *Flast* has not previously been expanded in the way that respondents urge. In the unlikely event that any of these executive actions did take place, Congress could quickly step in. And respondents make no effort to show that these improbable abuses could not be challenged in federal court by plaintiffs who would possess standing based on grounds other than taxpayer standing.
>
> — Justice Samuel Alito, plurality opinion, *Hein v. Freedom From Religion* (2007)

Question before the Court: Do taxpayers have Constitutional standing to challenge, under the Establishment Clause of the First Amendment, a Presidential Executive Order that offers indirect federal financial assistance through general appropriations, and only dispersed to groups or individuals within the government, when that assistance is given to faith-based or religious organizations?

Decision: 5–4 plurality. No, taxpayers do not have standing to bring Establishment Clause challenges against the Executive Branch. The precedent set by the Court's decision in *Flast v. Cohen* (1968) that granted taxpayers the right to file suit against the Federal Government permitted that right *only* against congressional expenditure, not Executive Order, and thus did not apply.

Antecedent Case Decisions:

- SEVENTH CIRCUIT COURT OF APPEALS, *Freedom From Religion Foundation v. Chao* (7th Circuit Court of Appeals, 2006), citation: 433 F.3d 989.

  Ruling: 2–1, the Foundation did have standing to sue, and the District Court's decision was reversed. The United States Government petitioned the Supreme Court for a writ of certiorari, which it approved.

- UNITED STATES DISTRICT COURT FOR THE WESTERN DISTRICT OF WISCONSIN, *Freedom From Religion Foundation v. Towey* (U.S. District Court for the Western District of Wisconsin, 2005), No. 04-C-381-S.

Ruling: The Foundation lacked standing to sue because the federal funding they argued as unconstitutional was not a result of congressional legislation, but of Presidential Executive Order.

Background

On January 29th, 2001, President George W. Bush created through Executive Order the White House Office of Faith-Based and Community Initiatives, the policy of which was described as follows:

> Faith-based and other community organizations are indispensable in meeting the needs of poor Americans and distressed neighborhoods. Government cannot be replaced by such organizations, but it can and should welcome them as partners. The paramount goal is compassionate results, and private and charitable community groups, including religious ones, should have the fullest opportunity permitted by law to compete on a level playing field, so long as they achieve valid public purposes, such as curbing crime, conquering addiction, strengthening families and neighborhoods, and overcoming poverty. This delivery of social services must be results oriented and should value the bedrock principles of pluralism, nondiscrimination, evenhandedness, and neutrality.[1]

Through subsequent Executive Orders, President Bush also set up a number of Agency Centers in departments across the Federal Government in an effort to 'enlist, equip, enable, empower, and expand the work of faith-based and other community organizations to the extent permitted by law.'[2] These included the Attorney General's office, the Department of Education, the Department of Labor, the Department of Health and Human Services, the Department of Housing and Urban Development,[3] the Department of Agriculture and the Agency for International Development,[4] the Departments of Commerce and Veterans Affairs, the Small Business Administration,[5] and the Department of Homeland Security.[6] In order to 'provide participants with information about the Federal funding process, available funding opportunities, and the requirements that come with the receipt of Federal funds,' as well as to offer 'an opportunity to inform State and local officials about equal treatment regulations and other central elements of the Faith-Based and Community Initiative,' these Agency Centers began sponsoring and hosting informative conferences.[7]

Then, in an Executive Order on December 12th, 2002, the President further clarified that such faith-based programs would be given equal consideration by stating that 'no organization should be discriminated against on the basis of religion or religious belief in the administration or distribution of Federal financial assistance under social service programs,' and that all organizations, both faith-based and secular, that received financial assistance, 'should be prohibited from discriminating against beneficiaries or potential beneficiaries of the social services programs on the basis of religion or religious belief.'[8] To pre-emptively combat any perceived First Amendment violations that might arise from the execution of the Office or the actions of the associated Agency Centers, he also clarified that:

> The Federal Government must implement Federal programs in accordance with the Establishment Clause and the Free Exercise Clause of the First Amendment to

> the Constitution. Therefore, organizations that engage in inherently religious activities, such as worship, religious instruction, and proselytization, must offer those services separately in time or location from any programs or services supported with direct Federal financial assistance, and participation in any such inherently religious activities must be voluntary for the beneficiaries of the social service program supported with such Federal financial assistance. [. . .] Accordingly, a faithbased [sic] organization that applies for or participates in a social service program supported with Federal financial assistance may retain its independence and may continue to carry out its mission, including the definition, development, practice, and expression of its religious beliefs, provided that it does not use direct Federal financial assistance to support any inherently religious activities, such as worship, religious instruction, or proselytization. Among other things, faith-based organizations that receive Federal financial assistance may use their facilities to provide social services supported with Federal financial assistance, without removing or altering religious art, icons, scriptures, or other symbols from these facilities. In addition, a faithbased [sic] organization that applies for or participates in a social service program supported with Federal financial assistance may retain religious terms in its organization's name, select its board members on a religious basis, and include religious references in its organization's mission statements and other chartering or governing documents.[9]

Two years later, in 2004, the Freedom From Religion Foundation, an Atheist/non-theist/secular organization devoted to safeguarding the separation of church and state, and three of its founding members, Anne Nicol Gaylor, Annie Laurie Gaylor, and Dan Barker, filed suit in the U.S. District Court for the Western District of Wisconsin against then acting Director, Jay F. Hein, as well as the Directors of the Agency Centers within the various government departments, claiming three allegations:

1. The Office and the named federal departments had violated the Establishment Clause by organizing national and regional conferences at which, as they claimed, faith-based organizations were 'singled out as being particularly worthy of federal funding because of their religious orientation';

2. The department officials named had engaged in 'myriad illegal activities,' such as 'making public appearances and giving speeches, throughout the United States, intended to promote and advocate for funding for faith-based organizations';

3. And finally, that Congressional appropriations were used to 'support the activities of the [Office and named officials].'[10]

The Foundation requested three outcomes: a declaratory ruling affirming that the actions of the Office and the named officials had violated the Establishment Clause; an injunction that would prohibit any further violations on behalf of the Office; and a Court Order that would require both it and the named officials to 'establish rules, regulations, prohibitions, standards and oversight' to guarantee this.[11]

In response, the named defendants requested a complete dismissal citing the Foundation's lack of standing as based on the precedence established by Chief Justice Earl Warren's decision for the Supreme Court in *Flast v. Cohen* (1968). Florance Flast – alongside other plaintiffs – had filed suit against then acting Secretary of Health, Education, and Welfare, Wilbur Cohen, claiming that his office's distribution of federal funding to religious schools was in violation of the Establishment Clause. In order to address this claim, Chief Justice Warren created a 'double-nexus' test so as to determine whether a taxpayer – or in that instance, a group of taxpayers – had suffered injury enough to warrant such judicial review:

> First, the taxpayer must establish a logical link between that status and the type of legislative enactment attacked. Thus, a taxpayer will be a proper party to allege the unconstitutionality only of exercises of congressional power under the taxing and spending clause of Article I, [section] 8, of the Constitution. It will not be sufficient to allege an incidental expenditure of tax funds in the administration of an essentially regulatory statute. [. . .] Secondly, the taxpayer must establish a nexus between that status and the precise nature of the constitutional infringement alleged. Under this requirement, the taxpayer must show that the challenged enactment exceeds specific constitutional limitations imposed upon the exercise of the congressional taxing and spending power, and not simply that the enactment is generally beyond the powers delegated to Congress by Article I, [section] 8.[12]

Only when both of these connections had been shown as occurring, would a litigant bringing the suit qualify as an individual (or group) with standing to do so under the 'cases and controversies' requirement of Article III of the Constitution. Because an allegation brought by a taxpayer would in essence describe a situation wherein his or her tax money was being 'extracted and spent in violation of specific constitutional protections against such abuses of legislative power,' this would qualify as a valid 'injury,' and thus further qualify for standing 'to secure judicial review.'[13] The Court's 8–1 decision established that Flast and her fellow appellants had standing, and the Court ruled in their favor.

From the perspective of the named defendants, the Foundation did not have such standing. The Flast Test, as they argued, dealt exclusively with taxpayers' standing in consideration of alleged violations wherein a government agency was providing federal funding to religious organizations, and while the Foundation's complaint directly called out such violations on behalf of the Office's distribution of such funding to those types of religious organizations, that distribution was controlled by Presidential Executive Order, meaning they were acting on his behalf. And since the Court's decision in *Flast* only dealt with acts of Congress, the Flast Test did not apply.

In his judgment for the District Court, Judge John C. Shabaz agreed, and dismissed the Foundation's complaint.

They appealed to the 7th Circuit Court of Appeals, which by a 2–1 margin, vacated and remanded that decision.[14] On appeal to the same Court for a re-hearing, Chief Judge Joel M. Flaum, on behalf of a 7–4 vote, denied the named defendants a full review, remarking: 'the obvious tension which has evolved in this area of jurisprudence [. . .] can only be resolved by the Supreme Court [and in] my judgment, the needed consideration of this important issue by that tribunal would be unnecessarily delayed by our further deliberation.'[15]

The Supreme Court granted certiorari, and on June 25th, 2007 ruled, 5–4, against the Foundation.

Like the Court's ruling in *Welsh v. United States* (1970), *Hein v. Freedom From Religion Foundation* was a plurality opinion, meaning that though a majority of the Justices agreed on how the Court should rule, they did not agree on the specifics as to why. In this instance, though, because newly appointed Chief Justice John Roberts and Justice Anthony

Kennedy agreed with Justice Alito that the Foundation's defense was built on a misguided broadening of the precedent set in *Flast v. Cohen*, it became the Court's opinion.

* * *

Before proceeding to the decision itself, it should also be noted here that though this was, and still is (so far), the only time the Freedom From Religion Foundation argued a case before the Supreme Court, it was neither the first time, nor the last, that it filed lawsuits directed at faith-based organizations.

In its first in 2003, the Foundation successfully challenged the State of Wisconsin's financial support of Faith Works, a Christian-based nine- to twelve-month residential treatment facility.[16] Then, in 2004, it successfully won its second against the Montana Faith-Health Cooperative, a group of fifteen faith-based organizations, which received federal funding through the Montana Office of Rural Health and Montana State University-Bozeman.[17] A year later, it won a similar case in Minnesota when it successfully halted a 'faith/health leadership' course that would provide devotional training in faith/health policies at the University of Minnesota.[18] In that same year, it filed suit in the U.S. District Court for the Western District of Wisconsin against the then acting Secretary of the Department of Health and Human Services, Tommy Thompson, and the Administration for Children and Families, which administered the Compassion Capital Fund program, that was initially formed to 'increase the effectiveness of faith-based and community organizations and enhance their ability to provide social services to those most in need.' The Foundation specifically targeted two grants supplied by the Compassion Capital Fund program: the first was extended to Emory University's Interfaith Health Program in 2002 in the form of $900,000 distributed between nine 'religious health conversion' foundations, who then awarded smaller increments to forty-nine faith-based organizations; and the second was an award of $225,000, provided between 2003 and 2006, to MentorKids USA, a Christian-based youth mentoring organization within the Mentoring Children of Prisoners program created by the Department of Health and Human Services. In his ruling on January 11th, 2005, Judge John C. Shabaz concluded that the Foundation's argument concerning Emory University's grant failed to produce 'any evidence' of constitutional violation, while their complaint concerning MentorKids did. In an unprecedented judgment, he vacated MentorKids' grant and denied them further funding.[19]

In April of 2006 the Foundation filed suit against the Department of Veteran Affairs alleging that the 'pastoral services' provided by the Veterans Health Administration proved an impermissible violation of the First Amendment. The case was once again heard by Judge John C. Shabaz, who ruled in January 2007 in favor of the Department of Veterans Affairs. The Foundation appealed to the 7th Circuit Court of Appeals, but the case was put on hold until the Supreme Court could submit its ruling in *Hein v. Freedom From Religion Foundation*. After that ruling was announced in 2007, the case was dismissed.[20]

This pattern continued. In 2005 and 2006 it filed two lawsuits against alleged constitutional violations within the prison system, the first to stop a faith-based initiative sponsored by the Federal Bureau of Prisons' Life Connections Program, and the second to contest a fundamentalist Christian ministry called Basic Life Principles within a women's prison in Grants, New Mexico, that was financially supported by Corrections Corporation of America, the nation's largest private prison provider. While the first resulted in the

Federal Bureau of Prisons suspending its grant program,[21] the second was withdrawn because of the Foundation's lack of standing.[22]

In 2007, two more cases ended the same way. While the Foundation was successful in challenging the first federally funded chaplaincy in the State of Indiana by the Family and Social Services Administration,[23] at the same time it lost its challenge against the federal funding of a Christian juvenile detention facility sponsored by the Lutheran Church/ Missouri Synod and the Evangelical Lutheran Church in America.[24] Like its challenges against the Department of Veterans Affairs and the Corrections Corporation of America, the latter was decided solely on the Supreme Court's decision in *Hein*.

* * *

Hein v. Freedom From Religion Foundation, Inc. (2007)

Full Title

Jay F. Hein, Director, White House Office of Faith-Based And Community Initiatives, et al., Petitioners v. Freedom From Religion Foundation, Inc., et al.

Official Citation

551 U.S. 587
Argued: February 28, 2007
Decided: June 25, 2007

Author

Justice Samuel Alito
(Plurality Opinion)

Syllabus

The President, by executive orders, created a White House office and several centers within federal agencies to ensure that faith-based community groups are eligible to compete for federal financial support. No congressional legislation specifically authorized these entities, which were created entirely within the Executive Branch, nor has Congress enacted any law specifically appropriating money to their activities, which are funded through general Executive Branch appropriations. Respondents, an organization opposed to Government endorsement of religion and three of its members, brought this suit alleging that petitioners, the directors of the federal offices, violated the Establishment Clause by organizing conferences that were designed to promote, and had the effect of promoting, religious community groups over secular ones. The only asserted basis for standing was that the individual respondents are federal taxpayers opposed to Executive Branch use of congressional appropriations for these conferences. The District Court dismissed the claims for lack of standing, concluding that under *Flast v. Cohen* (1968),[25] federal taxpayer standing is limited to Establishment Clause challenges to the constitutionality of exercises of congressional power under the taxing and spending clause of Article I, [section] 8. Because petitioners acted on the President's behalf and were not charged with administering a congressional program, the court held that the challenged activities did not authorize taxpayer standing under *Flast.* The Seventh Circuit reversed, reading *Flast* as granting federal taxpayers standing to challenge Executive Branch programs on Establishment Clause grounds so long as the activities are financed by a congressional appropriation, even where there is no statutory program and the funds are from appropriations for general administrative expenses. According to the court, a taxpayer has standing to challenge anything done by a federal agency so long as the marginal or incremental cost to the public of the alleged Establishment Clause violation is greater than zero.

Held

The judgment is reversed.

[*Freedom From Religion Foundation, Inc., et al., v. Elaine L. Chao, Secretary of Department of Labor, et al.* (2006), 7th Circuit Court of Appeals, citation: 433 F. 3d 989], *reversed.*

Opinion

JUSTICE ALITO announced the judgment of the Court and delivered an opinion in which THE CHIEF JUSTICE and JUSTICE KENNEDY join.

This is a lawsuit in which it was claimed that conferences held as part of the President's Faith-Based and Community Initiatives program violated the Establishment Clause of the First Amendment because, among other things, President Bush and former Secretary of Education Paige gave speeches that used 'religious imagery' and praised the efficacy of faith-based programs in delivering social services. The plaintiffs contend that they meet the standing requirements of Article III of the Constitution because they pay federal taxes.

It has long been established, however, that the payment of taxes is generally not enough to establish standing to challenge an action taken by the Federal Government. In light of the size of the federal budget, it is a complete fiction to argue that an unconstitutional federal expenditure causes an individual federal taxpayer any measurable economic harm. And if every federal taxpayer could sue to challenge any Government expenditure, the federal courts would cease to function as courts of law and would be cast in the role of general complaint bureaus.

In *Flast v. Cohen* (1968), we recognized a narrow exception to the general rule against federal taxpayer standing. Under *Flast*, a plaintiff asserting an Establishment Clause claim has standing to challenge a law authorizing the use of federal funds in a way that allegedly violates the Establishment Clause. In the present case, Congress did not specifically authorize the use of federal funds to pay for the conferences or speeches that the plaintiffs challenged. Instead, the conferences and speeches were paid for out of general Executive Branch appropriations. The Court of Appeals, however, held that the plaintiffs have standing as taxpayers because the conferences were paid for with money appropriated by Congress.

The question that is presented here is whether this broad reading of *Flast* is correct. We hold that it is not. We therefore reverse the decision of the Court of Appeals.

I

A

In 2001, the President issued an executive order creating the White House Office of Faith-Based and Community Initiatives within the Executive Office of the President.[26] The purpose of this new office was to ensure that 'private and charitable community groups, including religious ones [. . .] have the fullest opportunity permitted by law to compete on a level playing field, so long as they achieve valid public purposes' and adhere to 'the bedrock principles of pluralism, nondiscrimination, evenhandedness, and neutrality.'[27] The office was specifically charged with the task of eliminating unnecessary bureaucratic, legislative, and regulatory barriers that could impede such organizations' effectiveness and ability to compete equally for federal assistance.[28]

By separate executive orders, the President also created Executive Department Centers for Faith-Based and Community Initiatives within several federal agencies and departments.[i] These centers were given the job of ensuring that faith-based community groups would be eligible to compete for federal financial support without impairing their independence or autonomy, as long as they did 'not use direct Federal financial assistance to support any inherently religious activities, such as worship, religious instruction, or proselytization.'[29] To this end, the President directed that '[n]o organization should be discriminated against on the basis of religion or religious belief in the administration or distribution of Federal financial assistance under social service programs,'[30] and that '[a]ll organizations that receive Federal financial assistance under social services programs should be prohibited from discriminating against beneficiaries or potential beneficiaries of the social services programs on the basis of religion or religious belief.'[31] Petitioners, who have been sued in their official capacities, are the directors of the White House Office and various Executive Department Centers.

No congressional legislation specifically authorized the creation of the White House Office or the Executive Department Centers. Rather, they were 'created entirely within the executive branch [. . .] by Presidential executive order.'[32] Nor has Congress enacted any law specifically appropriating money for these entities' activities. Instead, their activities are funded through general Executive Branch appropriations. For example, the Department of Education's Center is funded from money appropriated for the Office of the Secretary of Education, while the Department of Housing and Urban Development's Center is funded through that Department's salaries and expenses account.[33]

B

The respondents are Freedom From Religion Foundation, Inc., a nonstock corporation 'opposed to government endorsement of religion,'[34] and three of its members. Respondents brought suit in the United States District Court for the Western District of Wisconsin, alleging that petitioners violated the Establishment Clause by organizing conferences at which faith-based organizations allegedly 'are singled out as being particularly worthy of federal funding [. . .], and the belief in God is extolled as distinguishing the claimed effectiveness of faith-based social services.'[35] Respondents further alleged that the content of these conferences sent a message to religious believers 'that

i See, *e.g.*, Exec. Order No. 13198, 3 CFR 750 (2001 Comp.); Exec. Order No. 13280, 3 CFR 262 (2002 Comp.); Exec. Order No. 13342, 3 CFR 180 (2004 Comp.); Exec. Order No. 13397, 71 Fed. Reg. 12275 (2006).

they are insiders and favored members of the political community' and that the conferences sent the message to nonbelievers 'that they are outsiders' and 'not full members of the political community.'[36] In short, respondents alleged that the conferences were designed to promote, and had the effect of promoting, religious community groups over secular ones.

The only asserted basis for standing was that the individual respondents are federal taxpayers who are 'opposed to the use of Congressional taxpayer appropriations to advance and promote religion.'[37] In their capacity as federal taxpayers, respondents sought to challenge Executive Branch expenditures for these conferences, which, they contended, violated the Establishment Clause.

C

The District Court dismissed the claims against petitioners for lack of standing.[38] It concluded that under *Flast*, federal taxpayer standing is limited to Establishment Clause challenges to the constitutionality of 'exercises of congressional power under the taxing and spending clause of Article I, [section] 8.'[39] Because petitioners in this case acted 'at the President's request and on the President's behalf' and were not 'charged with the administration of a congressional program,' the District Court concluded that the challenged activities were 'not "exercises of congressional power"' sufficient to provide a basis for taxpayer standing under *Flast*.[40]

A divided panel of the United States Court of Appeals for the Seventh Circuit reversed.[41] The majority read *Flast* as granting federal taxpayers standing to challenge Executive Branch programs on Establishment Clause grounds so long as the activities are 'financed by a congressional appropriation.'[42] This was the case, the majority concluded, even where 'there is no statutory program' enacted by Congress and the funds are 'from appropriations for the general administrative expenses, over which the President and other executive branch officials have a degree of discretionary power.'[43] According to the majority, a taxpayer has standing to challenge anything done by a federal agency or officer so long as 'the marginal or incremental cost to the taxpaying public of the alleged violation of the establishment clause' is greater than 'zero.'[44]

In dissent, Judge Ripple opined that the majority's decision reflected a 'dramatic expansion of current standing doctrine,'[45] that 'cuts the concept of taxpayer standing loose from its moorings.'[46] Noting that '[t]he executive can do nothing without general budget appropriations from Congress,'[47] he criticized the majority for overstepping *Flast*'s requirement that a 'plaintiff must bring an attack against a disbursement of public funds made in the exercise of *Congress*' taxing and spending power.'[48]

The Court of Appeals denied en banc review by a vote of seven to four.[49] Concurring in the denial of rehearing, Chief Judge Flaum expressed doubt about the panel decision, but noted that 'the obvious tension which has evolved in this area of jurisprudence [. . .] can only be resolved by the Supreme Court.'[50] We granted certiorari to resolve this question, and we now reverse.[51]

II

A

Article III of the Constitution limits the judicial power of the United States to the resolution of 'Cases' and 'Controversies,' and 'Article III standing [. . .] enforces the Constitution's case-or-controversy requirement.'[52] 'No principle is more fundamental to the judiciary's proper role in our system of government than the constitutional limitation of federal-court jurisdiction to actual cases or controversies.'[53]

'[O]ne of the controlling elements in the definition of a case or controversy under Article III' is standing.[54] The requisite elements of Article III standing are well established: 'A plaintiff must allege personal injury fairly traceable to the defendant's allegedly unlawful conduct and likely to be redressed by the requested relief.'[55]

The constitutionally mandated standing inquiry is especially important in a case like this one, in which taxpayers seek 'to challenge laws of general application where their own injury is not distinct from that suffered in general by other taxpayers or citizens.'[56] This is because '[t]he judicial power of the United States defined by Article III is not an unconditioned authority to determine the constitutionality of legislative or executive acts.'[57] The federal courts are not empowered to seek out and strike down any governmental act that they deem to be repugnant to the Constitution. Rather, federal courts sit 'solely, to decide on the rights of individuals,'[58] and must 'refrai[n] from passing upon the constitutionality of an act [. . .] unless obliged to do so in the proper performance of our judicial function, when the question is raised by a party whose interests entitle him to raise it.'[59] As we held over 80 years ago, in another case involving the question of taxpayer standing:

> We have no power *per se* to review and annul acts of Congress on the ground that they are unconstitutional. The question may be considered only when the justification for some direct injury suffered or threatened, presenting a justiciable issue, is made to rest upon such an act [. . .]. The party who invokes the power must be able to show not only that the statute is invalid but that he has sustained or is immediately in danger of sustaining some direct injury as the result of its enforcement, and not merely that he suffers in some indefinite way in common with people generally.[60]

B

As a general matter, the interest of a federal taxpayer in seeing that Treasury funds are spent in accordance with the Constitution does not give rise to the kind of redressable 'personal injury' required for Article III standing. Of course, a taxpayer has standing to challenge the *collection* of a specific tax assessment as unconstitutional; being forced to pay such a tax causes a real and immediate economic injury to the individual taxpayer.[61] But that is not the interest on which respondents assert standing here. Rather, their claim is that, having paid lawfully collected taxes into the Federal Treasury at some point, they have a continuing, legally cognizable interest in ensuring that those funds are not *used* by the Government in a way that violates the Constitution.

We have consistently held that this type of interest is too generalized and attenuated to support Article III standing. In *Frothingham*, a federal taxpayer sought to challenge federal appropriations for mothers' and children's health, arguing that federal involvement in this area intruded on the rights reserved to the States under the Tenth Amendment and would 'increase the burden of future taxation and thereby take [the plaintiff's] property without due process of law.'[62] We concluded that the plaintiff lacked the kind of particularized injury required for Article III standing:

> [I]nterest in the moneys of the Treasury [. . .] is shared with millions of others; is comparatively minute and indeterminable; and the effect upon future taxation,

> of any payment out of the funds, so remote, fluctuating and uncertain, that no basis is afforded for an appeal to the preventive powers of a court of equity.
>
> The administration of any statute, likely to produce additional taxation to be imposed upon a vast number of taxpayers, the extent of whose several liability is indefinite and constantly changing, is essentially a matter of public and not of individual concern.[63]

Because the interests of the taxpayer are, in essence, the interests of the public-at-large, deciding a constitutional claim based solely on taxpayer standing 'would be[,] not to decide a judicial controversy, but to assume a position of authority over the governmental acts of another and co-equal department, an authority which plainly we do not possess.'[64]

In *Doremus v. Board of Ed. of Hawthorne* (1952),[65] we reaffirmed this principle, explaining that 'the interests of a taxpayer in the moneys of the federal treasury are too indeterminable, remote, uncertain and indirect to furnish a basis for an appeal to the preventive powers of the Court over their manner of expenditure.' We therefore rejected a state taxpayer's claim of standing to challenge a state law authorizing public school teachers to read from the Bible because 'the grievance which [the plaintiff] sought to litigate [. . .] is not a direct dollars-and-cents injury but is a religious difference.'[66] In so doing, we gave effect to the basic constitutional principle that 'a plaintiff raising only a generally available grievance about government – claiming only harm to his and every citizen's interest in proper application of the Constitution and laws, and seeking relief that no more directly and tangibly benefits him than it does the public at large – does not state an Article III case or controversy.'[ii] [67]

C

In *Flast*, the Court carved out a narrow exception to the general constitutional prohibition against taxpayer standing. The taxpayer-plaintiff in that case challenged the distribution of federal funds to religious schools under the Elementary and Secondary Education Act of 1965, alleging that such aid violated the Establishment Clause. The Court set out a two-part test for determining whether a federal taxpayer has standing to challenge an allegedly unconstitutional expenditure:

> First, the taxpayer must establish a logical link between that status and the type of legislative enactment attacked. Thus, a taxpayer will be a proper party to allege the

ii See also *DaimlerChrysler Corp. v. Cuno* (2006), citation: 547 U. S. 332, ___ (slip opinion, at 8) ('Standing has been rejected' where 'the alleged injury is not "concrete and particularized," [. . .] but instead a grievance the taxpayer "suffers in some indefinite way in common with people generally"' (quoting *Lujan v. Defenders of Wildlife* (1992), citation: 504 U. S., 560)); *ASARCO Inc.* v. *Kadish* (1989), citation: 490 U. S. 605, 616 (opinion of Justice Kennedy) ('[G]eneralized grievances brought by concerned citizens [. . .] are not cognizable in the federal courts'); *Valley Forge Christian College v. Americans United for Separation of Church and State, Inc.* (1982), citation: 454 U. S. 464, 483 ('[A]ssertion of a right to a particular kind of Government conduct, which the Government has violated by acting differently, cannot alone satisfy the requirements of Art. III'); *United States v. Richardson* (1974), citation: 418 U. S. 166, 174 ('[A] taxpayer may not "employ a federal court as a forum in which to air his generalized grievances about the conduct of

> unconstitutionality only of exercises of congressional power under the taxing and spending clause of Article I, [section] 8, of the Constitution. It will not be sufficient to allege an incidental expenditure of tax funds in the administration of an essentially regulatory statute [. . .]. Secondly, the taxpayer must establish a nexus between that status and the precise nature of the constitutional infringement alleged. Under this requirement, the taxpayer must show that the challenged enactment exceeds specific constitutional limitations imposed upon the exercise of the congressional taxing and spending power and not simply that the enactment is generally beyond the powers delegated to Congress by Article I, [section] 8.[68]

The Court held that the taxpayer-plaintiff in *Flast* had satisfied both prongs of this test: The plaintiff's 'constitutional challenge [was] made to an exercise by Congress of its power under Article I, [section] 8, to spend for the general welfare,' and she alleged a violation of the Establishment Clause, which 'operates as a specific constitutional limitation upon the exercise by Congress of the taxing and spending power conferred by Article I, [section] 8.'[69]

III

A

Respondents argue that this case falls within the *Flast* exception, which they read to cover any 'expenditure of government funds in violation of the Establishment Clause.'[70] But this broad reading fails to observe 'the rigor with which the *Flast* exception to the *Frothingham* principle ought to be applied.'[71]

The expenditures at issue in *Flast* were made pursuant to an express congressional mandate and a specific congressional appropriation. The plaintiff in that case challenged disbursements made under the Elementary and Secondary Education Act of 1965.[72] That Act expressly appropriated the sum of $100 million for fiscal year 1966,[73] and authorized the disbursement of those funds to local educational agencies for the education of low-income students.[74] The Act mandated that local educational agencies receiving such funds 'ma[k]e provision for including special educational services and arrangements (such as dual enrollment, educational radio and television, and mobile educational services and equipment)' in which students enrolled in private elementary and secondary schools could participate.[75] In addition, recipient agencies were required to ensure that 'library resources, textbooks, and other instructional materials' funded through the grants 'be provided on an equitable basis for the use of children and teachers in private elementary and secondary schools.'[76]

government or the allocation of power in the Federal System"' (quoting *Flast v. Cohen* (1968), citation: 392 U. S. 83, 114 (Justice Stewart, concurring); some internal quotation marks omitted); *Schlesinger v. Reservists Comm. to Stop the War* (1974), citation: 418 U. S. 208, 217 ('Respondents seek to have the Judicial Branch compel the Executive Branch to act in conformity with the Incompatibility Clause [of the Constitution], an interest shared by all citizens [. . .]. And that claimed nonobservance, standing alone, would adversely affect only the generalized interest of all citizens in constitutional governance, and that is an abstract injury'); *Frothingham v. Mellon*, decided with *Massachusetts v. Mellon* (1923), citation: 262 U. S. 447, 488 ('The party who invokes the power [of judicial review] must be able to show not only that the statute is invalid but that he has sustained or is immediately in danger of sustaining some direct injury as the result of its enforcement, and not merely that he suffers in some indefinite way in common with people generally').

The expenditures challenged in *Flast*, then, were funded by a specific congressional appropriation and were disbursed to private schools (including religiously affiliated schools) pursuant to a direct and unambiguous congressional mandate.[iii] Indeed, the *Flast* taxpayer-plaintiff's constitutional claim was premised on the contention that if the Government's actions were 'within the authority and intent of the Act, the Act is to that extent unconstitutional and void.'[77] And the judgment reviewed by this Court in *Flast* solely concerned the question whether 'if [the challenged] expenditures are authorized by the Act the statute constitutes a 'law respecting an establishment of religion' and law 'prohibiting the free exercise thereof'' under the First Amendment.[78]

Given that the alleged Establishment Clause violation in *Flast* was funded by a specific congressional appropriation and was undertaken pursuant to an express congressional mandate, the Court concluded that the taxpayer-plaintiffs had established the requisite 'logical link between [their taxpayer] status and the type of legislative enactment attacked.' In the Court's words, '[t]heir constitutional challenge [was] made to an exercise by Congress of its power under Article I, [section] 8, to spend for the general welfare.'[79] But as this Court later noted, *Flast* 'limited taxpayer standing to challenges directed "only [at] exercises of congressional power"' under the Taxing and Spending Clause.[80]

B

The link between congressional action and constitutional violation that supported taxpayer standing in *Flast* is missing here. Respondents do not challenge any specific congressional action or appropriation; nor do they ask the Court to invalidate any congressional enactment or legislatively created program as unconstitutional. That is because the expenditures at issue here were not made pursuant to any Act of Congress. Rather, Congress provided general appropriations to the Executive Branch to fund its day-to-day activities.[iv] These appropriations did not expressly authorize, direct, or even mention the expenditures of which respondents complain. Those expenditures resulted from executive discretion, not congressional action.

We have never found taxpayer standing under such circumstances. In *Valley Forge*, we held that a taxpayer lacked standing to challenge 'a decision by [the federal Department of Health, Education and Welfare] to transfer a parcel of federal property' to a religious college because this transfer was 'not a congressional action.'[81] In fact, the connection to congressional action was closer in *Valley Forge* than it is here, because in that case, the 'particular Executive Branch action' being challenged was at least 'arguably authorized' by the Federal Property and Administrative Services Act of 1949, which permitted federal agencies to transfer surplus property to private entities.[82] Nevertheless, we found that the plaintiffs lacked standing because *Flast* 'limited taxpayer standing to

iii At around the time the Act was passed and *Flast* was decided, the great majority of nonpublic elementary and secondary schools in the United States were associated with a church. In 1965–1966, for example, 91.1 percent of all nonpublic elementary schools and 78.2 percent of all nonpublic secondary schools in the United States were religiously affiliated. Dept. of Health, Education, and Welfare, Statistics of Nonpublic Elementary and Secondary Schools 1965–66, p. 7 (1968). Congress surely understood that much of the aid mandated by the statute would find its way to religious schools.

iv See, *e.g.*, 119 Stat. 2472 (appropriating $53,830,000 'to be available for allocation within the Executive Office of the President').

challenges directed "only [at] exercises of congressional power"' under the Taxing and Spending Clause.[v] [83]

Similarly, in *Schlesinger v. Reservists Committee to Stop the War* (1974),[84] the taxpayer-plaintiffs contended that the Incompatibility Clause of Article I prohibited Members of Congress from holding commissions in the Armed Forces Reserve. We held that these plaintiffs lacked standing under *Flast* because they 'did not challenge an enactment under Article I, [section] 8, but rather the action of the Executive Branch in permitting Members of Congress to maintain their Reserve status.'[85] This was the case even though the plaintiffs sought to reclaim reservist pay received by those Members – pay that presumably was funded through Congress' general appropriations for the support of the Armed Forces: 'Such relief would follow from the invalidity of Executive action in paying persons who could not lawfully have been reservists, not from the invalidity of the statutes authorizing pay to those who lawfully were Reservists.'[86]

Bowen v. Kendrick (1988),[87] on which respondents rely heavily, is not to the contrary. In that case, we held that the taxpayer-plaintiffs had standing to mount an as-applied challenge to the Adolescent Family Life Act (AFLA), which authorized federal grants to private community service groups including religious organizations. The Court found 'a sufficient nexus between the taxpayer's standing as a taxpayer and the congressional exercise of taxing and spending power,' notwithstanding the fact that the [sic] 'the funding authorized by Congress ha[d] flowed through and been administered' by an Executive Branch official.[88]

But the key to that conclusion was the Court's recognition that AFLA was 'at heart a program of disbursement of funds pursuant to Congress' taxing and spending powers,' and that the plaintiffs' claims 'call[ed] into question how the funds authorized by Congress [were] being disbursed *pursuant to the AFLA's statutory mandate*.'[89] AFLA not only expressly authorized and appropriated specific funds for grant-making, it also expressly contemplated that some of those moneys might go to projects involving religious groups.[vi] [90] Unlike this case, *Kendrick* involved a 'program of disbursement of funds pursuant to Congress' taxing and spending powers' that 'Congress had created,' 'authorized,' and 'mandate[d].'[91]

Respondents attempt to paint their lawsuit as a *Kendrick*-style as-applied challenge, but this effort is unavailing for the simple reason that they can cite no statute whose application they challenge. The best they can do is to point to unspecified, lump-sum 'Congressional budget appropriations' for the general use of the Executive Branch – the allocation of

v *Valley Forge* also relied on a second rationale: that the authorizing Act was an exercise of Congress' power under the Property Clause of Article IV, [section] 3, [clause] 2, and not the Taxing and Spending Clause of Article I, [section] 8. *Valley Forge Christian College v. Americans United for Separation of Church and State, Inc.* (1982), 480. But this conclusion merely provided an additional – 'and perhaps redundan[t],' Ibid. – basis for denying a claim of standing that was already foreclosed because it was not based on any congressional action.

vi For example, the statute noted that the problems of adolescent premarital sex and pregnancy 'are best approached through a variety of integrated and essential services provided to adolescents and their families' by 'religious and charitable organizations,' among other groups. 42 U. S. C. [section] 300z(a)(8)(B) (1982 ed.). It went on to mandate that federally provided services in that area should 'emphasize the provision of support by other family members, religious and charitable organizations, voluntary associations, and other groups.' [section] 300z(a)(10)(c). And it directed that demonstration projects funded by the government 'shall [. . .] make use of support systems' such as religious organizations, [section] 300z–2(a), and required grant applicants to describe how they would 'involve religious and charitable organizations' in their projects, [section] 300z–5(a)(21)(B).

which 'is a[n] administrative decision traditionally regarded as committed to agency discretion.'[92] Characterizing this case as an 'as-applied challenge' to these general appropriations statutes would stretch the meaning of that term past its breaking point. It cannot be that every legal challenge to a discretionary Executive Branch action implicates the constitutionality of the underlying congressional appropriation. When a criminal defendant charges that a federal agent carried out an unreasonable search or seizure, we do not view that claim as an as-applied challenge to the constitutionality of the statute appropriating funds for the Federal Bureau of Investigation. Respondents have not established why the discretionary Executive Branch expenditures here, which are similarly funded by no-strings, lump-sum appropriations, should be viewed any differently.[vii]

In short, this case falls outside the [sic] 'the narrow exception' that *Flast* 'created to the general rule against taxpayer standing established in *Frothingham*.'[93] Because the expenditures that respondents challenge were not expressly authorized or mandated by any specific congressional enactment, respondents' lawsuit is not directed at an exercise of congressional power,[94] and thus lacks the requisite 'logical nexus' between taxpayer status 'and the type of legislative enactment attacked.'[95]

IV

A

1

Respondents argue that it is 'arbitrary' to distinguish between money spent pursuant to congressional mandate and expenditures made in the course of executive discretion, because 'the injury to taxpayers in both situations is the very injury targeted by the Establishment Clause and *Flast* – the expenditure for the support of religion of funds exacted from taxpayers.'[96] The panel majority below agreed, based on its observation that 'there is so much that executive officials could do to promote religion in ways forbidden by the establishment clause.'[97]

But *Flast* focused on congressional action, and we must decline this invitation to extend its holding to encompass discretionary Executive Branch expenditures. *Flast* itself distinguished the 'incidental expenditure of tax funds in the administration of an essentially regulatory statute,'[98] and we have subsequently rejected the view that taxpayer standing 'extends to "the Government as a whole, regardless of which branch is at work in a particular instance."'[99] Moreover, we have repeatedly emphasized that the *Flast* exception has a 'narrow application in our precedent,'[100] that only 'slightly lowered' the bar on taxpayer standing,[101] and that must be applied with 'rigor.'[102]

It is significant that, in the four decades since its creation, the *Flast* exception has largely been confined to its facts. We have declined to lower the taxpayer standing bar in suits

vii Nor is it relevant that Congress may have informally 'earmarked' portions of its general Executive Branch appropriations to fund the offices and centers whose expenditures are at issue here. See, *e.g.*, [House of Representatives Report] No. 107–342, p. 108 (2001). '[A] fundamental principle of appropriations law is that where "Congress merely appropriates lump-sum amounts without statutorily restricting what can be done with those funds, a clear inference arises that it does not intend to impose legally binding restrictions, and indicia in committee reports and other legislative history as to how the funds should or are expected to be spent do not establish any legal requirements on" the agency.' *Lincoln v. Vigil* (1993), citation: 508 U. S. 182, 192 (quoting *In re LTV Aerospace Corp.*, 55 [Comptroller General] 307, 319 (1975)); see also *TVA v. Hill* (1978), citation: 437 U. S. 153, 191 ('Expressions of committees dealing with requests for appropriations cannot be equated with statutes enacted by Congress').

alleging violations of any constitutional provision apart from the Establishment Clause.[103] We have similarly refused to extend *Flast* to permit taxpayer standing for Establishment Clause challenges that do not implicate Congress' taxing and spending power.[104] In effect, we have adopted the position set forth by Justice Powell in his concurrence in *Richardson* and have 'limit[ed] the expansion of federal taxpayer and citizen standing in the absence of specific statutory authorization to an outer boundary drawn by the *results* in *Flast* [. . .].'[105]

2

While respondents argue that Executive Branch expenditures in support of religion are no different from legislative extractions, *Flast* itself rejected this equivalence: 'It will not be sufficient to allege an incidental expenditure of tax funds in the administration of an essentially regulatory statute.'[106]

Because almost all Executive Branch activity is ultimately funded by some congressional appropriation, extending the *Flast* exception to purely executive expenditures would effectively subject every federal action – be it a conference, proclamation or speech – to Establishment Clause challenge by any taxpayer in federal court. To see the wide swathe of activity that respondents' proposed rule would cover, one need look no further than the amended complaint in this action, which focuses largely on speeches and presentations made by Executive Branch officials.[107] Such a broad reading would ignore the first prong of *Flast*'s standing test, which requires 'a logical link between [taxpayer] status and the type of legislative enactment attacked.'[108]

It would also raise serious separation-of-powers concerns. As we have recognized, *Flast* itself gave too little weight to these concerns. By framing the standing question solely in terms of whether the dispute would be presented in an adversary context and in a form traditionally viewed as capable of judicial resolution, *Flast* 'failed to recognize that this doctrine has a separation-of-powers component, which keeps courts within certain traditional bounds vis-à-vis the other branches, concrete adverseness or not.'[109] Respondents' position, if adopted, would repeat and compound this mistake.

The constitutional requirements for federal-court jurisdiction – including the standing requirements and Article III – 'are an essential ingredient of separation and equilibration of powers.'[110] 'Relaxation of standing requirements is directly related to the expansion of judicial power,' and lowering the taxpayer standing bar to permit challenges of purely executive actions 'would significantly alter the allocation of power at the national level, with a shift away from a democratic form of government.'[111] The rule respondents propose would enlist the federal courts to superintend, at the behest of any federal taxpayer, the speeches, statements, and myriad daily activities of the President, his staff, and other Executive Branch officials. This would 'be quite at odds with [. . .] *Flast*'s own promise that it would not transform federal courts into forums for taxpayers' "generalized grievances"' about the conduct of government,[112] and would 'open the Judiciary to an arguable charge of providing "government by injunction."'[113] It would deputize federal courts as 'virtually continuing monitors of the wisdom and soundness of Executive action,' and that, most emphatically, 'is not the role of the judiciary.'[114]

3

Both the Court of Appeals and respondents implicitly recognize that unqualified federal taxpayer standing to assert Establishment Clause claims would go too far, but neither the Court of Appeals nor respondents has identified a workable limitation. The Court of

Appeals, as noted, conceded only that a taxpayer would lack standing where 'the marginal or incremental cost to the taxpaying public of the alleged violation of the establishment clause' is 'zero.'[115] Applying this rule, the Court of Appeals opined that a taxpayer would not have standing to challenge a President's favorable reference to religion in a State of the Union address because the costs associated with the speech 'would be no greater merely because the President had mentioned Moses rather than John Stuart Mill.'[116]

There is reason to question whether the Court of Appeals intended for its zero-marginal-cost test to be taken literally, because the court, without any apparent inquiry into the costs of Secretary Paige's speech, went on to agree that the plaintiffs lacked standing to challenge that speech.[117] But if we take the Court of Appeals' test literally – *i.e.*, that any marginal cost greater than zero suffices – taxpayers might well have standing to challenge some (and perhaps many) speeches. As Judge Easterbrook observed: 'The total cost of presidential proclamations and speeches by Cabinet officers that touch on religion (Thanksgiving and several other holidays) surely exceeds $500,000 annually; it may cost that much to use Air Force One and send a Secret Service detail to a single speaking engagement.'[118] At a minimum, the Court of Appeals' approach (asking whether the marginal cost exceeded zero) would surely create difficult and uncomfortable line-drawing problems. Suppose that it is alleged that a speech writer or other staff member spent extra time doing research for the purpose of including 'religious imagery' in a speech. Suppose that a President or a Cabinet officer attends or speaks at a prayer breakfast and that the time spent was time that would have otherwise been spent on secular work.

Respondents take a somewhat different approach, contending that their proposed expansion of *Flast* would be manageable because they would require that a challenged expenditure be 'fairly traceable to the conduct alleged to violate the Establishment Clause.'[119] Applying this test, they argue, would 'scree[n] out [. . .] challenge[s to] the content of one particular speech, for example the State of the Union address, as an Establishment Clause violation.'[120]

We find little comfort in this vague and ill-defined test. As an initial matter, respondents fail to explain why the (often substantial) costs that attend, for example, a Presidential address are any less 'traceable' than the expenses related to the Executive Branch statements and conferences at issue here. Indeed, respondents concede that even lawsuits involving *de minimis* amounts of taxpayer money can pass their proposed 'traceability' test.[121]

Moreover, the 'traceability' inquiry, depending on how it is framed, would appear to prove either too little or too much. If the question is whether an allegedly unconstitutional executive action can somehow be traced to taxpayer funds *in general*, the answer will always be yes: Almost all Executive Branch activities are ultimately funded by *some* congressional appropriation, whether general or specific, which is in turn financed by tax receipts. If, on the other hand, the question is whether the challenged action can be traced to the contributions of a *particular* taxpayer-plaintiff, the answer will almost always be no: As we recognized in *Frothingham*, the interest of any individual taxpayer in a particular federal expenditure 'is comparatively minute and indeterminable [. . .] and constantly changing.'[122]

B

Respondents set out a parade of horribles that they claim could occur if *Flast* is not extended to discretionary Executive Branch expenditures. For example, they say, a federal agency could use its discretionary funds to build a house of worship or to hire clergy of one denomination and send them out to spread their faith. Or an agency could use its funds to make bulk purchases of Stars of David, crucifixes, or depictions of the star and crescent for use in its offices or for distribution to the employees or the general public. Of course, none of these things has happened, even though *Flast* has not previously been expanded in the way that respondents urge. In the unlikely event that any of these executive actions did take place, Congress could quickly step in. And respondents make no effort to show that these improbable abuses could not be challenged in federal court by plaintiffs who would possess standing based on grounds other than taxpayer standing.

C

Over the years, *Flast* has been defended by some and criticized by others. But the present case does not require us to reconsider that precedent. The Court of Appeals did not apply *Flast*; it extended *Flast*. It is a necessary concomitant of the doctrine of *stare decisis* that a precedent is not always expanded to the limit of its logic. That was the approach that then-Justice Rehnquist took in his opinion for the Court in *Valley Forge*, and it is the approach we take here. We do not extend *Flast*, but we also do not overrule it. We leave *Flast* as we found it.

Justice Scalia says that we must either overrule *Flast* or extend it to the limits of its logic. His position is not '[in]sane,' inconsistent with the 'rule of law,' or 'utterly meaningless.'[123] But it is wrong. Justice Scalia does not seriously dispute either

(1) that *Flast* itself spoke in terms of 'legislative enactment[s]' and 'exercises of congressional power,'[124] or

(2) that in the four decades since *Flast* was decided, we have never extended its narrow exception to a purely discretionary Executive Branch expenditure.

We need go no further to decide this case. Relying on the provision of the Constitution that limits our role to resolving the 'Cases' and 'Controversies' before us, we decide only the case at hand.

* * *

For these reasons, the judgment of the Court of Appeals for the Seventh Circuit is reversed.

It is so ordered.

* * *

Importance

Because the deciding factor in Justice Alito's opinion for the Court was based on whether or not the precedence set in *Flast v. Cohen* granted the Freedom From Religion Foundation standing to sue, like Justice Steven's decision in *Elk Grove v. Newdow* (2004), he did not address its Establishment Clause complaint. Which also means that, aside from a brief reference in Justice Souter's dissenting opinion about how any sort of governmental endorsement sends the message to 'nonadherents' that they are 'outsiders,' *Hein v. Freedom From Religion Foundation* did not discuss the First Amendment rights of the Foundation's representatives. So that, unlike *McCollum*, *Torcaso*, *Abington*, and *Welsh*, the discourse it provides does not offer in any way an insight into how they, and their Atheism, might be guaranteed First Amendment protection. This does not make it, however, any less important to the larger discussion herein of Atheism's role in helping re-shape the American religious landscape.

Rather, and again like *Elk Grove v. Newdow*, what it does provide is an insight into the Court's growing conservative narrative, and how that narrative continued to solidify its 'soft endorsement.' That is, where before we saw the theistic language in the Pledge of Allegiance deemed permissible as a product of 'ceremonial deism' in the concurrent opinions of Chief Justice Rehnquist and Justice O'Connor, in this instance the Federal Government was permitted to continue providing federal funding to religious organizations in order to ensure the President's use of ceremonial deism – such as in speeches that invoke God, or in Executive Orders that permit federal funding to religious groups – would not be 'filtered' through subsequent lawsuits concerning the possible Establishment Clause violations inherent in doing so. The result of which, of course, meant yet another re-conceptualization of the relationship between church and state. That this was made possible once more by representatives of an Atheist/secular organization claiming a First Amendment injury, is quite telling of the continued influence that such Americans have had on the broader notion of religion in America.

And this leads directly toward this decision's secondary importance.

The Freedom From Religion Foundation was created in 1978, a year after Anne Nicol Gaylor won her first legal battle in Madison, Wisconsin against the United States Post Office's use of a 'cancellation stamp,' that promoted a local Catholic organization. In the years that followed, it gained some moderate national recognition, unsuccessfully filing a lawsuit against President Ronald Reagan in 1982 that challenged the constitutionality of his proposed 'Year of the Bible,' and in 1993, alongside a chapter based in Denver Colorado, successfully halting the mayor's office from co-sponsoring a National Day of Prayer. It perhaps gained its most effective victory up to that point in 1996 in *Freedom From Religion Foundation v. Tommy Thompson*, wherein it successfully stopped the State of Wisconsin from endorsing a legal holiday for Good Friday.[125]

Since then, but especially in the last twenty years, it has brought numerous suits on behalf of perceived First Amendment violations, both winning and losing cases dealing with Christmas and Ten Commandment displays,[126] religious expression and proselytization in public schools,[127] the constitutionality of President Obama's promotion of the National Day of Prayer,[128] the constitutionality of the tax exempt status of ministers,[129] and, of course, the constitutionality of federal funding for religious-based social service organizations (see the list above).

According to its bylaws, the Foundation's central doctrine has always been focused on the promotion and preservation of the 'constitutional principle of separation of state and church,' as well as the education of the public in respect to 'matters related to nontheistic beliefs.'[130] And just like Madalyn Murray's American Atheists, it has accomplished this through a diverse public outreach campaign: publishing a freethought newspaper, *Freethought Today*, sponsoring high school, college, and grad student essay competitions, hosting annual national conventions, broadcasting podcasts and radio programs on its 'Freethought Radio,' and promoting its agenda via billboards and bus advertisement campaigns, as well as through differing media such as books, articles, music, and art.[131] As such, it has worked to define itself as an organization uniquely equipped for safeguarding the American rights of both freedom of and from religion, a responsibility, it has argued, exceptional to 'American freethinkers':

> The history of Western civilization shows us that most social and moral progress has been brought about by persons free from religion. In modern times the first to speak out for prison reform, for humane treatment of the mentally ill, for abolition of

> capital punishment, for women's right to vote, for death with dignity for the terminally ill, and for the right to choose contraception, sterilization and abortion have been freethinkers, just as they were the first to call for an end to slavery. The Foundation works as an umbrella for those who are free from religion and are committed to the cherished principle of separation of state and church.[132]

By means of this discourse we can perceive a sense of organized Atheism, and though it might not seem like the sort of structural attributes normatively associated with the definition of the term 'church,' it does offer a glimpse into how the individualized Atheists of the case decisions thus far discussed might bind themselves into a like-minded group working toward achieving the same doctrinal goal. And this epitomizes *Hein v. Freedom From Religion Foundation*'s secondary importance, perhaps best summarized by this question: does this sort of organized Atheism, built on a doctrinal foundation, and devoted to a distinct agenda, further push Atheism toward the category of American religion?

When considered alongside the final case decision presented and discussed herein, and in particular how that decision has further solidified the 'soft endorsement' supported by both *Elk Grove* and *Hein*, this question will become even more complex.

Notes

1 George W. Bush: 'Executive Order 13199 – Establishment of White House Office of Faith-Based and Community Initiatives,' January 29th, 2001.
2 Ibid.
3 George W. Bush: 'Executive Order 13198 – Agency Responsibilities With Respect to Faith-Based and Community Initiatives,' January 29th, 2001.
4 George W. Bush: 'Executive Order 13280 – Responsibilities of the Department of Agriculture and the Agency for International Development With Respect to Faith-Based and Community Initiatives,' December 12th, 2002.
5 George W. Bush: 'Executive Order 13342 – Responsibilities of the Departments of Commerce and Veterans Affairs and the Small Business Administration With Respect to Faith-Based and Community Initiatives,' June 1st, 2004.
6 George W. Bush: 'Executive Order 13397 – Responsibilities of the Department of Homeland Security With Respect to Faith-Based and Community Initiatives,' March 7th, 2006.
7 *Petition for Writ of Certiorari, Dennis Grace, Acting Director of The White House Office Of Faith-Based And Community Initiatives, Et Al., Petitioners v. Freedom From Religion Foundation, Inc., et al.* Appendix A, 9a. Citing the Office of Faith-Based and Community Initiatives website (now inactive): www.dtiassociates.com/FBCI/.
8 George W. Bush: 'Executive Order 13279 – Equal Protection of the Laws for Faith-Based and Community Organizations,' December 12th, 2002.
9 Ibid.
10 *Petition for Writ of Certiorari, Dennis Grace, Acting Director of The White House Office Of Faith-Based And Community Initiatives, Et Al., Petitioners v. Freedom From Religion Foundation, Inc., et al.*, 4.
11 Ibid.
12 *Flast v. Cohen* (1968), citation: 392 U.S. 83, 103.
13 Ibid., 106.
14 *Freedom From Religion v. Chao* (7th Circuit Court of Appeals, 2006), citation: 433 F.3d 989.
15 *Freedom From Religion v. Chao* (7th Circuit Court of Appeals, 2006), citation: 447 F.3d 988.
16 *Freedom From Religion Foundation v. McCallum* (7th Circuit Court of Appeals, 2003), citation: 324 F.3d 880.
17 *Freedom From Religion Foundation v. Montana Office of Rural Health* (U.S. District Court for the district of Montana, Butte Divisin, 2004), Docket No. CV-03-30-BU-RWA.
18 *Freedom From Religion Foundation et al. v. Dr. Robert Bruininks, et al.* (U.S. District Court, District of Minnesota, 2005), Civil No. 05-638 JNE/SRN.

19 *Freedom From Religion Foundation, Inc. v. Towey* (U.S. District Court for the Western District of Wisconsin, 2005), No. 04-C-381-S.
20 *Freedom From Religion Foundation v. Nicholson* (U.S. District Court for the Western District of Wisconsin, 2006), No. 06-C-212-S.
21 *Freedom From Religion Foundation v. Gonzales* (U.S. District Court for the Western District of Wisconsin, 2006), Case No. 06-C-0244-S.
22 *Freedom From Religion Foundation v. Secretary Joe R. Williams* (U.S. District Court for the District of New Mexico, 2006), Case No. CIV 05-1168.
23 *Freedom From Religion Foundation v. Roob* (U.S. District Court for the Southern District of Indiana, 2007), No. 1:07-CV-00559-DFH-JMS.
24 *Freedom From Religion Foundation v. Olson* (U.S. District Court for the Southwest Division of North Dakota, 2007), No. 1:07-cv-043.
25 *Flast* v. *Cohen* (1968), citation: 392 U.S. 83.
26 Executive Order No. 13199, Title 3, Code of Federal Regulations, 752 (2001 Comp.).
27 Ibid.
28 Ibid., 752–753.
29 Executive Order No. 13279, 3 CFR [section] 2(f), p. 260 (2002 Comp.).
30 Ibid., [section] 2(c), 260.
31 Ibid., [section] 2(d), 260.
32 *Freedom From Religion Foundation, Inc. v. Chao* (7th Circuit Court of Appeals, 2006), 997.
33 See Government Accountability Office, Faith-Based and Community Initiative: Improvements in Monitoring Grantees and Measuring Performance Could Enhance Accountability, GAO-06-616, p. 21 (June 2006), online at www.gao.gov/new.items/d06616.pdf (as visited June 25th, 2007, and available in Clerk of Court's case file); see also Amended Complaint in No. 04-C-381-S (Western District, Wisconsin.), [paragraph] 23, Application to Petition for Certiorari, 71a–72a.
34 Ibid., [section] 5, Application to Petition for Certiorari, 68a.
35 Ibid., [paragraph] 32, Application to Petition for Certiorari, 73a.
36 Ibid., [paragraph] 37, Application to Petition for Certiorari, 76a.
37 Ibid., [paragraph] 10, Application to Petition for Certiorari, 69a; see also Ibid., [paragraphs] 7–9, Application to Petition for Certiorari, 68a–69a.
38 See *Freedom From Religion Foundation, Inc.* v. *Towey*, No. 04-C-381-S (Western District, Wisconsin, 2004), Application to Petition for Certiorari, 27a–35a.
39 Application to Petition for Certiorari, 31a (quoting *Flast v. Cohen* (1968), 102).
40 Application to Petition for Certiorari, 33a–34a.
41 *Freedom From Religion Foundation, Inc. v. Chao* (7th Circuit Court of Appeals, 2006), 989.
42 Ibid., 997.
43 Ibid., 994.
44 Ibid., 995.
45 Ibid., 997.
46 Ibid., 998.
47 Ibid., 1000.
48 Ibid. (emphasis in original).
49 *Freedom From Religion Foundation, Inc. v. Chao* (7th Circuit Court of Appeals, 2006), 988.
50 Ibid.
51 549 U.S. ___ (2006).
52 *DaimlerChrysler Corp. v. Cuno* (2006), (slip opinion, at 6), quoting *Elk Grove Unified School District v. Newdow* (2004), citation: 542 U.S. 1, 11.
53 *Raines v. Byrd* (1997), citation: 521 U.S. 811, 818 (quoting *Simon v. Eastern Kentucky Welfare Rights Organization* (1976), citation: 426 U.S. 26, 37).
54 *ASARCO Inc. v. Kadish* (1989), 613 (opinion of Justice Kennedy).
55 *Allen v. Wright* (1984), 751.
56 *ASARCO Inc. v. Kadish* (1989), 613 (opinion of Justice Kennedy).
57 *Valley Forge Christian College v. Americans United for Separation of Church and State, Inc.* (1982), 471.
58 *Marbury v. Madison* (1803), citation: 5 U.S. (1 Cranch) 137, 170.
59 *Valley Forge Christian College v. Americans United for Separation of Church and State, Inc.* (1982), 474 (quoting *Blair v. United States* (1919), citation: 250 U.S. 273, 279).

60 *Frothingham v. Mellon*, decided with *Massachusetts v. Mellon* (1923), 488.
61 See, e.g., *Follett v. Town of McCormick* (1944), citation: 321 U.S. 573 (invalidating tax on preaching on First Amendment grounds).
62 *Frothingham v. Mellon*, decided with *Massachusetts v. Mellon* (1923), 486.
63 Ibid., 487.
64 Ibid., 489; see also *Alabama Power Co. v. Ickes* (1938), citation: 302 U.S. 464, 478–479.
65 *Doremus v. Board of Ed. of Hawthorne* (1952), citation: 342 U.S. 429, 433.
66 Ibid., 434.
67 *Lujan v. Defenders of Wildlife* (1992), 573–574.
68 *Flast v. Cohen* (1968), 102–103.
69 Ibid., 103–104.
70 Brief for Respondents 12.
71 *Valley Forge Christian College v. Americans United for Separation of Church and State, Inc.* (1982), 481.
72 Elementary and Secondary Education Act, Statute 79, 27.
73 [section] 201(b), Ibid., 36.
74 See *Flast v. Cohen* (1968), 86.
75 [section] 2, Elementary and Secondary Education Act, Statute 79, 30–31.
76 [section] 203(a)(3)(B), ibid., 37.
77 *Flast v. Cohen* (1968), 90.
78 *Flast* v. *Gardner* (Southern District of New York, 1967), citation: 271 F.Supp. 1, 2.
79 *Flast* v. *Cohen* (1968), 90.
80 *Valley Forge Christian College v. Americans United for Separation of Church and State, Inc.* (1982), 479.
81 Ibid.
82 Ibid., 479, footnote 15.
83 Ibid., 479 (quoting *Flast v. Cohen* (1968), 102).
84 *Schlesinger v. Reservists Committee to Stop the War* (1974), citation: 418 U.S. 208.
85 Ibid., 228.
86 Ibid., footnote 17. See also *United States v. Richardson* (1974), citation: 418 U.S. 166, 175.
87 *Bowen v. Kendrick* (1988), 589.
88 Ibid., 620, 619.
89 Ibid., 619–620 (emphasis added).
90 See ibid., 595–596; see also ibid., at 623 (Justice O'Connor, concurring, noting the 'partnership between governmental and religious institutions contemplated by the AFLA').
91 Ibid., 619–620.
92 *Lincoln v. Vigil* (1993), citation: 508 U.S. 182, 192.
93 *Bowen v. Kendrick* (1988), 618.
94 See *Valley Forge Christian College v. Americans United for Separation of Church and State, Inc.* (1982), 479.
95 *Flast v. Cohen* (1968), 102.
96 Brief for Respondents 13.
97 *Freedom From Religion Foundation, Inc. v. Chao* (7th Circuit Court of Appeals, 2006), 995.
98 *Flast v. Cohen* (1968), 102.
99 *Valley Forge Christian College v. Americans United for Separation of Church and State, Inc.* (1982), 484, footnote 20.
100 *DaimlerChrysler Corp. v. Cuno* (2006), (slip opinion, 12).
101 *United States v. Richardson* (1974), 173.
102 *Valley Forge Christian College v. Americans United for Separation of Church and State, Inc.* (1982), 481.
103 See *Tilton v. Richardson* (1971), citation: 403 U.S. 672 (no taxpayer standing to sue under Free Exercise Clause of First Amendment); *United States v. Richardson* (1974), 175 (no taxpayer standing to sue under Statement and Account Clause of Article I); *Schlesinger v. Reservists Committee to Stop the War* (1974), 228 (no taxpayer standing to sue under Incompatibility Clause of Article I); *DaimlerChrysler Corp. v. Cuno* (2006), (slip opinion, 13), no taxpayer standing to sue under Commerce Clause.
104 See *Valley Forge Christian College v. Americans United for Separation of Church and State, Inc.* (1982), 479–482 (no taxpayer standing to challenge Executive Branch action taken

pursuant to Property Clause of Article IV); see also *District of Columbia Common Cause v. District of Columbia* (District of Columbia Court of Appeals, 1988), citation: 858 F.2d 1, 3–4; *In re United States Catholic Conference* (2nd Circuit, 1989), citation: 885 F.2d 1020, 1028.

105 *United States v. Richardson* (1974), 196.
106 *Flast v. Cohen* (1968), 102.
107 See, e.g., Amended Complaint [paragraph] 32, Application to Petition for Certiorari, 73a (challenging Executive Branch officials' 'support of national and regional conferences'); ibid., [paragraph] 33, Application to Petition for Certiorari, 73a–75a (challenging content of speech by Secretary of Education); ibid., [paragraphs] 35, 36, Application to Petition for Certiorari, 76a (challenging content of Presidential speeches); ibid., [paragraph] 41, Application to Petition for Certiorari, 77a (challenging Executive Branch officials' 'public appearances' and 'speeches').
108 *Flast v. Cohen* (1968), 102.
109 *Lewis v. Casey* (1996), citation: 518 U.S. 343, 353, footnote 3; see also *Valley Forge Christian College v. Americans United for Separation of Church and State, Inc.* (1982), 471.
110 *Steel Company v. Citizens for Better Environment* (1998), citation: 523 U.S. 83, 101.
111 *United States v. Richardson* (1974), 188 (Justice Powell, concurring).
112 *DaimlerChrysler Corp. v. Cuno* (2006), (slip opinion, 12), quoting *Flast v. Cohen* (1968), 106.
113 *Schlesinger v. Reservists Committee to Stop the War* (1974), 222.
114 *Allen v. Wright* (1984), 760 (quoting *Laird* v. *Tatum* (1972), citation: 408 U.S. 1, 15).
115 *Freedom From Religion Foundation, Inc. v. Chao* (7th Circuit Court of Appeals, 2006), 995.
116 Ibid.
117 Ibid., 996.
118 *Freedom From Religion Foundation, Inc. v. Chao* (7th Circuit Court of Appeals, 2006), 989–990 (concurring in denial of rehearing en banc).
119 Brief for Respondents 17.
120 Ibid., 21.
121 Ibid., 20, footnote 6.
122 *Frothingham v. Mellon*, decided with *Massachusetts v. Mellon* (1923), 487.
123 Post, at 1 (opinion concurring in judgment).
124 392 U.S., at 102.
125 *Freedom From Religion Foundation v. Thompson* (U.S. District Court for the Western District of Wisconsin, 1996), 969.
126 *Freedom From Religion Foundation v. City of Marshfield* (7th Circuit Court of Appeals, 2000), citation: 203 F.3d 487; *Mercier v. Fraternal Order of Eagles* (7th Circuit Court of Appeals, 2005), citation: 395 F.3d 693; *Freedom From Religion Foundation, Inc. v. Manitowoc County* (U.S. District Court for the Eastern District of Wisconsin, 2010), Case No. 08-C-1105; *Freedom From Religion Foundation v. Connellsville Area School District* (U.S. District Court for the Western District of Pennsylvania, 2015), No. 2:12-cv-1406; *Freedom From Religion Foundation v. Weber* (9th Circuit Court of Appeals, 2015), Docket No. 9:12-cv-00019-DLC; *Freedom From Religion Foundation v. New Kensington-Arnold School District* (3rd Circuit Court of Appeals, 2016), Case No. 15-3083.
127 *Doe v. Porter* (6th Circuit Court of Appeals, 2004), citation: 370 F.3d 558; *Freedom From Religion Foundation v. Orange County School Board* (11th Circuit Court of Appeals, 2015), Docket No. 6:13-cv-00922-GKS-KRS.
128 *Freedom From Religion Foundation v. Obama* (7th Circuit Court of Appeals, 2011), No. 10–1973.
129 *Freedom From Religion Foundation v. Lew* (7th Circuit Court of Appeals, 2014), citation: 773 F.3d 815.
130 'About the Foundation/Why is the Foundation Concerned with State/Church Entanglement?' Available at: https://ffrf.org/faq/item/12602-why-is-the-foundation-concerned-with-state-church-entanglement? (Accessed October 21st, 2017).
131 'About the Foundation/What does the Foundation Do?' Available at: https://ffrf.org/faq/item/15001-what-does-the-foundation-do? (Accessed October 21st, 2017).
132 https://ffrf.org/about (Accessed November 5th, 2017).

10 *Town of Greece v. Galloway* (2014)

Argued: November 6th, 2013 – Decided: May 5th, 2014.

> That is not the country we are, because that is not what our Constitution permits. Here, when a citizen stands before her government, whether to perform a service or request a benefit, her religious beliefs do not enter into the picture. The government she faces favors no particular religion, either by word or by deed. And that government, in its various processes and proceedings, imposes no religious tests on its citizens, sorts none of them by faith, and permits no exclusion based on belief. When a person goes to court, a polling place, or an immigration proceeding – I could go on: to a zoning agency, a parole board hearing, or the DMV – government officials do not engage in sectarian worship, nor do they ask her to do likewise. They all participate in the business of government not as Christians, Jews, Muslims (and more), but only as Americans – none of them different from any other for that civic purpose. Why not, then, at a town meeting?
>
> Justice Elena Kagan, dissenting opinion,
> *Town of Greece v. Galloway*

Question before the Court: Does the offering of a prayer at a Town Board Meeting violate the Establishment Clause of the First Amendment, especially when that prayer is offered voluntarily, without payment, and is free from discriminatory content?

Decision: 5–4. No, the Establishment Clause was not designed to prohibit legislative prayer, especially when that prayer sets a 'proper deliberative mood,' as well as acknowledges the role of religion in American society.

Antecedent Case Decisions:

- SECOND CIRCUIT COURT OF APPEALS, May 17th, 2012.

  Ruling: The Court of Appeals reversed and remanded the District Court's ruling, finding in favor of Plaintiff-Appellants Susan Galloway and Linda Stephens. The Town Board appealed to the Supreme Court, which granted certiorari.

- UNITED STATES DISTRICT COURT FOR THE WESTERN DISTRICT OF NEW YORK, August 5th, 2010.

  Ruling: The District Court ruled in favor of the Town Board, arguing that they did not violate the First Amendment.

Background

The Town of Greece, in Monroe County, New York, is governed by a five-person Town Board of elected members who meet monthly to conduct official town business, including the approval of proposed ordinances, conducting public hearings, swearing in new town employees, and bestowing citizenship awards. Minor children have often participated in these meetings: Boy Scout Troops have led the pledge of allegiance, and local high school students, needing to fulfill state-mandated civics requirements, have attended. All meetings are open to the public.

After his election in 1999, the Town Supervisor, John Auberger, supplemented the traditional 'moment of silence' at the start of each Town Meeting with an invocation, given by a volunteer member of the local clergy. After calling roll, and the recitation of the Pledge of Allegiance, Auberger would invite the clergy member to the front of the room, where they would provide the invocation. After which, he would present them with a plaque, thanking them for being the Town Board's 'chaplain of the month.' The prayer itself, he argued, was meant to 'place [the] town board members in a solemn and deliberative frame of mind, invoke divine guidance in town affairs, and follow a tradition practiced by Congress and dozens of state legislatures.'[1]

In the eleven years that this practice took place, between 1999 and 2010, the Town Board used an informal selection process for choosing clergy members, never implementing an official procedure for either selecting volunteers, or for the purposes of reviewing the content of the invocations themselves. And no clergy member was ever paid for his or her services. In later affidavits, the Town Board clarified that anyone, not just clergy members, could volunteer to provide an invocation, including 'adherents of any religion, atheists, and the nonreligious,' and that no volunteer was ever rejected. Although it did admit that it failed to advertise that this opportunity was available to the town's residents.[2]

The religious organizations within the Town of Greece were predominately Christian-based, and neither the plaintiffs who brought the suit, nor the Town board, acknowledged at the time of the initial trial familiarity with any Mosques, Synagogues, Temples, or other non-Christian places of worship. As such, every invocation given between 1999 and 2008 was provided by a representative of a Christian denomination.

Throughout that time, three clerical employees of the Town's Office of Constituent Services, Linda Sofia, Geri Wagoner, and Michele Fiannaca, were responsible for contacting and appointing each month's chaplain.

From March 1999 to February 2005, Linda Sofia used a directory compiled by the Town of Greece Chamber of Commerce to contact local religious organizations in search of volunteers. She logged each organization that offered a chaplain, and how many times that organization's volunteer provided an invocation:

> Greece Assembly of God (14 times); First Bible Baptist Church (9 times); West Side Baptist Church (4 times); Holy Name of Jesus Church (2 times); Our Mother of Sorrows Church (8 times); St. John the Evangelist Church (1 time); St. Charles Borromeo Church (2 times); St. Lawrence Church (3 times); English Road Alliance Church (4 times); Shepherd's Heart Christian Fellowship (7 times); Hope Lutheran Church (1 time); Aldersgate United Methodist Church (4 times); Lakeshore Community Church (3 times); New Testament Christian Church (1 time); and John Knox Presbyterian Church (1 time).[3]

From March 2005 to late 2006, Geri Wagoner used a list composed by Linda Sofia, which she called her 'Town Board Chaplains List,' that included all the religious organizations that provided volunteers. In that time volunteers from these organizations provided an invocation:

> First Bible Baptist Church (1 time); West Side Baptist Church (1 time); Holy Name of Jesus (1 time); Our Lady of Mercy (1 time); Our Mother of Sorrows (1 time); St. John the Evangelist (1 time); St. Lawrence Church (1 time); English Road Alliance Church (1 time); Messiah Lutheran (1 time); Hope Lutheran Church (1 time); Park Ridge Free Methodist (1 time); Trinity Church of the Nazarene (1 time); Lakeshore Community Church (1 time); Calvary Chapel of Greece (2 times); Covenant Orthodox Presbyterian (1 time); and Lakeview Community Church (2 times).[4]

When Michele Fiannaca took over responsibilities from Geri Wagoner in January 2007, in addition to Linda Sofia's Town Board Chaplains List, and an updated list compiled by Geri Wagoner, she also utilized the Religious Services Directory, published in the *Greece Post*. Between January 2007 and December 2008 volunteers from these organizations provided an invocation:

> First Bible Baptist Church (3 times), Our Mother of Sorrows (2 times), St. John the Evangelist (1 time), New Testament Christian Church (1 time), Greece Assembly of God (3 times), St. Charles Borromeo (2 times), Morning Star Christian Fellowship (1 time), Lakeshore Community Church (1 time), Lakeview Community Church (1 time), Covenant Orthodox Presbyterian Church (1 time), St. Mark's Church (1 time), Our Lady of Mercy (1 time), The Savior's Chapel (1 time), Aldersgate United Methodist Church (1 time), and Baha'i Assembly of Greece (1 time).[5]

After the Plaintiffs in the case, Susan Galloway, a Jewish woman, and Linda Stephens, an Atheist, voiced their complaints to the Board in 2007, four non-Christian invocations were given: Dave Chikowsky, a Jewish laymen, offered two prayers on January 15th and July 15th, 2008; Jen Zarpentine, a Wiccan Priestess, offered a prayer on April 15th, 2008; and Thomas Lynch, the chairmen of the local Baha'i Temple, offered a prayer on December 16th, 2008.

As to the content of the prayers provided between 1999 and 2010, each varied significantly, depending on the chaplain who gave them. However, in their initial suit in the U.S. District Court for the Western District of New York, Galloway and Stephens argued that at least 73.6% of the prayers given during this time period were 'sectarian' in nature, though they also contended that that percentage went up to 90% in some years, and down to 58.3% in 2008.[6]

During its own review of the facts of the case, the 2nd Circuit Court of Appeals found that of the 130 invocations offered between 1999 and 2009 – 121 of which were transcribed – a substantial majority of them contained sectarian Christian language:

> Roughly two-thirds contained references to 'Jesus Christ,' 'Jesus,' 'Your Son,' or the 'Holy Spirit.' Within this subset, almost all concluded with a statement that the prayer had been given in Jesus Christ's name. Typically, prayer-givers stated something like, 'In Jesus's name we pray,' or 'We ask this in Christ's name.' Some prayer-givers

> elaborated further, describing Christ as 'our Savior,' 'God's only son,' 'the Lord,' or part of the Holy Trinity. One prayer, for example, was given 'in the name of the Lord and Savior Jesus Christ, who lives with you and the Holy Spirit, one God for ever and ever.' Other prayers, including ones not expressly made in Christ's name, spoke of 'the role of the Holy Spirit in our lives,' and celebrated Christ's birth and resurrection.[7]

The remaining third of the prayers used generic theistic terminology:

> Christian clergy delivered prayers referring to 'God of all creation,' 'Heavenly Father,' and God's 'kingdom of Heaven.' The lay Jewish prayer-giver spoke of 'God,' the 'Father,' and the 'Lord;' he also referenced, at one point, 'the songs of David, your servant.' The Baha'i prayer-giver referred generally to 'God,' concluding his prayer with the Baha'i greeting, 'Alláh–u–Abhá,' which loosely means 'God the All Glorious.' Finally, the Wiccan priestess invoked Athena and Apollo; she stated these were fitting deities given the Town's name.[8]

Citing personal offense to the prayer policy in general, and arguing that it merely 'promoted the Christian religion,' Galloway addressed the Town Board on September 18th, 2007. She later recalled saying something to this effect:

> I find that it is a promotion of religion when you have preachers come in here and say, 'in Jesus Christ our Lord,' or 'in the Holy Spirit.' [. . .] Supposedly we are considered a secular country, and thus we should not have a mingling of church and state. [. . .] I hope this will be addressed because this is not okay to have Christian religion introduced into our town board. There is a separation of church and state and it needs to be kept that way.[9]

The following month Galloway addressed the Board once more, this time joined by Stephens, at which point they were told that, if they wished, they were allowed to leave the meeting during the offending prayer.

In her deposition for the initial trial, Linda Stephens described herself as an Atheist, and as such she believed that the 'strict separation' between church and state should prohibit both sectarian and nonsectarian prayer, and that the invocations given at both the Town Board meetings, as well as the ones in Congress that the Town Board used as justification in permitting their own, were inappropriate violations of the First Amendment. She further clarified that her goal in filing the lawsuit was to stop *sectarian* prayers from being given, defining them, in her own words, as those that invoked a 'particular religion,' or the 'particulars of a particular religion,' such as the inclusion of the names 'Jesus,' 'Jesus Christ,' 'Holy Spirit,' or 'Allah.' In comparison, she defined *nonsectarian* prayers, which she found acceptable, as those that 'encompassed' the 'three major religions' (presumably the Abrahamic religions of Judaism, Christianity, and Islam), in which the usage of such terms as 'God,' 'Almighty,' 'Lord God,' and 'Father,' would be tolerable, though nonetheless inappropriate.[10]

On February 28th, 2008, after feeling their complaints were not taken seriously by the Town Board, Galloway and Stephens filed their initial suit with the Western District Court of New York, stating:

> The Board has neither suggested nor required that prayer-givers present inclusive, nonsectarian entreaties. As a result, the vast majority of prayers during the past four

> years have been explicitly Christian in content. By sponsoring persistently sectarian – and almost exclusively Christian – prayers, the Town Board has publicly aligned itself with a single faith. In so doing, the Board sends the message to non-Christians that they are unwelcome at Board meetings and that the Board does not represent non-Christian's concerns. Making non-Christians second-class citizens in the body politic runs afoul of the United States Constitution. [. . .] [The Board]'s practices of favoring Christian clergy and prayers at Town Board meetings have the purpose and effect of promoting, advancing, favoring and endorsing the Christian religion, and have a coercive effect on children present at Town Board meetings. These practices convey the message that the Christian religion is favored or preferred by the Town over other religions and over nonreligion. The practices send the message to adherents of the Christian religion that they are political insiders, and simultaneously send the message to non-Christians that they are political outsiders.[11]

They requested both a declaratory statement condemning the Board's promotion of Christianity, as well as an injunction to halt the sectarian invocations – though not the nonsectarian ones. As precedence in favor of their complaint, they cited the Supreme Court decisions *Marsh v. Chambers* (1983) and *County of Allegheny v. ACLU Greater Pittsburgh Chapter* (1989).

In response, the Town Board argued that Galloway and Stephens lacked standing to sue for four reasons: the injury they claimed was moot because they were never 'denied the opportunity to give an invocation' themselves, and that their exposure to the sectarian prayers could not have caused the distress they described because their content neither 'proselytized' nor 'disparaged' other religious faiths; their argument that certain religious organizations were excluded was invalid, as they were unaware of such exclusions until the facts of the litigation were made available by the litigation itself; they could not have been caused injury by prayers offered at meetings at which they did not attend; and their request to end the Board's offering of 'sectarian' prayers would ultimately prove unconstitutional as it would require the Board to 'excessively entangle' itself in church doctrine by forcing it to determine each prayer's 'sectarian nature.'[12]

The Board further contended that, in comparison to that approved by the Supreme Court in its decision in *Marsh v. Chambers*, its own invocation policy offered a much more inclusive option, as it was open to volunteers from varying denominations, it provided a different prayer in each session, and because no volunteer was ever excluded or rejected.[13]

In his ruling on August 5th, 2010, District Judge Charles J. Siragusa agreed with the Town Board, and in particular cited the unconstitutionality of requiring it to determine the 'illusory' differences between sectarian and nonsectarian prayer.

Galloway and Stephens appealed to the 2nd Circuit Court of Appeals.

In his decision for that Court, Circuit Judge Guido Calabresi reversed and remanded the District Court's ruling, citing that a 'reasonable objective observer' could see that the Town Board's prayer policy, however benevolent in its intentions, was a clear violation of the Establishment Clause:

> Occasional prayers recognizing the divinities or beliefs of a particular creed, in a context that makes clear that the town is not endorsing or affiliating itself with that creed or, more broadly, with religion or non-religion, are not offensive to the Constitution. Nor are we adopting a test that permits prayers in theory but makes it impossible for a town in practice to avoid Establishment Clause problems. To the contrary,

> it seems to us that a practice such as the one to which the town here apparently aspired – one that is inclusive of multiple beliefs and makes clear, in public word and gesture, that the prayers offered are presented by a randomly chosen group of volunteers, who do not express an official town religion, and do not purport to speak on behalf of all the town's residents or to compel their assent to a particular belief – is fully compatible with the First Amendment. What we do hold is that a legislative prayer practice that, however well-intentioned, conveys to a reasonable objective observer under the totality of the circumstances an official affiliation with a particular religion violates the clear command of the Establishment Clause. Where the overwhelming predominance of prayers offered are associated, often in an explicitly sectarian way, with a particular creed, and where the town takes no steps to avoid the identification, but rather conveys the impression that town officials themselves identify with the sectarian prayers and that residents in attendance are expected to participate in them, a reasonable objective observer would perceive such an affiliation.[14]

The Town Board appealed this decision to the Supreme Court, and their petition for a writ of certiorari was granted. Oral arguments were heard on November 6th, 2013, and the opinion of the Court was announced on May 5th, 2014. In a 5–4 decision, it found in favor of the Town Board, reversing the Court of Appeals' ruling.

Because Justice Kennedy's opinion for the Court relied so heavily on *Marsh v. Chambers* (1983), a brief discussion of it here is crucial.

* * *

Beginning in 1855, twelve years before it became a state, the Nebraska Unicameral Legislature began opening its daily sessions with a prayer provided by a chaplain. In 1973, the Rules of the Nebraska Legislature were amended so that Rule 1, section 2, under the title 'Officers and Employees,' included a chaplain. Rule 1, section 21 stated: 'The Chaplain shall attend and shall open with prayer each day's sitting of the Legislature.' In its current form (at the time of this writing), Rule 1, section 22 states: 'The Clerk's office shall arrange for prayer at the beginning of each day of the legislative session.' And under Rule 7, section 1, which describes the proceedings of the Legislature, it states that the 'order of business' must begin with a 'Prayer by the Chaplain.'

In 1980, Robert E. Palmer, a Presbyterian Minister, was serving as the 'duly selected' chaplain for the Nebraska Legislature, a position he had held since 1965. He was paid a salary of $319.75 per month, for each month in which the legislature was in session. His salary was provided by the general funds of the State of Nebraska, and was disbursed to him by the then acting State Treasurer, Frank Marsh.

In addition, each prayer was recorded in the Legislative Journal, and after an approved vote by the legislature, they were collected and published on three occasions, at public expense: 200 copies in 1975, 200 copies in 1978, and 100 copies in 1979. The total cost for all three publications came to $458.56. The prayers themselves were offered exclusively for the members of the Legislature, so that any interaction with the public was purely coincidental.

Ernest Chambers,[15] an elected Nebraska State Senator and member of the Nebraska Unicameral Legislature representing District 11, filed suit with the United States District Court for the District of Nebraska in 1979, citing as defendants Frank Marsh, Robert E.

Palmer, and the members of the Executive Board of the Legislative Council. He claimed that the chaplaincy practice violated the Establishment Clause, citing three abuses: the compensation paid to the chaplain using public funds, the publication of the prayer books using the same, and the offering of the prayers in general.

The District Court ruled in 1980 that the Nebraska Legislature's chaplaincy practice did not violate the Constitution as it pertained to the daily invocations provided by the chaplain, but did conclude that the salary given him for doing so, as well as the publication of the prayer books, did.

Marsh, Palmer, and the Executive Board appealed that decision to the 8th Circuit Court of Appeals in 1981. Writing for that Court, Circuit Judge Gerald Heaney applied the Lemon Test and found the chaplaincy practice failed all three prongs, arguing that the employment of the same chaplain for sixteen years, as well as the publication of his invocations, represented a promotion of a particular religious expression, and that the use of federal funds to support this led to a clear entanglement between church and state. Consequently, he affirmed the District Court's decision in respect to the chaplain's salary and the publication of the prayer books, and reversed its decision in regard to the prayers themselves, thus prohibiting the practice to continue.

Marsh, Palmer, and the Executive Board appealed once more to the Supreme Court, which limited its consideration only to the question of the constitutionality of the invocations themselves. In a 6–3 decision, it found in favor of Marsh et al., arguing that the prayers did not violate the Establishment Clause.

Chief Justice Warren Burger wrote the decision for the Court, in which he famously dismissed using the Lemon Test to reach his conclusion. Instead, his argument leaned heavily on 'history' and 'tradition.'

> The opening of sessions of legislative and other deliberative public bodies with prayer is deeply embedded in the history and tradition of this country. From colonial times through the founding of the Republic and ever since, the practice of legislative prayer has coexisted with the principles of disestablishment and religious freedom. In the very courtrooms in which the United States District Judge and later three Circuit Judges heard and decided this case, the proceedings opened with an announcement that concluded, 'God save the United States and this Honorable Court.' The same invocation occurs at all sessions of this Court.[16]

This tradition, he established, began with the First Continental Congress. Starting in 1774, it adopted an invocation process for the opening of each session. Then, on April 7th, 1789, while meeting in the First Congress of the United States, the Senate appointed a committee that would consider the 'manner of electing Chaplains.'[17] The House of Representatives did the same two days later. By the end of the month the Senate had elected its first Chaplain, again followed by the House of Representatives a week later. A statute that would provide payment for these chaplains was enacted on September 22nd, 1789.[18] Three days later, Congress approved the final wording of the Bill of Rights, including the First Amendment. Clearly, Chief Justice Burger argued, this timeline of events proved that the 'men who wrote the First Amendment Religion Clauses did not view paid legislative chaplains and opening prayers as a violation of that Amendment, for the practice of opening sessions with prayer has continued without interruption ever since that early session of Congress.'[19]

As such, he concluded thus:

> In light of the unambiguous and unbroken history of more than 200 years, there can be no doubt that the practice of opening legislative sessions with prayer has become part of the fabric of our society. To invoke Divine guidance on a public body entrusted with making the laws is not, in these circumstances, an 'establishment' of religion or a step toward establishment; it is simply a tolerable acknowledgment of beliefs widely held among the people of this country.[20]

This conclusion, and the reasoning behind it, not only echoes the conservative ideology that permitted the theistic language in the Pledge of Allegiance in *Elk Grove v. Newdow*, it also directly inspired Justice Anthony Kennedy's similar decision for the Court here in *Town of Greece v. Galloway.*

* * *

Town of Greece v. Galloway (2014)

Full Title

Town Of Greece, New York, Petitioner v. Susan Galloway et al.

Official Citation

572 U. S. ____
Argued: November 6, 2013
Decided: May 5, 2014

Author

Justice Anthony Kennedy

Syllabus

Since 1999, the monthly town board meetings in Greece, New York, have opened with a roll call, a recitation of the Pledge of Allegiance, and a prayer given by clergy selected from the congregations listed in a local directory. While the prayer program is open to all creeds, nearly all of the local congregations are Christian; thus, nearly all of the participating prayer givers have been too. Respondents, citizens who attend meetings to speak on local issues, filed suit, alleging that the town violated the First Amendment's Establishment Clause by preferring Christians over other prayer givers and by sponsoring sectarian prayers. They sought to limit the town to 'inclusive and ecumenical' prayers that referred only to a 'generic God.' The District Court upheld the prayer practice on summary judgment, finding no impermissible preference for Christianity; concluding that the Christian identity of most of the prayer givers reflected the predominantly Christian character of the town's congregations, not an official policy or practice of discriminating against minority faiths; finding that the First Amendment did not require Greece to invite clergy from congregations beyond its borders to achieve religious diversity; and rejecting the theory that legislative prayer must be nonsectarian. The Second Circuit reversed, holding that some aspects of the prayer program, viewed in their totality by a reasonable observer, conveyed the message that Greece was endorsing Christianity.

Held

The judgment is reversed.

[*Susan Galloway and Linda Stephens, Plaintiffs–Appellants, v. Town of Greece, Defendant–Appellee, and John Auberger, in his Official Capacity as Town of Greece Supervisor, Defendant* (2012), Second Circuit Court of Appeals, citation: 681 F. 3d 20], reversed.

Justice Kennedy delivered the opinion of the Court, except as to Part II–B, concluding that the town's prayer practice does not violate the Establishment Clause.

(a) Legislative prayer, while religious in nature, has long been understood as compatible with the Establishment Clause.[21] In [*Marsh v. Chambers* (1983)], the Court concluded that it was not necessary to define the Establishment Clause's precise boundary in order to uphold Nebraska's practice of employing a legislative chaplain because history supported the conclusion that the specific practice was permitted. The First Congress voted to appoint and pay official chaplains shortly after approving language for the First Amendment, and both Houses have maintained the office virtually uninterrupted since then.[22] A majority of the States have also had a consistent practice of legislative prayer.[23] There is historical precedent for the practice of opening local legislative meetings with prayer as well. *Marsh* teaches that the Establishment Clause must be interpreted 'by reference to historical practices and understandings.'[24] Thus, any test must acknowledge a practice that was accepted by the Framers and has withstood the critical scrutiny of time and political change. The Court's inquiry, then, must be to determine whether the prayer practice in the town of Greece fits within the tradition long followed in Congress and the state legislatures.

(b) Respondents' insistence on nonsectarian prayer is not consistent with this tradition. The prayers in *Marsh* were consistent with the First Amendment not because they espoused only a generic theism but because the Nation's history and tradition have shown that prayer in this limited context could 'coexis[t] with the principles of disestablishment and religious freedom.'[25] Dictum in County of Allegheny suggesting that *Marsh* permitted only prayer with no overtly Christian references is irreconcilable with the facts, holding, and reasoning of *Marsh*, which instructed that the 'content of the prayer is not of concern to judges,' provided 'there is no indication that the prayer opportunity has been exploited to proselytize or advance any one, or to disparage any other, faith or belief.'[26] To hold that invocations must be nonsectarian would force the legislatures sponsoring prayers and the courts deciding these cases to act as supervisors and censors of religious speech, thus involving government in religious matters to a far greater degree than is the case under the town's current practice of neither editing nor approving prayers in advance nor criticizing their content after the fact. Respondents' contrary arguments are unpersuasive. It is doubtful that consensus could be reached as to what qualifies as a generic or nonsectarian prayer. It would also be unwise to conclude that only those religious words acceptable to the majority are permissible, for the First Amendment is not a majority rule and government may not seek to define permissible categories of religious speech. In rejecting the suggestion that legislative prayer must be nonsectarian, the Court does not imply that no constraints remain on its content. The relevant constraint derives from the prayer's place at the opening of legislative sessions, where it is meant to lend gravity to the occasion and reflect values long part of the Nation's heritage. From the Nation's earliest days, invocations have been addressed to assemblies comprising many different creeds, striving for the idea that people of many faiths may be united in a community of tolerance and devotion, even if they disagree as to religious doctrine. The prayers delivered in Greece do not fall outside this tradition. They may have invoked, e.g., the name of Jesus, but they also invoked universal themes, e.g., by calling for a 'spirit of cooperation.' Absent a pattern of prayers that over time denigrate, proselytize, or betray an impermissible government purpose, a challenge based solely on the content of a particular prayer will not likely establish a constitutional violation.[27] Finally, so long as the town maintains a policy of nondiscrimination, the Constitution does not require it to search beyond its borders for non-Christian prayer givers in an effort to achieve religious balancing.

Justice Kennedy, joined by [Chief Justice John G. Roberts] and Justice Alito, concluded in Part II–B that a fact-sensitive inquiry that considers both the setting in which the prayer arises and the audience to whom it is directed shows that the town is not coercing its citizens to engage in a religious observance. The prayer opportunity is evaluated against the backdrop of a historical practice showing that prayer has become part of the Nation's heritage and tradition. It is presumed that the reasonable observer is acquainted with this tradition and understands that its purposes are to lend gravity to public proceedings and to acknowledge the place religion holds in the lives of many private citizens. Furthermore, the principal audience for these invocations is not the public, but the lawmakers themselves. And those lawmakers did not direct the public to participate, single out dissidents for opprobrium, or indicate that their decisions might be influenced by a person's acquiescence in the prayer opportunity. Respondents claim that the prayers gave them offense and made them feel excluded and disrespected, but offense does not equate to coercion. In contrast to *Lee v. Weisman* (1992),[28] where the Court found coercive a religious invocation at a high school graduation,[29] the record here does not suggest that citizens are dissuaded from leaving the meeting room during the prayer, arriving late, or making a later protest. That the prayer in Greece is delivered during the opening ceremonial portion of the town's meeting, not the policymaking portion, also suggests that its purpose and effect are to acknowledge religious leaders and their institutions, not to exclude or coerce nonbelievers.

Justice Thomas, joined by Justice Scalia as to Part II, agreed that the town's prayer practice does not violate the Establishment Clause, but concluded that, even if the Establishment Clause were properly incorporated against the States through the Fourteenth Amendment, the Clause is not violated by the kind of subtle pressures respondents allegedly suffered, which do not amount to actual legal coercion. The municipal prayers in this case bear no resemblance to the coercive state establishments that existed at the founding, which exercised government power in order to exact financial support of the church, compel religious observance, or control religious doctrine.

[Justice Kennedy] delivered the opinion of the Court, except as to Part II–B. [Justices Roberts and Alito] joined the opinion in full, and [Justices Scalia and Thomas] joined except as to Part II–B. [Justice Alito] filed a concurring opinion, in which [Justice Scalia] joined. [Justice Thomas] filed an opinion concurring in part and concurring in the judgment, in which [Justice Scalia] joined as to Part II. [Justice Breyer] filed a dissenting opinion. [Justice Kagan] filed a dissenting opinion, in which [Justices Ginsburg, Breyer, and Sotomayor] joined.

Opinion

Justice Kennedy delivered the opinion of the Court, except as to Part II–B.

The Court must decide whether the town of Greece, New York, imposes an impermissible establishment of religion by opening its monthly board meetings with a prayer. It must be concluded, consistent with the Court's opinion in *Marsh v. Chambers* (1983), that no violation of the Constitution has been shown.

I

Greece, a town with a population of 94,000, is in upstate New York. For some years, it began its monthly town board meetings with a moment of silence. In 1999, the newly elected town supervisor, John Auberger, decided to replicate the prayer practice he had found meaningful while serving in the county legislature. Following the roll call and recitation of the Pledge of Allegiance, Auberger would invite a local clergyman to the front of the room to deliver an invocation. After the prayer, Auberger would thank the minister for serving as the board's 'chaplain for the month' and present him with a commemorative plaque. The prayer was intended to place town board members in a solemn and deliberative frame of mind, invoke divine guidance in town affairs, and follow a tradition practiced by Congress and dozens of state legislatures.[30]

The town followed an informal method for selecting prayer givers, all of whom were unpaid volunteers. A town employee would call the congregations listed in a local directory until she found a minister available for that month's meeting. The town eventually compiled a list of willing 'board chaplains' who had accepted invitations and agreed to return in the future. The town at no point excluded or denied an opportunity to a would-be prayer giver. Its leaders maintained that a minister or layperson of any persuasion, including an atheist, could give the invocation. But nearly all of the congregations in town were Christian; and from 1999 to 2007, all of the participating ministers were too.

Greece neither reviewed the prayers in advance of the meetings nor provided guidance as to their tone or content, in the belief that exercising any degree of control over the prayers would infringe both the free exercise and speech rights of the ministers.[31] The town instead left the guest clergy free to compose their own devotions. The resulting prayers often sounded both civic and religious themes. Typical were invocations that asked the divinity to abide at the meeting and bestow blessings on the community:

> Lord we ask you to send your spirit of servanthood upon all of us gathered here this evening to do your work for the benefit of all in our community. We ask you to bless our elected and appointed officials so they may deliberate with wisdom and act with courage. Bless the members of our community who come here to speak before the board so they may state their cause with honesty and humility. [. . .] Lord we ask you to bless us all, that everything we do here tonight will move you to welcome us one day into your kingdom as good and faithful servants. We ask this in the name of our brother Jesus. Amen.[32]

Some of the ministers spoke in a distinctly Christian idiom; and a minority invoked religious holidays, scripture, or doctrine, as in the following prayer:

> Lord, God of all creation, we give you thanks and praise for your presence and action in the world. We look with anticipation to the celebration of Holy Week and Easter.

> It is in the solemn events of next week that we find the very heart and center of our Christian faith. We acknowledge the saving sacrifice of Jesus Christ on the cross. We draw strength, vitality, and confidence from his resurrection at Easter. [. . .] We pray for peace in the world, an end to terrorism, violence, conflict, and war. We pray for stability, democracy, and good government in those countries in which our armed forces are now serving, especially in Iraq and Afghanistan. [. . .] Praise and glory be yours, O Lord, now and forever more. Amen.[33]

Respondents Susan Galloway and Linda Stephens attended town board meetings to speak about issues of local concern, and they objected that the prayers violated their religious or philosophical views. At one meeting, Galloway admonished board members that she found the prayers 'offensive,' 'intolerable,' and an affront to a 'diverse community.'[34] After respondents complained that Christian themes pervaded the prayers, to the exclusion of citizens who did not share those beliefs, the town invited a Jewish layman and the chairman of the local Baha'i temple to deliver prayers. A Wiccan priestess who had read press reports about the prayer controversy requested, and was granted, an opportunity to give the invocation.

Galloway and Stephens brought suit in the United States District Court for the Western District of New York. They alleged that the town violated the First Amendment's Establishment Clause by preferring Christians over other prayer givers and by sponsoring sectarian prayers, such as those given 'in Jesus' name.'[35] They did not seek an end to the prayer practice, but rather requested an injunction that would limit the town to 'inclusive and ecumenical' prayers that referred only to a 'generic God' and would not associate the government with any one faith or belief.[36]

The District Court on summary judgment upheld the prayer practice as consistent with the First Amendment. It found no impermissible preference for Christianity, noting that the town had opened the prayer program to all creeds and excluded none. Although most of the prayer givers were Christian, this fact reflected only the predominantly Christian identity of the town's congregations, rather than an official policy or practice of discriminating against minority faiths. The District Court found no authority for the proposition that the First Amendment required Greece to invite clergy from congregations beyond its borders in order to achieve a minimum level of religious diversity.

The District Court also rejected the theory that legislative prayer must be nonsectarian. The court began its inquiry with the opinion in *Marsh v. Chambers* (1983), 463 U.S. 783, which permitted prayer in state legislatures by a chaplain paid from the public purse, so long as the prayer opportunity was not 'exploited to proselytize or advance any one, or to disparage any other, faith or belief.'[37] With respect to the prayer in Greece, the District Court concluded that references to Jesus, and the occasional request that the audience stand for the prayer, did not amount to impermissible proselytizing. It located in *Marsh* no additional requirement that the prayers be purged of sectarian content. In this regard the court quoted recent invocations offered in the U. S. House of Representatives 'in the name of our Lord Jesus Christ,'[38] and situated prayer in this context as part a long tradition. Finally, the trial court noted this Court's statement in *County of Allegheny v. American Civil Liberties Union, Greater Pittsburgh Chapter* (1989), that the prayers in *Marsh* did not offend the Establishment Clause 'because the particular chaplain had "removed all references to Christ."'[39] But the District Court did not read that statement to mandate that legislative prayer be nonsectarian, at least in circumstances where the town permitted clergy from a variety of faiths to give invocations. By welcoming many viewpoints, the District Court concluded, the town would be unlikely to give the impression that it was affiliating itself with any one religion.

The Court of Appeals for the Second Circuit reversed.[40] It held that some aspects of the prayer program, viewed in their totality by a reasonable observer, conveyed the message that Greece was endorsing Christianity. The town's failure to promote the prayer opportunity to the public, or to invite ministers from congregations outside the town limits, all but 'ensured a Christian viewpoint.'[41] Although the court found no inherent problem in the sectarian content of the prayers, it concluded that the 'steady drumbeat' of Christian prayer, unbroken by invocations from other faith traditions, tended to affiliate the town with Christianity.[42] Finally, the court found it relevant that guest clergy sometimes spoke on behalf of all present at the meeting, as by saying 'let us pray,' or by asking audience members to stand and bow their heads: 'The invitation [. . .] to participate in the prayer [. . .] placed audience members who are nonreligious or adherents of non-Christian religion in the awkward position of either participating in prayers invoking beliefs they did not share or appearing to show disrespect for the invocation.'[43] That board members bowed their heads or made the sign of the cross further conveyed the message that the town endorsed Christianity. The Court of Appeals emphasized that it was the 'interaction of the facts present in this case,' rather than any single element, that rendered the prayer unconstitutional.[44]

Having granted certiorari to decide whether the town's prayer practice violates the Establishment Clause, the Court now reverses the judgment of the Court of Appeals.

II

In *Marsh v. Chambers* (1983), the Court found no First Amendment violation in the Nebraska Legislature's practice of opening its sessions with a prayer delivered by a chaplain paid from state funds. The decision concluded that legislative prayer, while religious in nature, has long been understood as compatible with the Establishment Clause. As practiced by Congress since the framing of the Constitution, legislative prayer lends gravity to public business, reminds lawmakers to transcend petty differences in pursuit of a higher purpose, and expresses a common aspiration to a just and peaceful society.[45] The Court has considered this symbolic expression to be a 'tolerable acknowledgement of beliefs widely held,'[46] rather than a first, treacherous step towards establishment of a state church.

Marsh is sometimes described as 'carving out an exception' to the Court's Establishment Clause jurisprudence, because it sustained legislative prayer without subjecting the practice to 'any of the formal "tests" that have traditionally structured' this inquiry.[47] The Court in *Marsh* found those tests unnecessary because history supported the conclusion that legislative invocations are compatible with the Establishment Clause. The First Congress made it an early item of business to appoint and pay official chaplains, and both the House and Senate have maintained the office virtually uninterrupted since that time.[48] When *Marsh* was decided, in 1983, legislative prayer had persisted in the Nebraska Legislature for more than a century, and the majority of the other States also had the same, consistent practice.[49] Although no information has been cited by the parties to indicate how many local legislative bodies open their meetings with prayer, this practice too has historical precedent.[50]

Yet *Marsh* must not be understood as permitting a practice that would amount to a constitutional violation if not for its historical foundation. The case teaches instead that the Establishment Clause must be interpreted 'by reference to historical practices and understandings.'[51] That the First Congress provided for the appointment of chaplains only days after approving language for the First Amendment demonstrates that the Framers considered legislative prayer a benign acknowledgment of religion's role in society.[52] In the 1850's, the judiciary committees in both the House and Senate reevaluated the practice of official chaplaincies after receiving petitions to abolish the office. The committees concluded that the office posed no threat of an establishment because lawmakers were not compelled to attend the daily prayer;[53] no faith was excluded by law, nor any favored;[54] and the cost of the chaplain's salary imposed a vanishingly small burden on taxpayers.[55] *Marsh* stands for the proposition that it is not necessary to define the precise boundary of the Establishment Clause where history shows that the specific practice is permitted. Any test the Court adopts must acknowledge a practice that was accepted by the Framers and has withstood the critical scrutiny of time and political change.[56] A test that would sweep away what has so long been settled would create new controversy and begin anew the very divisions along religious lines that the Establishment Clause seeks to prevent.[57]

The Court's inquiry, then, must be to determine whether the prayer practice in the town of Greece fits within the tradition long followed in Congress and the state legislatures. Respondents assert that the town's prayer exercise falls outside that tradition and transgresses the Establishment Clause for two independent but mutually reinforcing reasons. First, they argue that *Marsh* did not approve prayers containing sectarian language or themes, such as the prayers offered in Greece that referred to the 'death, resurrection, and ascension of the Savior Jesus Christ,'[58] and the 'saving sacrifice of Jesus Christ on the cross.'[59] Second, they argue that the setting and conduct of the town board meetings create social pressures that force non-adherents to remain in the room or even feign participation in order to avoid offending the representatives who sponsor the prayer and will vote on matters citizens bring before the board. The sectarian content of the prayers compounds the subtle coercive pressures, they argue, because the nonbeliever who might tolerate ecumenical prayer is forced to do the same for prayer that might be inimical to his or her beliefs.

A

Respondents maintain that prayer must be nonsectarian, or not identifiable with any one religion; and they fault the town for permitting guest chaplains to deliver prayers that 'use overtly Christian terms' or 'invoke specifics of Christian theology.'[60] A prayer is fitting for the public sphere, in their view, only if it contains the 'most general, nonsectarian reference to God,'[61] and eschews mention of doctrines associated with any one faith.[62] They argue that prayer which contemplates 'the workings of the Holy Spirit, the events of Pentecost, and the belief that God "has raised up the Lord Jesus" and "will raise us, in our turn, and put us by His side"' would be impermissible, as would any prayer that reflects dogma particular to a single faith tradition.[63]

An insistence on nonsectarian or ecumenical prayer as a single, fixed standard is not consistent with the tradition of legislative prayer outlined in the Court's cases. The Court found the prayers in *Marsh* consistent with the First Amendment not because they espoused only a generic theism but because our history and tradition have shown that prayer in this limited context could 'coexis[t] with the principles of disestablishment and religious freedom.'[64] The Congress that drafted the First Amendment would have been accustomed to invocations containing explicitly religious themes of the sort respondents find objectionable. One of the Senate's first chaplains, the Rev. William White, gave prayers in a series that included the Lord's Prayer, the Collect for Ash Wednesday, prayers for peace and grace, a general thanksgiving, St. Chrysostom's Prayer, and a prayer seeking 'the grace of our Lord Jesus Christ, &c.'[65] The decidedly Christian nature of these prayers must not be dismissed as the relic of a time when our Nation was less pluralistic than it is today. Congress continues to permit its appointed and visiting chaplains to express themselves in a religious idiom. It acknowledges our growing diversity not by proscribing sectarian content but by welcoming ministers of many creeds.[66]

The contention that legislative prayer must be generic or nonsectarian derives from dictum in *County of Allegheny*, that was disputed when written and has been repudiated by later cases. There the Court held that a crèche placed on the steps of a county courthouse to celebrate the Christmas season violated the Establishment Clause because it had 'the effect of endorsing a patently Christian message.'[67] Four dissenting Justices disputed that endorsement could be the proper test, as it likely would condemn a host of traditional practices that recognize the role religion plays in our society, among them legislative prayer and the 'forthrightly religious' Thanksgiving proclamations issued by nearly every President since Washington.[68] The Court sought to counter this criticism by recasting *Marsh* to permit only prayer that contained no overtly Christian references:

> However history may affect the constitutionality of nonsectarian references to religion by the government, history cannot legitimate practices that demonstrate the government's allegiance to a particular sect or creed. [. . .] The legislative prayers involved in *Marsh* did not violate this principle because the particular chaplain had 'removed all references to Christ.'[69]

This proposition is irreconcilable with the facts of *Marsh* and with its holding and reasoning. *Marsh* nowhere suggested that the constitutionality of legislative prayer turns on the neutrality of its content. The opinion noted that Nebraska's chaplain, the Rev. Robert E. Palmer, modulated the 'explicitly Christian' nature of his prayer and 'removed all references to Christ' after a Jewish law-maker complained.[70] With this footnote, the Court did no more than observe the practical demands placed on a minister who holds a permanent, appointed position in a legislature and chooses to write his or her prayers to appeal to more members, or at least to give less offense to those who object.[71] *Marsh* did not suggest that Nebraska's prayer practice would have failed had the chaplain not acceded to the legislator's request. Nor did the Court imply the rule that prayer violates the Establishment Clause any time it is given in the name of a figure deified by only one faith or creed.[72] To the contrary, the Court instructed that the 'content of the prayer is not of concern to judges,' provided 'there is no indication that the prayer opportunity has been exploited to proselytize or advance any one, or to disparage any other, faith or belief.'[73]

To hold that invocations must be nonsectarian would force the legislatures that sponsor prayers and the courts that are asked to decide these cases to act as supervisors and censors of religious speech, a rule that would involve government in religious matters to a far greater degree than is the case under the town's current practice of neither editing or approving prayers in advance nor criticizing their content after the fact.[74] Our Government is prohibited from prescribing prayers to be recited in our public institutions in order to promote a preferred system of belief or code of moral behavior.[75] It would be but a few steps removed from that prohibition for legislatures to require chaplains to redact the religious content from their message in order to make it acceptable for the public sphere.

Government may not mandate a civic religion that stifles any but the most generic reference to the sacred any more than it may prescribe a religious orthodoxy.[76]

Respondents argue, in effect, that legislative prayer may be addressed only to a generic God. The law and the Court could not draw this line for each specific prayer or seek to require ministers to set aside their nuanced and deeply personal beliefs for vague and artificial ones. There is doubt, in any event, that consensus might be reached as to what qualifies as generic or nonsectarian. Honorifics like 'Lord of Lords' or 'King of Kings' might strike a Christian audience as ecumenical, yet these titles may have no place in the vocabulary of other faith traditions. The difficulty, indeed the futility, of sifting sectarian from nonsectarian speech is illustrated by a letter that a lawyer for the respondents sent the town in the early stages of this litigation. The letter opined that references to 'Father, God, Lord God, and the Almighty' would be acceptable in public prayer, but that references to 'Jesus Christ, the Holy Spirit, and the Holy Trinity' would not.[77] Perhaps the writer believed the former grouping would be acceptable to monotheists. Yet even seemingly general references to God or the Father might alienate nonbelievers or polytheists.[78] Because it is unlikely that prayer will be inclusive beyond dispute, it would be unwise to adopt what respondents think is the next-best option: permitting those religious words, and only those words, that are acceptable to the majority, even if they will exclude some.[79] The First Amendment is not a majority rule, and government may not seek to define permissible categories of religious speech. Once it invites prayer into the public sphere, government must permit a prayer giver to address his or her own God or gods as conscience dictates, unfettered by what an administrator or judge considers to be nonsectarian.

In rejecting the suggestion that legislative prayer must be nonsectarian, the Court does not imply that no constraints remain on its content. The relevant constraint derives from its place at the opening of legislative sessions, where it is meant to lend gravity to the occasion and reflect values long part of the Nation's heritage. Prayer that is solemn and respectful in tone, that invites lawmakers to reflect upon shared ideals and common ends before they embark on the fractious business of governing, serves that legitimate function. If the course and practice over time shows that the invocations denigrate nonbelievers or religious minorities, threaten damnation, or preach conversion, many present may consider the prayer to fall short of the desire to elevate the purpose of the occasion and to unite lawmakers in their common effort. That circumstance would present a different case than the one presently before the Court.

The tradition reflected in *Marsh* permits chaplains to ask their own God for blessings of peace, justice, and freedom that find appreciation among people of all faiths. That a prayer is given in the name of Jesus, Allah, or Jehovah, or that it makes passing reference to religious doctrines, does not remove it from that tradition. These religious themes provide particular means to universal ends. Prayer that reflects beliefs specific to only some creeds can still serve to solemnize the occasion, so long as the practice over time is not 'exploited to proselytize or advance any one, or to disparage any other, faith or belief.'[80]

It is thus possible to discern in the prayers offered to Congress a commonality of theme and tone. While these prayers vary in their degree of religiosity, they often seek peace for the Nation, wisdom for its lawmakers, and justice for its people, values that count as universal and that are embodied not only in religious traditions, but in our founding documents and laws. The first prayer delivered to the Continental Congress by the Rev. Jacob Duché on Sept. 7, 1774, provides an example:

> Be Thou present O God of Wisdom and direct the counsel of this Honorable Assembly; enable them to settle all things on the best and surest foundations; that the scene of blood may be speedily closed; that Order, Harmony, and Peace be effectually restored, and the Truth and Justice, Religion and Piety, prevail and flourish among the people.
>
> Preserve the health of their bodies, and the vigor of their minds, shower down on them, and the millions they here represent, such temporal Blessings as Thou seest expedient for them in this world, and crown them with everlasting Glory in the world to come. All this we ask in the name and through the merits of Jesus Christ, Thy Son and our Saviour, Amen.[81]

From the earliest days of the Nation, these invocations have been addressed to assemblies comprising many different creeds. These ceremonial prayers strive for the idea that people of many faiths may be united in a community of tolerance and devotion. Even those who dis-agree as to religious doctrine may find common ground in the desire to show respect for the divine in all aspects of their lives and being. Our tradition assumes that adult citizens, firm in their own beliefs, can tolerate and perhaps appreciate a ceremonial prayer delivered by a person of a different faith.[82]

The prayers delivered in the town of Greece do not fall outside the tradition this Court has recognized. A number of the prayers did invoke the name of Jesus, the Heavenly Father, or the Holy Spirit, but they also invoked universal themes, as by celebrating the changing of the seasons or calling for a 'spirit of cooperation' among town leaders.[83] Among numerous examples of such prayer in the record is the invocation given by the Rev. Richard Barbour at the September 2006 board meeting:

> Gracious God, you have richly blessed our nation and this community. Help us to remember your generosity and give thanks for your goodness. Bless the elected leaders of the Greece Town Board as they conduct the business of our town this evening. Give them wisdom, courage, discernment and a single-minded desire to serve the common good. We ask your blessing on all public servants, and especially on our police force, firefighters, and emergency medical personnel. [. . .] Respectful of every religious tradition, I offer this prayer in the name of God's only son Jesus Christ, the Lord, Amen.[84]

Respondents point to other invocations that disparaged those who did not accept the town's prayer practice. One guest minister characterized objectors as a 'minority' who are 'ignorant of the history of our country,'[85] while another lamented that other towns did not have 'God-fearing' leaders.[86] Although these two remarks strayed from the rationale set out in *Marsh*, they do not despoil a practice that on the whole reflects and embraces our tradition. Absent a pattern of prayers that over time denigrate, proselytize, or betray an impermissible government purpose, a challenge based solely on the content of a prayer will not likely establish a constitutional violation. *Marsh*, indeed, requires an inquiry into the prayer opportunity as a whole, rather than into the contents of a single prayer.[87]

Finally, the Court disagrees with the view taken by the Court of Appeals that the town of Greece contravened the Establishment Clause by inviting a predominantly Christian set of ministers to lead the prayer. The town made reasonable efforts to identify all of the congregations located within its borders and represented that it would welcome a prayer by any minister or layman who wished to give one. That nearly all of the congregations in town turned out to be Christian does not reflect an aversion or bias on the part of town leaders against minority faiths. So long as the town maintains a policy of nondiscrimination, the Constitution does not require it to search beyond its borders for non-Christian prayer givers in an effort to achieve religious balancing. The quest to promote 'a "diversity" of religious views' would require the town 'to make wholly inappropriate judgments about the number of religions [it] should sponsor and the relative frequency with which it should sponsor each,'[88] a form of government entanglement with religion that is far more troublesome than the current approach.

B

Respondents further seek to distinguish the town's prayer practice from the tradition upheld in *Marsh* on the ground that it coerces participation by non-adherents. They and some amici contend that prayer conducted in the intimate setting of a town board meeting differs in fundamental ways from the invocations delivered in Congress and state legislatures, where the public remains segregated from legislative activity and may not address the body except by occasional invitation. Citizens attend town meetings, on the other hand, to accept awards; speak on matters of local importance; and petition the board for action that may affect their economic interests, such as the granting of permits, business licenses, and zoning variances. Respondents argue that the public may feel subtle pressure to participate in prayers that violate their beliefs in order to please the board members from whom they are about to seek a favorable ruling. In their view the fact that board members in small towns know many of their constituents by name only increases the pressure to conform.

It is an elemental First Amendment principle that government may not coerce its citizens 'to support or participate in any religion or its exercise.'[89] On the record in this case the Court is not persuaded that the town of Greece, through the act of offering a brief, solemn, and respectful prayer to open its monthly meetings, compelled its citizens to engage in a religious observance. The inquiry remains a fact-sensitive one that considers both the setting in which the prayer arises and the audience to whom it is directed.

The prayer opportunity in this case must be evaluated against the backdrop of historical practice. As a practice that has long endured, legislative prayer has become part of our heritage and tradition, part of our expressive idiom, similar to the Pledge of Allegiance, inaugural prayer, or the recitation of 'God save the United States and this honorable Court' at the opening of this Court's sessions.[90] It is presumed that the reasonable observer is acquainted with this tradition and understands that its purposes are to lend gravity to public proceedings and to acknowledge the place religion holds in the lives of many private citizens, not to afford government an opportunity to proselytize or force truant constituents into the pews.[91] That many appreciate these acknowledgments of the divine in our public institutions does not suggest that those who disagree are compelled to join the expression or approve its content.[92]

The principal audience for these invocations is not, indeed, the public but lawmakers themselves, who may find that a moment of prayer or quiet reflection sets the mind to a higher purpose and thereby eases the task of governing. The District Court in *Marsh* described the prayer exercise as 'an internal act' directed at the Nebraska Legislature's 'own members,'[93] rather than an effort to promote religious observance among the public.[94] To be sure, many members of the public find these prayers meaningful and wish to join them. But their purpose is largely to accommodate the spiritual needs of lawmakers and connect them to a tradition dating to the time of the Framers. For members of town boards and commissions, who often serve part-time and as volunteers, ceremonial prayer may also reflect the values they hold as private citizens. The prayer is an opportunity for them to show who and what they are without denying the right to dissent by those who disagree.

The analysis would be different if town board members directed the public to participate in the prayers, singled out dissidents for opprobrium, or indicated that their decisions might be influenced by a person's acquiescence in the prayer opportunity. No such thing occurred in the town of Greece. Although board members themselves stood, bowed their heads, or made the sign of the cross during the prayer, they at no point solicited similar gestures by the public. Respondents point to several occasions where audience members were asked to rise for the prayer. These requests, however, came not from town leaders but from the guest ministers, who presumably are accustomed to directing their congregations in this way and might have done so thinking the action was inclusive, not coercive.[95] Respondents suggest that constituents might feel pressure to join the prayers to avoid irritating the officials who would be ruling on their petitions, but this argument has no evidentiary support. Nothing in the record indicates that town leaders allocated benefits and burdens based on participation in the prayer, or that citizens were received differently depending on whether they joined the invocation or quietly declined. In no instance did town leaders signal disfavor toward nonparticipants or suggest that their stature in the community was in any way diminished. A practice that classified citizens based on their religious views would violate the Constitution, but that is not the case before this Court.

In their declarations in the trial court, respondents stated that the prayers gave them offense and made them feel excluded and disrespected. Offense, however, does not equate to coercion. Adults often encounter speech they find disagreeable; and an Establishment Clause violation is not made out any time a person experiences a sense of affront from the expression of contrary religious views in a legislative forum, especially where, as here, any member of the public is welcome in turn to offer an invocation reflecting his or her own convictions.[96] If circumstances arise in which the pattern and practice of ceremonial, legislative prayer is alleged to be a means to coerce or intimidate others, the objection can be addressed in the regular course. But the showing has not been made here, where the prayers neither chastised dissenters nor attempted lengthy disquisition on religious dogma. Courts remain free to review the pattern of prayers over time to determine whether they comport with the tradition of solemn, respectful prayer approved in *Marsh*, or whether coercion is a real and substantial likelihood. But in the general course legislative bodies do not engage in impermissible coercion merely by exposing constituents to prayer they would rather not hear and in which they need not participate.[97]

This case can be distinguished from the conclusions and holding of *Lee v. Weisman* (1992). There the Court found that, in the context of a graduation where school authorities maintained close supervision over the conduct of the students and the substance of the ceremony, a religious invocation was coercive as to an objecting student.[98] Four Justices dissented in *Lee*, but the circumstances the Court confronted there are not present in this case and do not control its outcome. Nothing in the record suggests that members of the public are dissuaded from leaving the meeting room during the prayer, arriving late, or even, as happened here, making a later protest. In this case, as in *Marsh*, board members and constituents are 'free to enter and leave with little comment and for any number of reasons.'[99] Should nonbelievers choose to exit the room during a prayer they find distasteful, their absence will not stand out as disrespectful or even noteworthy. And should they remain, their quiet acquiescence will not, in light of our traditions, be interpreted as an agreement with the words or ideas expressed. Neither choice represents an unconstitutional imposition as to mature adults, who 'presumably' are 'not readily susceptible to religious indoctrination or peer pressure.'[100]

In the town of Greece, the prayer is delivered during the ceremonial portion of the town's meeting. Board members are not engaged in policymaking at this time, but in more general functions, such as swearing in new police officers, inducting high school athletes into the town hall of fame, and presenting proclamations to volunteers, civic groups, and senior citizens. It is a moment for town leaders to recognize the achievements of their constituents and the aspects of community life that are worth celebrating. By inviting ministers to serve as chaplain for the month, and welcoming them to the front of the room alongside civic leaders, the town is acknowledging the central place that religion, and religious institutions, hold in the lives of those present. Indeed, some congregations are not simply spiritual homes for town residents but also the provider of social services for citizens regardless of their beliefs.[101] The inclusion of a brief, ceremonial prayer as part of a larger exercise in civic recognition suggests that its purpose and effect are to acknowledge religious leaders and the institutions they represent rather than to exclude or coerce nonbelievers.

Ceremonial prayer is but a recognition that, since this Nation was founded and until the present day, many Americans deem that their own existence must be understood by precepts far beyond the authority of government to alter or define and that willing participation in civic affairs can be consistent with a brief acknowledgment of their belief in a higher power, always with due respect for those who adhere to other beliefs. The prayer in this case has a permissible ceremonial purpose. It is not an unconstitutional establishment of religion.

* * *

The town of Greece does not violate the First Amendment by opening its meetings with prayer that comports with our tradition and does not coerce participation by nonadherents.

The judgment of the U. S. Court of Appeals for the Second Circuit is reversed.

It is so ordered.

* * *

Importance

The result of the Court's decision in *Town of Greece v. Galloway* was felt on a national level. While its decision in *Marsh v. Chambers* bent slightly the permissibility of a type of sectarian prayer within the context of a strictly governmental environment, the permission granted here entirely broke through the wall of separation that once divided these two entities. With much broader implications, particularly in that it not only authorized a government endorsement of religious speech, inspiring an influx of sectarian prayer policy enactments and amendments nationwide, it also provided the opportunity for that speech to change, altering in the process what might have once been normatively understood as 'American prayer' by motivating an equally nationwide campaign of non-theistic volunteer 'chaplains' willing to offer non-theistic invocations for the first time.

And these two outcomes represent its principal importance.

Shortly after the announcement of the Court's decision, a number of similar town legislative bodies began instigating or amending their own prayer policies. In Roanoke County, Virginia, for example, a County Supervisor unsuccessfully attempted to draft legislation that would only permit Christian prayers at the start of county board meetings. Also in Virginia, Chesterfield County's Board of Supervisors amended their own prayer policy to only permit invocations given by members of monotheistic religious organizations. In Dillsboro, North Carolina, town officials announced they would begin implementing a prayer policy for the first time, which they would limit to only Christian prayers. Also in North Carolina, Lincoln County Commissioner, Carroll Mitchem declared a year after the Court's decision that non-Christians, especially Muslims, would be excluded from offering any prayers at all. In nearby Rowan County, chaplains repeatedly dismissed continued complaints about the sectarian nature of their prayers, even after the ACLU filed a lawsuit to stop them. In Sussex County, Delaware, the County Council replaced its decades-long opening recitation of the Lord's Prayer, which was halted by a Federal Trial Court in 2012, with a reading of Psalm 23. In Carroll County, Maryland, County Commissioners returned to reciting sectarian prayers after an injunction to halt them by District Judge William D. Quarles Jr. was overturned by *Town of Greece v. Galloway*. And then in October 2015, the Cleveland County School Board in Cleveland County, North Carolina, voted to begin offering invocations at the start of their meetings for the first time. They designed their own policy after the one in the Town of Greece, and invited any volunteer clergy member the opportunity to offer the prayer. In February 2016, that clergy member was Tony Brown, a reverend with the North Carolina Piedmont Church of Wicca.

The same thing occurred two years earlier in November 2014 in Huntsville, Alabama, when Blake Kirk, a Priest of the Oak, Ash, and Thorn tradition of Wicca, offered the invocation at the Huntsville City Council Meeting. Kirk's prayer was the result of the City Council's agreement to be more inclusive of its City's diverse religious background, albeit inspired by the threat of a lawsuit from the Freedom from Religion Foundation. On September 25th, 2014, they went one step further by inviting Kelly McCauley, an Atheist, to provide that evening's invocation.

This trend continued.

The Central Florida Freethought Community kept until January 2016 a running tally of all invocations provided by Atheists and humanists. Prior to May 2014, they recorded nineteen such invocations from March 25th, 2004 to April 4th, 2014, in the states of Arizona, Colorado, Florida, Georgia, Louisiana, Maine, Massachusetts, Michigan, North Carolina, North Dakota, Oklahoma, South Carolina, and Washington. In the State of Florida alone, it counted fifty invocations given between June 2014 and August 2017. Between June 2014 and December 2015, it recorded these invocations nationwide:

- June 2nd, 2014 – Ted Utchen, Wheaton, Illinois
- June 10th, 2014 – Tim Earl, Portage, Wisconsin
- June 12th, 2014 – Justin Vacula, Wilkes-Barre, Pennsylvania
- June 15th, 2014 – Michelle Ritt, Dane County, Wisconsin
- June 17th, 2014 – Joe Beck, Martin County, Florida
- July 15th, 2014 – Dan Courtney, Town of Greece, New York
- July 15th, 2014 – Phil Katrovitz, Vero Beach, Florida
- July 17th, 2014 – Linda Allewalt, Shelbyville, Kentucky
- August 5th, 2014 – Joseph Rhinehart, Largo, Florida

- August 5th, 2014 – Amanda Novotny, Sioux Falls, South Dakota
- August 12th, 2014 – Brooke Mulder, Glendale, Arizona
- August 12th, 2014 – Eric Williams, Colorado Springs, Colorado
- August 20th, 2014 – Dave Kovar, Clearwater, Florida
- September 4th, 2014 – Gloria Julius, St. Petersburg, Florida
- September 8th, 2014 – Robert Ray, Marysville, Washington
- September 25th, 2014 – David Suhor, Escambia County, Florida
- September 25th, 2014 – Kelly McCauley, Huntsville, Alabama
- December 2nd, 2014 – David Marcus, El Paso, Texas
- December 2nd, 2014 – Preston Smith, Lake Worth, Florida
- January 6th, 2015 – George Gold, Chico, California
- April 7th, 2015 – Cheryl Kolbe, Clark County, Washington
- April 13th, 2015 – Robert Ray, Washington State House of Representatives
- April 15th, 2015 – Deana Weaver, Pennsylvania State Senate
- April 16th, 2015 – Cheryl Kolbe, Yamhill County, Oregon
- April 28th, 2015 – Peter Wood, Leon County, Florida
- June 8th, 2015 – Robert Ray, Clark County, Washington
- June 8th, 2015 – Ryan Davis, Sparks, Nevada.
- July 16th, 2015 – Warren Geltch, Orange County Board of County Commissioners
- September 10th, 2015 – Loren Kahle, Longwood, Florida
- December 28th, 2015 – Steven Belstra, Grandville, Michigan[102]

On July 25th, 2014, this trend came full circle when Dan Courtney, a local resident in the Town of Greece, gave a secular invocation before its Town Meeting. He was joined by Ronald Lindsay, the Executive Director of the Center for Inquiry, Gregory M. Lipper, the Senior Litigation Counsel for Americans United, Susan Galloway and Linda Stephens, Annie Laurie Gaylor of the Freedom from Religion Foundation, and David Niose of the American Humanist Association. Focusing on the sacred principles set forth in the Declaration of Independence, he said:

> Freethinkers, atheists, non-believers, whatever label you wish, this group comprises a significant part of our population. I am honored to be providing an invocation on their behalf, and on behalf of all the citizens of the town of Greece. On July 4th, 1776, the 56 men, who pledged their lives to the document that changed the course of history, agreed to the central tenet that, 'Governments are instituted among Men, deriving their just powers from the consent of the governed.' More than 238 years later this central premise still echoes, however faintly, from the town hall to the white columned halls of Washington. Yet this premise, this foundation necessary for a free and flourishing society, is today, more than ever, under assault. This central pillar of a free society; this notion that is deeply heretical to authoritarian culture, proclaims that it is from the people that moral authority is derived. It is that within us, the citizens, that knowledge and wisdom must emerge. The preservation of this premise does not come from accepting the status quo, but by asserting our rights and exercising our duties. That this premise still endures testifies to its truth, and we can say with confidence that it is in seeking the counsel of our conscience that we find the beginning of wisdom. It is in the exercise of our duty as citizens that we find the beginning of knowledge. We, as citizens, the beginning and the end, the alpha and the omega of our destiny are not, as the great philosopher Immanuel Kant warned,

> mere means to the ends of another, but we are ends in ourselves. This basic premise, this profound idea, guides us such that we need not kneel to any king, and we need not bow to any tyrant. So I ask all officials present here, as guarantors of our founder's revolutionary proclamation, to heed the counsel of the governed; to seek the wisdom of all citizens, and to honor the enlightened wisdom and the profound courage of those 56 brave men. Thank you.[103]

The language of this invocation, as well as the continued acceptance of freethinkers, Atheists, and humanists as valid chaplains across America,[104] speaks to the leading implication of the Court's decision in *Town of Greece v. Galloway*. And while the decision itself, as a discursive entity, provides for us an insight into the Court's further division across ideological lines – the five Justices in the majority were Catholic, while three of the Justices in the minority were Jewish – it also provides an insight into how these same freethinkers, Atheists, and humanists are continuing to re-shape the larger meaning of 'religion' in America. And this is due to the fact that, though this decision seemed, on the surface at least, to benefit Christian-Americans over non-Christian or Atheist ones, the resulting inclusion of the latter in prayer policies nationwide has had the opposite effect. Rather like a reversal of the result of *Abington v. Schempp*: where in that instance, prayers were removed from public schools because of their unconstitutionality, in this one, because they were deemed constitutional, their very content changed to accommodate the religious diversity of those people permitted to offer them. To clarify this point more specifically, consider this statement from the joint conclusion by Chief Justice Roberts and Justices Kennedy and Alito:

> Ceremonial prayer is but a recognition that, since this Nation was founded and until the present day, many Americans deem that their own existence must be understood by precepts far beyond the authority of government to alter or define and that willing participation in civic affairs can be consistent with a brief acknowledgment of their belief in a higher power, always with due respect for those who adhere to other beliefs. The prayer in this case has a permissible ceremonial purpose. It is not an unconstitutional establishment of religion.[105]

With the inclusion of non-Christian, Atheist, and generally secular invocations at Town Meetings nationwide, the traditional notions cited here as justification for legislative prayer have begun to evolve. And with that evolution the 'higher power' acknowledged within the language of those prayers has likewise started to change. The end result being that what might have once been thought of as an easily defined American tradition of invoking a higher power in order to establish a 'solemn and deliberative mood,' is now no longer so simple. Especially now that the higher power invoked by chaplains nationwide is being described in wholly secular terms.

Notes

1 *Town of Greece v. Galloway* (2014), citation: 572 U.S. ___.
2 *Town of Greece v. Galloway* (2nd Circuit Court of Appeals, 2012), citation: 681 F.3d 20.
3 *Galloway v. Town of Greece* (United States District Court for the Western District of New York, 2010), citation: 732 F.Supp.2d 195.
4 Ibid.
5 Ibid.

6 Plaintiff's Statement of Facts, cited in *Galloway v. Town of Greece* (U.S. District Court for the Western District of New York, 2010).
7 *Town of Greece v. Galloway* (2nd Circuit Court of Appeals, 2012).
8 Ibid.
9 Plaintiff's Statement of Facts, paragraph 411, cited in *Galloway v. Town of Greece* (U.S. District Court for the Western District of New York, 2010).
10 Deposition of Linda Stephens, 12–36, cited in Plaintiff's Statement of Facts, paragraph 411, cited in *Galloway v. Town of Greece* (U.S. District Court for the Western District of New York, 2010).
11 Plaintiff's Complaint, paragraphs 1–3, cited in *Galloway v. Town of Greece* (U.S. District Court for the Western District of New York, 2010).
12 Defendant's Memo of Law, 9, cited in *Galloway v. Town of Greece* (U.S. District Court for the Western District of New York, 2010).
13 Ibid., 18.
14 *Town of Greece v. Galloway* (2nd Circuit Court of Appeals, 2012), 34.
15 In its decision, the District Court described Chambers as 'not a Christian,' which was both accurate, and incomplete. Chambers is (at the time of this writing) the longest-serving State Senator in Nebraska, having served since 1971, excluding the term between 2009 and 2013 in which a Term Limit amendment forced him out of office in 2008. He was re-elected in 2012. He is also the longest-serving African-American. Over the years he has been described as 'non-Christian,' 'nonreligious,' and an 'Atheist.' In 2008 he filed a lawsuit against God, partly to seek an injunction that would cease God's 'harmful activities,' and partly to prove a point concerning the ease with which the public could file such frivolous lawsuits. In 2014 he unsuccessfully introduced a bill that would require churches to pay taxes. In 2005 he received the Freedom from Religion Foundation's 'Hero of the First Amendment Award,' as well as its 'Emperor Has No Clothes Award' in 2015, which celebrates individuals who 'speak plainly' about the shortcomings of religion by public figures. In 2016 he was awarded the American Humanist Association's Lifetime Achievement Award. Regardless of all of this, though, he has also openly rejected the label 'Atheist,' stating for example in his acceptance speech for the 'Emperor Has No Clothes' award:

> You know why I will not accept the term atheist? I've never referred to myself as an atheist and when other people hang that label on me, I tell them there are only two labels I accept: my name, which my mother gave me, and black.

Furthermore, in neither the 8th Circuit Court of Appeals decision, nor the one made by the Supreme Court, was Chambers described as anything other than 'Senator' or 'respondent.' Which means that they were decided with respect to the constitutionality of the Legislature's prayer policy, rather than his beliefs. As such, because the more distinct Atheism of Linda Stephens played a direct part in the Court's decision in *Town of Greece v. Galloway*, it offers a much more accessible discourse concerning its discussion of American Atheism than *Marsh*, which is why I chose not to include the latter, in full, within this book.

16 *Marsh v. Chambers* (1983), 463 U.S. 783, 786.
17 *Marsh v. Chambers* (1983), 788; citing *Senate Journal*, 1st Congress, 1st Session, 10 (1820 ed.).
18 *Marsh v. Chambers* (1983), 788; citing the *2nd Annals of Congress*, 2180; section 4, 1 Statute, 71.
19 *Marsh v. Chambers* (1983), 788.
20 Ibid., 792.
21 See *Marsh v. Chambers* (1983).
22 See *Marsh v. Chambers* (1983), 787–789, and footnote 10.
23 Ibid., 788–790, and footnote 11.
24 *County of Allegheny v. American Civil Liberties Union, Greater Pittsburgh Chapter* (1989), citation: 492 U.S. 573.
25 *Marsh v. Chambers* (1983), 786.
26 Ibid., 794–795.
27 See ibid., 794–795.
28 *Lee v. Weisman* (1992), citation: 505 U.S. 577. *Lee v. Weisman* dealt with the question of whether or not a public school could sponsor a religious leader (in this instance a Rabbi) in

conducting even non-sectarian prayer. The Court ruled that the Establishment Clause forbids such things.

29 Ibid., 592–594.

30 App. 22a–25a. In Justice Kennedy's opinion, citations to the initial application delivered to the court are made under the distinction 'App.' They will continue in this style in this transcription.

31 Ibid., 22a.

32 Ibid., 45a.

33 Ibid., 88a–89a.

34 Complaint in No. 08-cv-6088 (WDNY), [paragraph] 66.

35 *Galloway v. Town of Greece* (United States District Court for the Western District of New York, 2010), citation: 732 F.Supp.2d 195, 203.

36 Ibid., 210, 241.

37 *Marsh v. Chambers* (1983), 794–795.

38 For example, The 156th Congressional Record, H5205, June 30, 2010.

39 *County of Allegheny v. American Civil Liberties Union, Greater Pittsburgh Chapter* (1989), 603.

40 *Town of Greece v. Galloway* (2nd Circuit Court of Appeals, 2012), citation: 681 F.3d 20, 34.

41 Ibid., 30–31.

42 Ibid., 32.

43 Ibid.

44 Ibid., 33.

45 See *Lynch v. Donnelly* (1984), citation: 465 U.S. 668, 693 (Justice O'Connor, concurring); and A. Adams and C. Emmerich, *A Nation Dedicated to Religious Liberty* (Philadelphia: University of Pennsylvania Press, 1990), 83.

46 *Marsh v. Chambers* (1983), 792.

47 Ibid., 796, and 813 (Justice Brennan, dissenting).

48 See ibid., 787–789, and footnote 10; as well as Noah Feldman, *Divided by God* (New York: Farrar, Strauss, and Giroux, 2005), 109. Also see *Marsh v. Chambers* (1983), 791–792, and footnote 12 (noting dissenting views among the Framers); and Elizabeth Fleet, 'Madison's "Detached Memoranda,"' (*William and Mary Quarterly*, 3rd Series, Vol. 3, No. 4, 1946), 558–559 (hereinafter 'Madison's Detached Memoranda').

49 *Marsh v. Chambers* (1983), 788–790, and footnote 11.

50 See the *Reports of Proceedings of the City Council of Boston* for the year commencing January 1st, 1909, and ending February 5th, 1910, pp. 1–2 (1910), particularly Rev. Arthur Little: 'And now we desire to invoke Thy presence, Thy blessing, and Thy guidance upon those who are gathered here this morning.' Compare this to *Marsh v. Chambers* (1983), 792: 'In light of the unambiguous and unbroken history of more than 200 years, there can be no doubt that the practice of opening legislative sessions with a prayer has become part of the fabric of our society.'

51 *County of Allegheny v. American Civil Liberties Union, Greater Pittsburgh Chapter* (1989), 670 (Justice Kennedy, concurring in judgment in part and dissenting in part).

52 David P. Currie, *The Constitution in Congress: The Federalist Period 1789–1801* (Chicago: University of Chicago Press, 1997), 12–13.

53 *Report of the Committee of the Senate* (32nd Congress, 2nd Session, No. 376, 1853), 2.

54 Ibid., 3.

55 *House Report* (33rd Congress, 1st Session, No. 124, 1854), 6.

56 *County of Allegheny v. American Civil Liberties Union, Greater Pittsburgh Chapter* (1989), 670 (opinion of Justice Kennedy); see also *Abington v. Schempp* (1963), citation: 374 U.S. 203, 294 (Justice Brennan, concurring: '[T]he line we must draw between the permissible and the impermissible is one which accords with history and faithfully reflects the understanding of the Founding Fathers').

57 See *Van Orden v. Perry* (2005), citation: 545 U.S. 677–704 (Justice Breyer, concurring in judgment).

58 App. 129a.

59 Ibid., 88a.

60 *Brief for Respondents*, 20.

61 Ibid., 33 (quoting Michael J. Meyerson, *Endowed by Our Creator: The Birth of Religious Freedom in America* (New Haven: Yale University Press, 2012), 11–12.
62 *Brief for Respondents*, 32–33.
63 Ibid., 34 (quoting App. 89a, and citing ibid., 56a, 123a, and 134a).
64 *Marsh v. Chambers* (1983), 786.
65 Letter from W. White to H. Jones (December 29th, 1830), in Bird Wilson, *Memoir of the Life of the Right Reverend William White, D.D., Bishop of the Protestant Episcopal Church in the State of Pennsylvania* (Philadelphia: James Kay, Jun. & Brother, 1839), 322; see also *New Hampshire Patriot & State Gazette*, December 15th, 1823, p. 1 (describing a Senate prayer addressing the 'Throne of Grace'); *Congressional Globe*, 37th Congress, 1st Session, 1861, 2 (reciting the Lord's Prayer).
66 See, e.g., 160 Congressional Record, S1329, March 6th, 2014 (Dalai Lama: 'I am a Buddhist monk – a simple Buddhist monk – so we pray to Buddha and all other Gods'); 159 Congressional Record, H7006, November 13th, 2013 (Rabbi Joshua Gruenberg: 'Our God and God of our ancestors, Everlasting Spirit of the Universe'); 159 Congressional Record, H3024, June 4th, 2013 (Satguru Bodhinatha Veylanswami: Hindu scripture declares, without equivocation, that the highest of high ideals is to never knowingly harm anyone'); 158 Congressional Record, H5633, August 2nd, 2012 (Imam Nayyar Imam: 'The final prophet of God, Muhammad, peace be upon him, stated: "The leaders of a people are a representation of their deeds"').
67 *County of Allegheny v. American Civil Liberties Union* (1989), 601.
68 Ibid., 670–671.
69 Ibid., 603 (quoting *Marsh v. Chambers* (1983), 793, footnote 14; footnote omitted).
70 *Marsh v. Chambers* (1983), 793, footnote 14.
71 See Jeremy G. Mallory, 'An Officer of the House Which Chooses Him, and Nothing More: How Should *Marsh v. Chambers* Apply to Rotating Chaplains?' (*The University of Chicago Law Review*, Vol. 73, Iss. 4, 2006), 1445.
72 See *Van Orden v. Perry* (2005), 688, footnote 8 (recognizing that the prayers in *Marsh* were 'often explicitly Christian' and rejecting the view that this gave rise to an establishment violation).
73 *Marsh v. Chambers* (1983), 794–795.
74 Cf. *Hosanna-Tabor Evangelical Lutheran Church and School v. EEOC* (2012), citation: 565 U. S. ___ (slip decision, 13–14).
75 *Engel v. Vitale* (1962), 430.
76 See *Lee v. Weisman* (1992), 590 ('The suggestion that government may establish an official or civic religion as a means of avoiding the establishment of a religion with more specific creeds strikes us as a contradiction that cannot be accepted'); *Abington v. Schempp* (1963), 306 (Justice Goldberg, in concurrence, arguing that 'untutored devotion to the concept of neutrality' must not lead to 'a brooding and pervasive devotion to the secular').
77 App. 21a.
78 *McCreary County v. American Civil Liberties Union of Kentucky* (2005), citation: 545 U.S. 844, 893 (Justice Scalia, dissenting).
79 See *Torcaso v. Watkins* (1961), 495.
80 *Marsh v. Chambers* (1983), 794–795.
81 William J. Federer, *America's God and Country: Encyclopedia of Quotations* (St. Louis: Amerisearch, 2000), 137.
82 See 'Letter from John Adams to Abigail Adams (Sept. 16, 1774),' in Charles Francis Adams, *Familiar Letters of John Adams and His Wife Abigail Adams, During the Revolution* (New York: Hurd and Houghton, 1876), 37–38.
83 App. 31a, 38a.
84 Ibid., 98a–99a.
85 Ibid., 108a.
86 Ibid., 79a.
87 *Marsh v. Chambers* (1983), 794–795.
88 *Lee v. Weisman* (1992), 617 (Justice Souter, concurring).
89 *County of Allegheny v. American Civil Liberties Union, Greater Pittsburgh Chapter* (1989), 659 (Justice Kennedy, concurring in judgment in part and dissenting in part); see also *Van Orden*

v. Perry (2005), 683 (plurality opinion, recognizing that our 'institutions must not press religious observances upon their citizens').

90 See *Lynch v. Donnelly* (1984), 693 (Justice O'Connor, concurring).

91 See *Salazar v. Buono* (2010), citation: 559 U.S. 700–721 (plurality opinion); and *Santa Fe Independent School District v. Doe* (2000), citation: 530 U.S. 290, 308.

92 *West Virginia Board of Education v. Barnette* (1943), citation: 319 U.S. 624, 642.

93 *Chambers v. Marsh* (1980), 588.

94 See also *Lee v. Weisman* (1992), 630, footnote 8 (Justice Souter, concurring: describing *Marsh* as a case 'in which government officials invoke[d] spiritual inspiration entirely for their own benefit'); *Atheists Of Florida, Inc. v. City Of Lakeland, Florida* (11th Circuit Court of Appeals, 2013), citation: 713 F.3d 577, 583 (quoting a city resolution providing for prayer 'for the benefit and blessing of' elected leaders); 'Madison's Detached Memoranda,' 558 (characterizing prayer in Congress as 'religious worship for national representatives'); and the Brief for U.S. Senator Marco Rubio et al. as Amici Curiae 30–33; Brief for 12 Members of Congress as Amici Curiae 6.

95 See App. 69a ('Would you bow your heads with me as we invite the Lord's presence here tonight?'); ibid., 93a ('Let us join our hearts and minds together in prayer'); ibid., 102a ('Would you join me in a moment of prayer?'); ibid., 110a ('Those who are willing may join me now in prayer').

96 See *Elk Grove v. Newdow* (2004), citation: 542 U.S. 1, 44 (Justice O'Connor, concurring: 'The compulsion of which Justice Jackson was concerned [. . .] was of the direct sort – the Constitution does not guarantee citizens a right entirely to avoid ideas with which they disagree').

97 See *County of Allegheny v. American Civil Liberties Union, Greater Pittsburgh Chapter* (1989), 670 (Justice Kennedy, concurring in judgment in part and dissenting in part).

98 *Lee v. Weisman* (1992), 592–594; see also *Santa Fe Independent School District v. Doe* (2000), 312.

99 *Lee v. Weisman* (1992), 597.

100 *Marsh v. Chambers* (1983), 792 (internal quotation marks and citations omitted).

101 See App. 31a (thanking a pastor for his 'community involvement'); and ibid., 44a (thanking a deacon 'for the job that you have done on behalf of our community').

102 Available from the Central Florida Freethought Society webpage under the title 'Invocations': http://cflfreethought.org/invocations (Accessed September 12th, 2017). See also their Facebook page with recent updates: www.facebook.com/cflfreethought.

103 Antonia Blumberg, 'Atheist Invocation In New York Town Meeting Speaks To Shared American Identity,' *The Huffington Post*: www.huffingtonpost.com/2014/07/16/atheist-invocation-greece_n_5591757.html (Accessed September 12th, 2017).

104 See 'Operation Inclusion' as sponsored by Americans United for the Separation of Church and State: www.au.org/content/operation-inclusion; and the American Humanist Society's campaign to ensure chaplains are available throughout the United States: http://thehumanist society.org/invocations/listing/ (Accessed September 12th, 2017).

105 *Town of Greece v. Galloway* (2014).

Part III

Conclusions and consequences

Conclusion

Atheism, an American Religion

Your petitioners are atheists and they define their beliefs as follows. An atheist loves his fellow man instead of god. An atheist believes that heaven is something for which we should work now – here on earth for all men together to enjoy. An atheist believes that he can get no help through prayer but that he must find in himself the inner conviction and strength to meet life, to grapple with it, to subdue it, and enjoy it. An atheist believes that only in a knowledge of himself and a knowledge of his fellow man can he find the understanding that will help to a life of fulfillment. He seeks to know himself and his fellow man rather than to know a god. An atheist believes that a hospital should be built instead of a church. An atheist believes that a deed must be done instead of a prayer said. An atheist strives for involvement in life and not escape into death. He wants disease conquered, poverty vanquished, war eliminated. He wants man to understand and love man. He wants an ethical way of life. He believes that we cannot rely on a god or channel action into prayer nor hope for an end of troubles in a hereafter. He believes that we are our brother's keepers and are keepers of our own lives; that we are responsible persons and the job is here and the time is now.

— Madalyn Murray, petition for writ of certiorari, *Murray v. Curlett*

Atheism, religion, and the United States Supreme Court

The First Amendment to the United States Constitution is quite clear on how 'religion' should be treated in America:

> *Congress shall make no law respecting an establishment of religion, or prohibiting the free exercise thereof.*

But it is also quite vague on what religion actually 'is.'

And perhaps that was the point. Perhaps after the violent and philosophical conflicts that led to the creation of the United States, the men who gathered to draft the First Amendment meant to leave this definition open because they realized that any definition, no matter how practical, would always be deficient.

Instead, they left that job to the American Judiciary, and while there has been on occasion a Justice or two who has taken it upon him or herself to define what they, personally, felt was the 'essence' of religion, what the Court as a whole has done is simply *describe* the religions of the American people, how they practice them, what they mean in their lives, how they affect others, and so on, within the context of the face-to-face crucible that is American judicial review.

And that is where the value of analyzing discourse may most readily be sourced.

We can take these descriptions, as discourse, and analyze them and develop a clearer sense of what might constitute something like 'American religion,' devoid of any sort of prejudice or partiality.

And it works the very same with American Atheism, as each of the case decisions herein have collectively given us a *description* of that.

More than that, though, they have presented an Atheism that is a very distinct type, so that, where I might not conclude here with a 'definition' of the term 'in general,' I do have the ability to conclude here with, if nothing else, a more clarified understanding about how the Atheists in each of these decisions have been treated with respect to their First Amendment rights, as well as how in that process the Court has described them in reference to their relationship with American religion.

In *McCollum v. Board of Education*, Vashti McCollum defended her son's right not to be excluded or ostracized because of his Atheism, and in so doing, was responsible for having removed the practice of sectarian religious education from public schools nationwide.

In *Torcaso v. Watkins*, Roy Torcaso defended his right not to declare a belief in the existence of God in order to swear an oath as a notary public, and in so doing, ensured no such practice would be required nationwide.

In *Abington v. Schempp*, Madalyn Murray defended her son's right not to be excluded or ostracized for his own Atheism, in the same way as James McCollum, and in so doing, was responsible for having removed the practice of Bible recitation and prayer from public schools nationwide.

In *Welsh v. United States*, Elliot Ashton Welsh defended his right to conscientiously object to war, as well as military service in general, regardless of the fact that his 'religious training and belief' was seemingly antithetical to that required for such a distinction by the United States Government. And in so doing, he caused the Supreme Court to re-conceptualize the very meaning of 'religious training and belief' so that it henceforth included doctrines associated with agnosticism and Atheism.

In *Elk Grove v. Newdow*, Michael Newdow defended his daughter's right not to be indoctrinated by religious language, in his argument that the phrase 'under God' in the Pledge of Allegiance represented a violation of her, and his, First Amendment right of religious disestablishment. And in so doing, he provided an outlet for the Court to further solidify its permissibility of such violations in the name 'ceremonial deism.'

In *Hein v. Freedom from Religion Foundation*, the three representatives of the Freedom From Religion Foundation defended the rights of their members, as well as Atheist, humanist, and agnostic American taxpayers nationwide, from financially supporting faith-based social service programs. And in so doing, they provided the Court another opportunity to re-conceptualize the relationship between church and state in America so as to create a more welcoming place for the former within the latter.

And in *Town of Greece v. Galloway*, Susan Galloway and Linda Stephens defended their right not to feel compelled to participate during prayer invocations at the opening of their town's Town Meetings. And in so doing, they instigated a federal acceptance of such prayers nationwide, which in turn has had the result of re-conceptualizing both the meaning and practice of such invocations in order to accommodate the diversity of American religious and non-religious beliefs, including Atheism.

In that each of these examples represents both a constitutional interpretation of Atheism, and thus a re-conceptualization of American religion, what they additionally offer is an opportunity to address here the two thesis questions that I posed in the Introduction:

> If American Atheists are granted the same First Amendment religion protections as other Americans, whose religious beliefs are defined by their adherence to the doctrine, myths, and rituals of ideologies such as Christianity, Judaism, Islam, et al., would American Atheism, by means of these protections, be transformed into an equally accepted American religion? And if so, how would that transformation alter the very meaning of the concept 'American religion,' when the doctrine, myths, and rituals that define an Atheist's adherence to Atheism appear antithetical to the meaning that we have always imparted upon that concept?

This Conclusion will consider both of these questions.

Atheism, an American religion: discursive examples

Answering the question, *is Atheism an American religion*, requires a bit of a summary review of the discourses discussed throughout this book, beginning with a discursive trend inaugurated by Justice Hugo Black in his decision for the Court in *Torcaso v. Watkins*, and his inclusion of 'secular humanism' in a definition of American religions that did not teach 'what would generally be considered a belief in the existence of God.' More accurately, though, this trend actually begins with his concluding statement in *Torcaso v. Watkins*, to which this definition was attached:

> We repeat and again reaffirm that neither a State nor the Federal Government can constitutionally force a person 'to profess a belief or disbelief in any religion.' Neither can constitutionally pass laws or impose requirements which aid all religions as against ***non-believers***, and neither can aid those religions based on a belief in the existence of God as against those religions founded on different beliefs [emphasis mine].[1]

This reference here to 'non-believers' is then repeated seven years later in Justice Fortas' decision for the Court in *Epperson v. Arkansas* (1968).

> Government in our democracy, state and national, must be neutral in matters of religious theory, doctrine, and practice. It may not be hostile to any religion or to the advocacy of ***no-religion***, and it may not aid, foster, or promote one religion or religious theory against another or even against the militant opposite. The First Amendment mandates governmental neutrality between religion and religion, and between religion and ***nonreligion*** [emphases mine].[2]

More specific terminology then appears in Justice Stevens' decision for the Court in *Wallace v. Jaffree* (1985):

> Just as the right to speak and the right to refrain from speaking are complementary components of a broader concept of individual freedom of mind, so also the individual's freedom to choose his own creed is the counterpart of his right to refrain from accepting the creed established by the majority. At one time, it was thought that this

> right merely proscribed the preference of one Christian sect over another, but would not require equal respect for the conscience of the ***infidel***, the ***atheist***, or the adherent of a non-Christian faith such as Islam or Judaism. But when the underlying principle has been examined in the crucible of litigation, the Court has unambiguously concluded that the individual freedom of conscience protected by the First Amendment embraces the right to select any religious faith or ***none at all*** [emphases mine].[3]

And returns to a broader concept in Justice O'Connor's concurrent opinion to *McCreary County v. ACLU* (2005):

> Government may not coerce a person into worshiping against her will, nor prohibit her from worshiping according to it. It may not prefer one religion over another or promote religion over ***nonbelief*** [emphasis mine].[4]

When coupled together with the language of the seven case decisions presented herein, what this discursive trend also reveals is an ideological one, a slow acceptance by the Court of 'non-believers' and 'Atheists' alongside American Christians, Jews, Muslims, and so on, as equal partners deserving of the same rights and protections granted by the First Amendment.

But, we might ask, is this judicial equivalency enough to define these non-believers and Atheists as acting 'religiously' in their beliefs, so that their non-belief and Atheism might then be defined as an American religion?

After all, if the Court treats an Atheist the same as an adherent to a more traditionally defined religion, and by doing so re-conceptualizes the very meaning of 'religion,' does this not mean that the Court has, in essence, re-conceptualized 'Atheism' in the same way? Did we not see this exemplified in the language used by the Court in case decisions such as *Torcaso v. Watkins* or *Welsh v. United States*, where it began to consider the Free Exercise rights of Atheistic non-believers, alongside their Establishment Clause ones?

To address these questions properly, let us look here at a few more examples where the answer might be a bit less ambiguous.

In 2014, District Judge Ancer L. Haggerty, writing for the U.S. District Court for the District of Oregon, Portland Division, ruled in favor of Jason Michael Holden, an inmate within the Federal Correctional Facility in Sheridan, Oregon, who had requested that Humanism, which he identified as his religion, be included in the prison's list of accepted religious preferences. At the time of his request, that list included: Atheist, Adventist, American Indian, Buddhist, Catholic, Church of Christ, Hindu, Jehovah's Witness, Jewish, Messianic, Moorish Science Temple, Mormon, Muslim, Nation of Islam, No Preference, Non-Trinitarian, Orthodox, Other, Pagan, Protestant, Rastafarian, Santeria, Sikh, and Unknown. It also acknowledged the following sub-groups: Spanish Protestant, Native American Church, Native American (Hawaiian), Druid, and Odinist/Asatru. The prison denied his request, and he filed suit. In his decision for the Court, Judge Haggerty defended Holden's complaint that denying his request (which was somewhat moot by the time the Court heard his case, as the prison had officially accepted it by then) was a violation of the Establishment Clause, citing specifically the precedence set by Justice Black's definition in *Torcaso v. Watkins*:

> In *Torcaso v. Watkins*, the Supreme Court said that the government must not 'aid those religions based on a belief in the existence of God as against those religions founded on different beliefs.' Among these latter religions, in a footnote the Court

> included Secular Humanism. Therefore, the Court finds that Secular Humanism is a religion for Establishment Clause purposes and that plaintiffs have alleged sufficient facts to state a claim for relief that is plausible on its face.[5]

In that same year, the 7th Circuit Court of Appeals ruled in favor of the Center for Inquiry, and specifically, the Center's leader in the State of Indiana, Reba Boyd Wooden, in a case dealing with Indiana's policy of marriage solemnization, which limited the legality of conducting a marriage to legislative and judicial officials, or to clergy members of specific 'theistic' religious organizations. Any person who performed a marriage in the State, who did not qualify as one of these types of officials, was in violation of State law. As a 'secular celebrant' in the employ of the Center for Inquiry, which for the purposes of the case defined itself as a 'humanist group' that promoted 'ethical living without belief in a deity,' Wooden had filed suit initially with the U.S. District Court for the Southern District of Indiana requesting an injunction that would permit celebrants, such as her, the same rights as those individuals permitted to conduct marriages. That Court denied her request, arguing three points: any individual could obtain a 'clergy' credential from an organization like the Universal Life Church, and thus qualify to officiate marriages in the state; the Center for Inquiry could request to be defined as a 'religion,' which the state would likely accept; and any 'extra-legal' ceremonies could be conducted, as long as they were followed up by a solemnization conducted by a secular judicial or legislative official. Wooden rejected these options as unacceptable, particularly because none would depict an 'official' marriage ceremony, and because they would also erroneously define the humanism of the Center for Inquiry as a religion. So she appealed to the 7th Circuit.

Judge Frank H. Easterbrook wrote the decision for that Court, in which he argued that the State's restrictive list of qualified individuals represented a Constitutional violation where one type of religious belief (theistic) was privileged over another (non-theistic). What this also created, he concluded, was a dangerous sense of hypocrisy, wherein disingenuous individuals could take advantage of privileges not accessible to genuine ones:

> These examples, and the state's willingness to recognize marriages performed by hypocrites, show that the statute violates the Equal Protection Clause of the Fourteenth Amendment as well as the First Amendment. It is irrational to allow humanists to solemnize marriages if, and only if, they falsely declare that they are a 'religion.' It is absurd to give the Church of Satan, whose high priestess avows that her powers derive from having sex with Satan, and the Universal Life Church, which sells credentials to anyone with a credit card, a preferred position over Buddhists, who emphasize love and peace. A marriage solemnized by a self-declared hypocrite would leave a sour taste in the couple's mouths; like many others, humanists want a ceremony that celebrates their values, not the 'values' of people who will say or do whatever it takes to jump through some statutory hoop.[6]

As such, he reversed the District Court's ruling for the sake of First Amendment 'neutrality,' which in turn classified the humanism of the Center for Inquiry as equal to the religious beliefs of the other 'religious leaders' permitted on the state's list of approved officiants.

However, where these case decisions express an increasing plasticity in the Federal Judiciary's conception of humanism as a 'religious ideology,' they in no way broke the sort of conceptual ground as did the 7th Circuit Court of Appeals' decision in *Kaufman v. McCaughtry* (2005), which directly classified Atheism as an inmate's religion.[7] As such, I will use it to directly address the first of my two thesis questions here.

* * *

By permission of the guidelines of the Department of Corrections for the State of Wisconsin, the Waupun Correctional Institution created 'umbrella religious groups' to accommodate the different religious beliefs of its inmates. These groups could only be run by designated chaplains, approved spiritual leaders, or outside volunteers. Inmates were not permitted to lead them. And in order to better coordinate the attendance of these groups, the institution required incoming inmates to declare, in writing, their preferred religious designation.

James J. Kaufman, who was convicted in 1997 of 1st Degree Sexual Assault of a Child, and in 1998 of possession of child pornography and sexual exploitation of a child, became an inmate with the Waupun Correctional Institution on February 12th, 2002. So that he could attend the Pagan religious group, and under the guidance of the acting Chaplain, Jamyi Witch, he signed on March 12th, 2002 a 'religious preference form' that designated his preferred religious belief as 'Wiccan.' Dissatisfied with the group, and after discussions with Witch about Atheism, Kaufman expressed interest in creating a religious group for those inmates who did not believe in God or gods. As a supplementary description, he defined Atheism as a 'communal type of thing,' with 'no hierarchy or power structure,' and an Atheist as an individual who derives his or her 'ethics' from society, history, and personal experience, and as 'someone who does not believe in the supernatural or in any gods, does not believe in rituals and prayer, basically believes in what you can see and test through science or through your own observations.'[8] On September 3rd, 2002, he submitted the appropriate request form for the creation of a new religious group, crossing out all references to 'religion,' and included a list of resources and further information about Atheist organizations for the benefit of the prison officials who approved such requests. On his form, he described the proposed group as follows:

> I request that a group be formed for atheists within the institution, for the purpose of study and education. Every atheist has the right to determine his own ideas; to express his beliefs in teaching and practice; to assemble for purposes of learning and instructions; to educate others interested in atheism; and to promote a more thorough understanding of all religions, their origins, and their histories. The proposed group should meet once each week, for discussion and learning about the principles and practices which atheism is based upon. Even Atheism falls under this right [of free exercise]. Atheists are entitled to the same freedoms of movement, assembly, and speech, as those inmates who profess a religion.[9]

Because Kaufman was, at the time, the only inmate that had expressed interest in an Atheist group, Witch recommended that the request be denied, which it was, citing the second of three criteria required for the approval of new religious groups:

1. Whether the request is motivated by religious beliefs;
2. Whether other inmates with common ethical, moral or intellectual views share the interest in forming a new religious group; and
3. Whether there is volunteer support to lead the group.[10]

On September 15th, 2002, Kaufman submitted a new request, broadening the description of the group to accommodate 'humanism' and 'free thinking,' with the larger objective of:

> [Stimulating] and [promoting] Freedom of Thought and inquiry concerning religious beliefs, creeds, dogmas, tenets, rituals, and practices. To educate and provide information and literature on all religions, including their origins and history. To teach a progressive life stance, Free of Supernaturalism, to encourage critical thinking between fact and legend.[11]

The prison's Warden, Gary McCaughtry, once again rejected Kaufman's request on September 19th, stating that the Institution was not forming new religious groups at the time.

On November 14th, 2002, Kaufman submitted his request one final time, but it too was denied. In response, he filed suit with the U.S. District Court for the Western District of Wisconsin, claiming that with their rejections, McCaughtry and Witch had violated both religion clauses of the First Amendment.

Writing for the Court, Chief District Judge Barbara Crabb ruled that Kaufman's Free Exercise right was not violated, arguing that, even if his Atheism qualified as a religion – which she based on an assertion made by Judge Richard Posner in his decision in *Reed v. Great Lakes Companies, Inc.* (7th Circuit Court of Appeals, 2003), where he stated, 'if we think of religion as taking a position on divinity, then atheism is indeed a form of religion'[12] – his claim ultimately failed because he could not prove that McCaughtry and Witch had imposed a 'substantial burden' on the practice of his Atheism through their rejection of his request.

As to the Establishment Clause question, she used the definition of religion as applied by the Religious Land Use and Institutionalized Persons Act, as well as the Lemon Test, to conclude that McCaughtry and Witch's rejection did not violate Kaufman's rights. With respect to the first, she argued that the specificity of RLUIPA's definition – 'any exercise of religion, whether or not compelled by, or central to, a system of religious belief' – provided a clearer interpretation of 'religious exercise' than did the First Amendment, which in turn proved that McCaughtry and Witch's rejection of Kaufman's request merely represented the fact that his group did not properly denote a 'system of religious belief.' And then, by applying the Lemon Test to the three-point criteria required of the creation of new religious groups, via that definition, she found that both the first and second prongs were satisfied.[13]

After Judge Crabb's ruling, Kaufman appealed to the 7th Circuit Court of Appeals. Writing for that Court, Judge Diane Wood affirmed the District Court's ruling with respect to his Free Exercise complaint, but reversed and remanded its decision in regard to his Establishment one. How she came to these conclusions is especially pertinent to the discussion at hand.

She began with the Free Exercise question. While she agreed with the District Court that Kaufman failed to prove that he was restricted from exercising his beliefs, or was in some significant way burdened by his not being able to convene with other Atheists to do so, where it had failed, she argued, was in not acknowledging the judicial precedence that would have treated his Atheism as his religion. In citing many of the case decisions presented herein, she briefly detailed this precedence in order to clarify what the Supreme Court defined as 'religion':

> The Supreme Court has said that a religion, for purposes of the First Amendment, is distinct from a 'way of life,' even if that way of life is inspired by philosophical beliefs or other secular concerns.[14] A religion need not be based on a belief in the existence of a supreme being (or beings, for polytheistic faiths),[15] nor must it be a mainstream faith.[16] Without venturing too far into the realm of the philosophical, we have suggested in the past that when a person sincerely holds beliefs dealing with issues of 'ultimate concern' that for her occupy a 'place parallel to that filled by [. . .] God in traditionally religious persons,' those beliefs represent her religion.[17]

And then, by relying on the language of the Court's decision in *McCreary County v. ACLU* (2005) – 'the principle that the First Amendment mandates government neutrality between religion and religion, and between religion and nonreligion'[18] – as well as that in *Wallace v. Jaffree* (1985) – 'the Court has unambiguously concluded that the individual freedom of conscience protected by the First Amendment embraces the right to select any religious faith or none at all'[19] – she further justified her description of Kaufman's Atheism as his religion:

> Atheism is, among other things, a school of thought that takes a position on religion, the existence and importance of a supreme being, and a code of ethics. As such, we are satisfied that it qualifies as Kaufman's religion for purposes of the First Amendment claims he is attempting to raise.[20]

She then used this description as a basis for her answer to the case's Establishment Clause question:

> The problem with the district court's analysis is that the court failed to recognize that Kaufman was trying to start a 'religious' group, in the sense we discussed earlier. Atheism is Kaufman's religion, and the group that he wanted to start was religious in nature even though it expressly rejects a belief in a supreme being. As he explained in his application, the group wanted to study freedom of thought, religious beliefs, creeds, dogmas, tenets, rituals, and practices, all presumably from an atheistic perspective. It is undisputed that other religious groups are permitted to meet at Kaufman's prison, and the defendants have advanced no secular reason why the security concerns they cited as a reason to deny his request for an atheist group do not apply equally to gatherings of Christian, Muslim, Buddhist, or Wiccan inmates. The defendants argue that all they are doing is accommodating religious groups as a whole, as they are required to do under the [Religious Land Use and Institutionalized Persons Act]. But the defendants have not answered Kaufman's argument that by accommodating some religious views, but not his, they are promoting the favored ones. Because the defendants failed even to articulate – much less support with evidence – a secular reason why a meeting of atheist inmates would pose a greater security risk than meetings of inmates of other faiths, their rejection of Kaufman's request cannot survive the first part of the Lemon test.[21]

While Judge Wood's description here of Kaufman's Atheism as his religion offers a wonderful discursive contribution to the discussion throughout this book, it was not the final word on the matter.

In September 2009, Kaufman was transferred to the Stanley Correctional Institution, and in October he once again submitted a request to form an Atheist religious group. It was denied by the Warden, Jeffrey Pugh. On November 13th, he requested approval to wear a 'Knowledge Thought Ring,' a silver ring with the word 'knowledge' engraved on it. His request was denied. On December 24th, 2009 he re-submitted his request for the creation of an Atheist religious group. It was again denied. Throughout this process he had arranged for donated books on Atheism to be made available to his fellow inmates, but they were not. So he once again filed suit with the U.S. District Court for the Western District of Wisconsin, and once again Judge Barbara Crabb ruled against him with respect to all of his First Amendment complaints.[22]

He appealed, again, to the 7th Circuit Court of Appeals, where Judge Diane Wood once again affirmed all parts of the District Court's decision, except for his Establishment Clause complaint, which she reversed and remanded.

While all of this might merely seem like a repeat of his previous case, there is one difference that stands out as worthy of a brief discussion.

Pugh and the other named defendants defended their rejection of Kaufman's request because, as they argued, he was one of only two inmates who had ever expressed interest in Atheism. In his District Court complaint, he rejected this claim as misleading, as the prison actively ignored 'write-in' religions on the prisoner's religious designation form. Which meant that any form wherein an inmate might write 'Atheism' or one of its cognates, such as 'humanist,' 'secular,' 'freethinker,' or 'non-theist,' would be automatically re-characterized as 'No Preference.' Which further meant that the prison had no factual means of knowing how many Atheists, and so on, it held at any given time. Moreover, Kaufman also challenged their assumption that he was unique in his interests by relying on larger American religious demographics. In his brief for the case, for example, he cited the U.S. Census Bureau, the New York Times 2004 Almanac, and the 2003 World Almanac, which all suggested that 10–14% of the United States population self-identified as Atheistic. He also pointed out that in December 2011, a little over a year after his first request was denied, the Stanley Correctional Institution had a total of 1,465 inmates, with 178 identifying as Catholic, 236 as Muslim, 166 as Pagan, 517 as Protestant, 28 as Eastern Religion, 67 as Jewish, and 67 as Native American. Which in his estimation left 206 with unknown affiliations, or, 14% of the total inmate population. This, he claimed, suggested that at the very least, there were more than just two inmates who might find value in having an Atheist religious group that they could attend.

In her own defense of his claim in her decision for the 7th Circuit Court of Appeals, Judge Wood supplemented Kaufman's argument here with the results of a PEW Forum survey on Religion and Public Life, titled *Religion in Prisons: A 50-State Survey of Prison Chaplains*, that confirmed many of his assumptions.

> According to the survey, 1.7% of prisoners identify as Jewish and Pagan, and 0.9% identify as Buddhist, while '[o]n average, chaplains say that about 11% of the inmate population is atheist, agnostic or has no particular religious affiliation.' If only one-tenth of this 11% category would select the 'atheist' option if it were included among the umbrella groups, there would be a comparable number of atheists to Pagans, Jews, and Buddhists. If this is the case, then there may be no objective basis for refusing to create an umbrella atheist group, unless the prison could show that the expansion from seven to eight groups was somehow prohibitive. Because we have no evidence on this, we cannot determine how much weaker (if at all) the inmates'

> interest in an atheist group is, nor are we in a position to say whether the prison's justification is compatible with the Establishment Clause.[23]

Of course, she also conceded, these numbers meant nothing unless confirmed by the prison, which could only be done if it conducted a credible survey of its own, or began adding options such as 'Atheist,' 'humanist,' or 'agnostic' to its religious preference forms.

After passing her judgment, Kaufman's case was remanded back to the District Court, where in June of 2014 Judge Crabb once again dismissed his claims, overruling Judge Wood's decision by arguing his Establishment Clause complaint was invalid for two reasons:

> First, despite the opportunity to conduct additional discovery, [Kaufman] still [had] not adduced any evidence that more than two prisoners were interested in forming a study group. [. . .] Second, even if I assume that there were more atheist prisoners in 2009 and that defendants should have allowed prisoners to designate atheism as a religious preference, this would not have stopped atheist prisoners in 2009 from contacting defendants to let them know that the prisoners were interested in forming a study group.[24]

Because Kaufman was released in May of 2012, the case went no further.[25]

* * *

Kaufman's struggle here for religious recognition tells two stories. In fact, it tells the same two stories that have been told throughout this book: Atheism's growing acceptance as a position granted equal treatment with respect to the First Amendment, and its place as a religious belief alongside others within the changing landscape of American religion.

What's more though, these two stories symbolize the foundation of my two thesis questions, the first of which, *is Atheism an American religion?*, can be answered here – by repeating Judge Wood's own response – with a defensible 'yes.' After all, in her conception of the term for the benefit of efficiently considering his constitutional rights, and as a 'school of thought' that took a position on religion, Atheism was Kaufman's religion 'for purposes of the First Amendment claims he [was] attempting to raise.'[26]

Which brings me to my next question: *how would the transformation of Atheism into an American religion alter the very meaning of American religion?*

To address *this* question, we need to consider a few more discursive examples.

Atheism, an American religion: consequences

Answering the question, *how does defining Atheism as an American religion alter American religion?*, requires a similar review of another discursive trend, in this instance dealing with the relationship between the United States Government and the religious beliefs of its people, and how the complexity of that relationship is made all the more complicated by time and tradition, especially with respect to how the former transforms the latter.

And the Supreme Court plays a significant role both in applying and recording this transformation.

Which is especially true of its function in shaping 'ceremonial deism,' the Judiciary's companion concept to American civil religion,[27] perhaps best defined by Justice O'Connor in her concurrence to Justice Steven's decision for the Court in *Lynch v. Donnelly*:

> There are no *de minimis* violations of the Constitution – no constitutional harms so slight that the courts are obliged to ignore them. Given the values that the Establishment Clause was meant to serve, however, I believe that government can, in a discrete category of cases, acknowledge or refer to the divine without offending the Constitution. This category of 'ceremonial deism' most clearly encompasses such things as the national motto ('In God We Trust'), religious references in traditional patriotic songs such as the Star-Spangled Banner, and the words with which the Marshal of this Court opens each of its sessions ('God save the United States and this honorable Court'). These references are not minor trespasses upon the Establishment Clause to which I turn a blind eye. Instead, their history, character, and context prevent them from being constitutional violations at all [emphasis in original].[28]

Ceremonial deism equates to a sense of constitutional permissibility, of accepting things that would otherwise comprise an endorsement or establishment of religion, through an acknowledgment of the significance that such a benign religiousness has played in shaping the doctrine and narrative of 'America.' And this begins, as above, with a discursive trend once again inaugurated by Justice Hugo Black.

In a footnote to his decision for the Court in *Engel v. Vitale* (1962), which ruled as unconstitutional a prayer composed by the State Board of Regents of the State of New York, and adopted by the State's public school system, Justice Black described this permissibility as such:

> There is, of course, nothing in the decision reached here that is inconsistent with the fact that school children and others are officially encouraged to express love for our country by reciting historical documents such as the Declaration of Independence which contain references to the Deity or by singing officially espoused anthems which include the composer's professions of faith in a Supreme Being, or with the fact that there are many manifestations in our public life of belief in God. Such patriotic or ceremonial occasions bear no true resemblance to the unquestioned religious exercise that the State of New York has sponsored in this instance.[29]

A year after that, in Justice Brennan's expansive concurrence to Justice Tom C. Clark's decision for the Court in *Abington v. Schempp* (1963), where he quoted Chief Justice Earl Warren's decision in *McGowan v. Maryland* (1961), he added to this a sense of 'interweaving' between the religious and the secular, again made permissible by time and tradition:

> As we said in *McGowan v. Maryland*, 'the "Establishment" Clause does not ban federal or state regulation of conduct whose reason or effect merely happens to coincide or harmonize with the tenets of some or all religions.' This rationale suggests that the use of the motto 'In God We Trust' on currency, on documents and public buildings and the like may not offend the clause. It is not that the use of those four words can be dismissed as 'de minimis' – for I suspect there would be intense

> opposition to the abandonment of that motto. The truth is that we have simply interwoven the motto so deeply into the fabric of our civil polity that its present use may well not present that type of involvement which the First Amendment prohibits. This general principle might also serve to insulate the various patriotic exercises and activities used in the public schools and elsewhere which, whatever may have been their origins, no longer have a religious purpose or meaning. The reference to divinity in the revised pledge of allegiance, for example, may merely recognize the historical fact that our Nation was believed to have been founded 'under God.' Thus, reciting the pledge may be no more of a religious exercise than the reading aloud of Lincoln's Gettysburg Address, which contains an allusion to the same historical fact.[30]

And then in a more contemporary context, we saw this same sort of 'permissibility-in-the-name-of-tradition' applied in the Court's decision in *Town of Greece v. Galloway*, wherein Justice Anthony Kennedy compared the acceptability of the legislative prayer policies in both the Town of Greece and the Nebraska State Legislature:

> In *Marsh v. Chambers*, the Court found no First Amendment violation in the Nebraska Legislature's practice of opening its sessions with a prayer delivered by a chaplain paid from state funds. The decision concluded that legislative prayer, while religious in nature, has long been understood as compatible with the Establishment Clause. As practiced by Congress since the framing of the Constitution, legislative prayer lends gravity to public business, reminds lawmakers to transcend petty differences in pursuit of a higher purpose, and expresses a common aspiration to a just and peaceful society. The Court has considered this symbolic expression to be a 'tolerable acknowledgement of beliefs widely held,' rather than a first, treacherous step towards establishment of a state church.[31]

And it is here, in Justice Kennedy's estimation of an otherwise Establishment Clause violation as a 'tolerable acknowledgment of beliefs widely held,' where we find a critical defect in ceremonial deism as a whole, a double-edged quality that leads to even more complex permissibilities, such as defining American Atheism as a religion, and the consequences that result from that.

The Establishment Clause was not designed merely to protect religious and non-religious Americans from government endorsements, it was meant to likewise protect the sanctity of religion from any governmental definition in the first place, as, after all, an endorsement is just that. And this is where we might, for the sake of argument, reproach the use of ceremonial deism of doing just that. As an example, consider the Court's decision in *Salazar v. Buono* (2010), a case that dealt with, among other things, the placement of a 'Latin cross' on government property in 1934, as a war memorial to the casualties of World War I.

A former Mojave National Preserve employee, Frank Buono, filed the initial lawsuit with the U.S. District Court for the Central District of California in 2001, claiming that the cross, regardless of its initial intent, was a religious symbol, and thus represented an Establishment Clause violation. The District Court ruled in his favor, and a long and tumultuous judicial and legislative battle ensued. Eventually, the case found its way to the Supreme Court where, in a plurality 5–4 opinion – also drafted by Justice Anthony Kennedy – the cross was permitted to stay.[32]

And there are two features of this decision that stand out as examples of the defect of ceremonial deism. The first is a re-conceptualization by Justice Kennedy of the cross's overall religious meaning:

> But a Latin cross is not merely a reaffirmation of Christian beliefs. It is a symbol often used to honor and respect those whose heroic acts, noble contributions, and patient striving help secure an honored place in history for this Nation and its people. Here, one Latin cross in the desert evokes far more than religion. It evokes thousands of small crosses in foreign fields marking the graves of Americans who fell in battles, battles whose tragedies are compounded if the fallen are forgotten.[33]

The second comes from a back-and-forth discussion between Justice Antonin Scalia and Peter Eliasberg, who argued before the Court on behalf of Frank Buono on October 7th, 2009. Eliasberg was in the midst of explaining the original intention of the cross's placement by the local chapter of the Veterans of Foreign Wars, as designated by a plaque that was placed alongside it, when Justice Scalia interrupted him.[34]

CHIEF JUSTICE ROBERTS: What else . . . what else does the plaque say.

ELIASBERG: The plaque says: 'This cross,' in big letters, 'erected in honor of the dead of foreign wars.' I think it would be very—

CHIEF JUSTICE ROBERTS: And that's it? Nothing else?

ELIASBERG: Nothing else. I think it would be very odd indeed for the VFW to feel that it was free to take down the cross and put up, for example, a statue of a soldier which would honor *all* of the people who fought for America in World War I, not just Christians, and say: Well, we were free to do that because even though there's the sign that says, this cross is designated to honor all the—

JUSTICE SCALIA: The cross doesn't honor non-Christians who fought in the war? Is that . . . is that . . .

ELIASBERG: I believe that's actually correct.

JUSTICE SCALIA: Where does it say that?

ELIASBERG: It doesn't say that, but a cross is the predominant symbol of Christianity and it signifies that Jesus is the son of God and died to redeem mankind for our sins, and I believe that's why the Jewish war veterans—

JUSTICE SCALIA: It's erected as a war memorial. I assume it is erected in honor of all of the war dead. It . . . It's the . . . the cross is the . . . is the most common symbol of . . . of . . . of the resting place of the dead, and it doesn't seem to me . . . what would you have them erect? A cross . . . some, some, conglomerate of a cross, a Star of David, and you know, a Muslim half moon and star?

ELIASBERG: Well, Justice Scalia, if I may go to your first point. The cross is the most common symbol of the resting place of Christians. I have been in Jewish cemeteries. There is never a cross on a tombstone of a Jew. [Laughter] So it is the most common symbol to honor Christians.

JUSTICE SCALIA: I don't think you can leap from that to the conclusion that the only war dead that that cross honors are the Christian war dead. I think that's an outrageous conclusion.

ELIASBERG: Well, my . . . the point of my point here is to say that there is a reason the Jewish war veterans came in and said we don't feel honored by this cross. This cross can't honor us because it is a religious symbol of another religion.[35]

The critical defect that these two features represent is the 'de-sacralization,' or rather the *secularization*, of religious symbols and phrases endorsed by ceremonial deism in order to permit their unconstitutional placement on government property. A 'removal' of the religious meaning inherent in these types of representations by means of 'history' and 'tradition.' And this defect is central to the very definition of ceremonial deism itself. Such as in Justice O'Connor's argument that because these things have been 'in place for a significant portion of the Nation's history,' and have thus been 'observed by enough persons' that they can 'fairly be called ubiquitous,'[36] or in Justice Brennan's contention that through 'rote repetition,' they have lost 'any significant religious content.'[37] By 'removing' the sacred nature of these types of religious objects – such as the cross in *Salazar v. Buono*, or the phrase 'under God' in the Pledge of Allegiance – the Court's use of ceremonial deism has worked to secularize things once conventionally thought of as 'religious,' merely for the benefit of weakening the separation between church and state. So that, in this way, it has also begun to entirely re-conceptualize the very meaning of 'American religion' by making secular the sacred signifiers that once defined that concept. And while this process is terribly complex, especially in regard to how it also re-conceptualizes the Court's role in interpreting the First Amendment, it becomes even more so when we add Atheism into the equation.

If, by the acceptance that Atheists deserve equal First Amendment protection as other religious Americans, and, based on the precedent set by judicial decisions such as *Kaufman v. McCaughtry*, we perceive Atheism as the religion of the Atheists discussed herein, then Atheism-as-religion adds to this already complex discourse a whole new level of intricacy. After all, if what was once understood as 'sacred' is now 'secular' for the sake of Establishment Clause circumvention, and what was once understood as 'Atheistic' is now 'religious' for the sake of Establishment Clause implementation, then what constitutes 'American religion,' at least within the context of the Judiciary's understanding of it, becomes a truly exceptional concept.

Final conclusions and questions without answers

As a final conclusive statement, there is an additional level of complexity here that should be addressed with respect to American Atheism being 'defined' as a religion, and it derives from this question:

> Does defining Atheism as a religion require a re-evaluation of instances where it has clearly violated the Establishment Clause?

As an example of my meaning here, consider this passage from the Supreme Court's decision in *Edwards v. Aguilar* (1987), wherein a Louisiana law that mandated the teaching of 'creation science' alongside the theory of evolution, within the State's public school system, was found to be in violation of the First Amendment:

> The sponsor of the Creationism Act, [Louisiana State Senator Bill P. Keith], explained during the legislative hearings that his disdain for the theory of evolution resulted from the support that evolution supplied to views contrary to his own religious beliefs. According to Senator Keith, the theory of evolution was consonant with the 'cardinal principle[s] of religious humanism, secular humanism, theological liberalism, aetheistism [sic].' The state senator repeatedly stated that scientific evidence

> supporting his religious views should be included in the public school curriculum to redress the fact that the theory of evolution incidentally coincided with what he characterized as religious beliefs antithetical to his own.[38]

And then also consider Justice Scalia's dissent to Justice Brennan's decision for the Court in the same:

> The censorship of creation science has at least two harmful effects. First, it deprives students of knowledge of one of the two scientific explanations for the origin of life, and leads them to believe that evolution is proven fact; thus, their education suffers, and they are wrongly taught that science has proved their religious beliefs false. Second, it violates the Establishment Clause. The United States Supreme Court has held that secular humanism is a religion. Thus, by censoring creation science and instructing students that evolution is fact, public school teachers are now advancing religion in violation of the Establishment Clause.[39]

Added to this are the arguments made by the citizens of Mobile, Alabama in *Smith v. Board of School Commissioners of Mobile County* (11th Circuit Court of Appeals, 1987), in their fight to have removed from the Mobile County School District textbooks that, according to them, forced on their children the religious doctrine of Secular Humanism through the promotion of science, history, and the arts. Which we could also equate with the complaint filed by John E. Peloza in *Peloza v. Capistrano School District* (9th Circuit Court of Appeals, 1994), where he unsuccessfully requested an injunction against the teaching of evolution in the public school system in Capistrano County, California, because as the 'religious doctrine' of Secular Humanism, he saw its implementation as a violation of the Establishment Clause in equal measure to that considered in *McCollum v. Board of Education* and *Abington v. Schempp.*

In each of these cases, the central complaint pertained to an unconstitutional permissibility of a specific religious doctrine through the teaching of certain disciplines. And while the Courts that reviewed these complaints found them to be untenable, we might appropriately ask here if those verdicts were either fair or correct. After all, as the religious doctrine of Secular Humanism and Atheism, which have both been defended by the American Judiciary as religions, could we not argue here that secular textbooks about science, history, or art are just as 'religious,' and thus equally prohibited in public schools, alongside manuscripts such as the Bible?

Perhaps this question might be more easily addressed in relation to another example.

Elliot Ashton Welsh was, if nothing else, an Atheist-leaning agnostic. And yet, he was granted conscientious objector status in *Welsh v. United States* regardless of the fact that his 'religious training and belief' was predicated on a devotion to the ethics and morals he had gleaned from history and philosophy, two secular disciplines. Which meant that in its decision in his favor, the Court had, by accepting these things as the basis of his 'ultimate concern,' transformed them into the doctrine of his personal religion. They became 'beliefs' that, in his mind, constituted a place parallel to that filled by 'God' in the mind of another. A transformation, like the cross in *Salazar v. Buono* – albeit in the opposite direction – from secular to sacred. A sort of 'ceremonial deism' in reverse.

And in this way, if we were to take the Court's discourse across all of the decisions discussed herein as evidence that Atheism is indeed an American religion, then would we not likewise need to sincerely re-evaluate complaints expressed by individuals like Senator

Keith or John Peloza, especially with respect to the constitutionality of public school curriculum that might once have been conventionally thought of as entirely a-religious? And if so, wouldn't we also need to re-consider an appropriate way forward, such as either permitting a fair and balanced representation of religious texts like the Bible alongside textbooks on science, history, and art, or the removal of both in order to guarantee no excessive entanglement occurs between church and state?

These questions, alongside all the others that I have asked throughout this book, collectively represent the consequences of 'defining' American Atheism as an American religion, not just in theological or philosophical terms, but in legal ones as well. Which speaks additionally to another aspect of its exceptionalism. For if it were to be, officially, defined as such, doing so would require an even larger re-evaluation, in this instance of the very notion of the 'wall of separation' between church and state in America, especially since the principles that define Atheism – as we have seen described throughout the discourses presented herein – espouse much of the secular thinking on one side of that wall, in direct ideological opposition to the religious beliefs on the other.

This is not to say, of course, that doing so would be either 'good' or 'bad.' Passing such judgments is not my concern here. Rather, my point in asking these questions – and thus demanding that you consider them – has been merely to initiate a reflective dialogue of sorts. To force you to think about the details and facts inherent in these types of questions, and in that way to engage with the broader issues and concerns often overlooked by mere 'definitions' of concepts like religion and Atheism.

And as I argued at the conclusion of Chapter One, merely providing a definition for these things, or even working toward *defending* one's definition of them, is far less valuable than providing the discourses that feed them. For it is through an analysis of that discourse that we find the true 'essence' of signifiers like religion and Atheism. In seeing first-hand how they have been used by both insiders and outsiders, how they have been 'filled with meaning' in that process, and thus how they have been 'defined.' And this book has offered plenty of material for doing just that.

Of course, it would also be the height of carelessness not to reiterate here that this is only possible when we first create boundaries around our discursive fields. Which also demands a reiteration of the fact that while the outcomes of such analyses might lead us toward answering the questions I have asked throughout this book, those answers can only function within the context in which they have been formed. So that, while I might conclude here by stating something along the lines of, *American Atheism is a unique religious position dictated by a reactionary relationship to the beliefs and actions of other religious Americans*, this can only be understood in relation to the discourses found herein. And that is because words like 'religious position' and 'relationship' only make sense when we connect them to signifying components such as the First Amendment rights of Atheists like Vashti McCollum, Elliot Welsh, or James Kaufman, and the relationship these rights have had on shaping both their Atheism, as well as the religious beliefs against which they were compared, within the Court's treatment of both.

Outside of this context, these things lose their meaning.

Which also means that perhaps the better route toward understanding a concept like 'Atheism' is through a *collection* of these sorts of analyses, where contextually bound descriptions might come together to form a larger, more comprehensive one. So that, if we wanted to know how the 'religious nature' of the Atheists in this book relate to those found in other examples – such as the doctrines, myths, and rituals of certain exceptional American Atheist churches, like the Church of the Flying Spaghetti Monster or the

United Church of Bacon[40] – we could do that through analytical cross-comparison. And in that way begin to put together the complex pieces that collectively give meaning to the larger notion of 'American Atheism.'

Notes

1 *Torcaso v. Watkins* (1961), 367 U.S. 488, 495.
2 *Epperson v. Arkansas* (1968), citation: 393 U.S. 97, 104.
3 *Wallace v. Jaffree* (1985), citation: 472 U.S. 38, 52–53.
4 Justice O'Connor, concurring in *McCreary County v. ACLU* (2005), citation: 545 U.S. 844.
5 *American Humanist Association v. Bureau of Prisons* (U.S. District Court for Oregon, Portland Division, 2014), No. 3:14-cv-00565-HA.
6 *Center for Inquiry, Inc. v. Marion Circuit Court Clerk* (7th Circuit Court of Appeals, 2014), No. 12-3751.
7 See also *Warner v. Orange County Department of Probation* (2nd Circuit Court of Appeals, 1997), citation: 115 F.3d 1068. Though similar to the issue in *Kaufman v. McCaughtry*, *Warner v. Orange County* did not break as significant ideological ground as the former. In this instance, the 2nd Circuit Court of Appeals affirmed a ruling by the U.S. District Court for the Southern District of New York which argued that Robert Warner, an Atheist, had the constitutional right to absent himself from an Alcoholics Anonymous group that promoted a particular religious belief, even when his attendance was demanded by his conviction.
8 Kaufman's definition, cited in *Kaufman v. McCaughtry* (U.S. District Court for the Western District of Wisconsin, 2004), citation: WL 257133.
9 *Kaufman v. McCaughtry* (U.S. District Court for the Western District of Wisconsin, 2006), citation: 422 F.Supp.2d 1016, 1018.
10 Ibid.
11 Ibid., 1019.
12 *Reed v. The Great Lakes Companies, Inc.* (7th Circuit Court of Appeals, 2003), No. 02-3371.
13 *Kaufman v. McCaughtry* (U.S. District Court for the Western District of Wisconsin, 2004), No. 03-C-027-C.
14 *Wisconsin v. Yoder* (1972), citation: 406 U.S. 205, 215–216.
15 *Torcaso v. Watkins* (1961), citation: 367 US 488, 495 and footnote 11; see also *Malnak v. Yogi* (3rd Circuit Court of Appeals, 1979), citation: 592 F.2d 197, 200–215 (Judge Adams, concurring); and *Theriault v. Silber* (5th Circuit Court of Apealls, 1977), citation: 547 F.2d 1279, 1281 (per curiam).
16 *Thomas v. Review Board* (1981), citation: 450 U.S. 707, 714; see also *Lindell v. McCallum* (7th Circuit Court of Appeals, 2003), citation: 352 F.3d 1107, 1110.
17 *Fleischfresser v. Directors of School District 200* (7th Circuit Court of Appeals, 1994), citation: 15 F.3d 680, 688, footnote 5 (internal citation and quotation omitted); see also *Welsh v. United States* (1970), citation: 398 U.S. 333, 340; and *United States v. Seeger* (1965), citation: 380 U.S. 163, 184–188.
18 *McCreary County v. ACLU* (2005), citation: 545 U.S. 844.
19 Quoting *Wallace v. Jaffree* (1985).
20 *Kaufman v. MacCaughtry* (7th Circuit Court of Appeals, 2005), No. 04-1914.
21 Ibid.
22 *Kaufman v. Pugh* (U.S. District Court for the Western District of Wisconsin, 2011), No. 11-cv-168-bbc.
23 Citing *Religion in Prisons: A 50-State Survey of Prison Chaplains*, The PEW Forum on Religion and Public Life, available at: www.pewforum.org/SocialWelfare/ prison-chaplainsperspectives.aspx (accessed October 21st, 2017). *Kaufman v. Pugh* (7th Circuit court of Appeals, 2013), citation: 733 F.3d 692.
24 *Kaufman v. Pugh* (U.S. District Court for the Western District of Wisconsin, 2014), No. 11-cv-168-bbc.
25 He did, however, file suit in 2014 in the United States District Court for the District of Columbia requesting a reversal of a decision by the United States Citizenship and Immigration Services that did not permit him the right to renounce his American citizenship. He lost in

March 2016. See *Kaufman v. Johnson* (U.S. District Court for the District of Columbia, 2016), citation: 170 F.Supp.3d 71.

26 *Kaufman v. MacCaughtry* (7th Circuit Court of Appeals, 2005), No. 04-1914.

27 See also Robert N. Bellah, 'Civil Religion in America' (*Journal of the American Academy of Arts and Sciences*, Vol. 96, No. 1, 1967), 1–21; and Richard V. Pierard and Robert Dean Linder, *Civil Religion and the Presidency* (Grand Rapids: Zondervan, 1988).

28 Justice O'Connor, concurring in *Elk Grove v. Newdow* (2004), citation: 542 U.S. 1. (Parenthetical citations removed).

29 *Engel v. Vitale* (1962), citation: 370 U.S. 421, footnote 21.

30 Justice Brennan, concurring in *Abington v. Schempp* (1963), citation: 374 U.S. 203, 303–304.

31 *Town of Greece v. Galloway* (2014), citation: 572 U.S. ___ (Parenthetical citations removed).

32 After the case was remanded back to the 9th Circuit Court of Appeals, the original cross was stolen, and since the entire discussion of the Supreme Court's decision centered around that specific cross, no new one could be legally erected as a replacement.

33 *Salazar v. Buono* (2010), citation: 559 U.S. 700.

34 *Salazar v. Buono* (2010), citation: 559 U.S. 700, Oral Argument of 7 October 2009, recording and transcript available at: www.oyez.org/cases/2009/08-472 (accessed October 14th, 2017).

35 Justice Scalia and Eliasberg continued this discussion later on in the latter's argument, shifting from this debate to the idea that a national memorial, such as America's National Cemeteries, would better alleviate issues of governmental endorsement if, like an open forum, they accepted the placement of myriad symbols that might more properly represent the religious diversity of those interred there. Which is interesting in its own way, as there are currently 66 emblems available for headstone adornment in America's National Cemeteries, ranging from more traditional religious ones for Christianity, Judaism, Hinduism, Islam, Buddhism, et al., to secular ones such as the 'infinity' symbol or the 'sand hill crane,' as well as emblems for Humanism and Atheism. See, www.cem.va.gov/hmm/emblems.asp (accessed October 3rd, 2017).

36 Justice O'Connor, concurring in *Elk Grove v. Newdow* (2004).

37 Justice Brennan, dissenting in *Lynch v. Donnelly* (1984), citation: 465 U.S. 668, 716.

38 *Edwards v. Aguillard*, citation: 482 U.S. 578, 592.

39 Justice Antonin Scalia, dissenting in *Edwards v. Aguillard*, 623–624.

40 See Ethan G. Quillen, 'The Satirical Sacred: New Atheism, Parody Religion, and the Argument from Fictionalization,' in Philip Quadrio, Christopher R. Cotter, and Jonathan Tuckett, eds. *New Atheism: Critical Perspectives and Contemporary Debates* (Dordrecht: Springer, 2017).

Bibliography

Melanie E. Brewster, ed., *Atheists in America* (New York: Columbia University Press, 2014).

Richard Cimino and Christopher Smith, *Atheist Awakening: Secular Activism and Community in America* (Oxford: Oxford University Press, 2014).

Derek H. Davis, 'Is Atheism a Religion? Recent Judicial Perspectives on the Constitutional Meaning of "Religion"' (*Journal of Church & State*, Vol. 47, No. 4, 2005), 707–723.

Bruce E. Hunsberger, *Atheists: A Groundbreaking Study of America's Nonbelievers* (New York: Prometheus Books, 2006).

Ethan G. Quillen, 'The Satirical Sacred: New Atheism, Parody Religion, and the Argument from Fictionalization,' in Philip Quadrio, Christopher R. Cotter, and Jonathan Tuckett, eds. *New Atheism: Critical Perspectives and Contemporary Debates* (Dordrecht: Springer, 2017).

Leigh Eric Schmidt, *Village Atheists: How America's Unbelievers Made Their Way in a Godly Nation* (Princeton: Princeton University Press, 2016).

David A. Williamson and George Yancey, *There is No God: Atheists in America* (Lanham: Rowman and Littlefield, 2013).

Index

www.ingramcontent.com/pod-product-compliance
Ingram Content Group UK Ltd.
Pitfield, Milton Keynes, MK11 3LW, UK
UKHW050754180926
475701UK00007B/1043